GENOCIDE

and the Politics of Memory

Herbert Hirsch

GENO

THE UNIVERSITY OF NORTH CAROLINA PRESS *Chapel Hill & London*

CIDE

and the Politics of Memory

Studying Death to Preserve Life

© 1995

The University of

North Carolina Press

All rights reserved

Manufactured in the

United States of

America

The paper in this

book meets the guidelines

for permanence and

durability of the

Committee on

Production Guidelines

for Book Longevity

of the Council on

Library Resources.

Library of Congress Cataloging-in-Publication Data

Hirsch, Herbert, 1941–

Genocide and the politics of memory: studying death
to preserve life / by Herbert Hirsch.

p.   cm.

Includes bibliographical references and index.

ISBN 0-8078-2198-5 (alk. paper).—

ISBN 0-8078-4505-1 (pbk. : alk. paper)

1. Genocide.   2. Memory—Social aspects.

3. Social conflict—Psychological aspects.   I. Title.

HV6322.7.H55   1995

304.6′63—dc20   94-29750

CIP

99   98   97   96   95   5   4   3   2   1

To hope for the future

and, therefore, to my children

and all children, for they

are the carriers of memory

and the repositories of hope.

Whenever man has thought it necessary to create

a memory for himself, his effort has been attended

with torture, blood, sacrifice.

Friedrich Nietzsche, *The Birth of Tragedy and the*

Genealogy of Morals (1956)

Like Rumkowski, we too are so dazzled by power

and money as to forget our essential fragility, forget

that all of us are in the ghetto, that the ghetto is

fenced in, that beyond the fence stand the lords of

death, and not far away the train is waiting.

Primo Levi, *Moments of Reprieve* (1987)

CONTENTS

PREFACE

Memory is inescapable. It is, in fact, the capacity to remember, the ability to use our brains to create or re-create our past, that is said to separate human beings from their fellow inhabitants on the planet. This ability to remember, however, does not necessarily mean that all of us are aware of our past or even of events swirling around us.

When I was growing up in a small town in Pennsylvania, I knew very little about events going on around me—significant events that were to shape the world we live in today. What I did know was largely a series of indistinct impressions with little or no substance. Personally, I had experienced some vague and nonlethal manifestations of anti-Semitism, but of cruelty, repression, and mass extermination I knew little. As I began to become more aware of my surroundings and as I started to study history and politics, it dawned on me that a great deal of human energy was devoted to attempts to destroy other humans. Why, I asked myself, are humans so willing, now and in the past, to kill each other in large numbers?

My interest in this question was crystallized by the events that occurred in 1978 in Jonestown, Guyana, where 950 followers of the "Reverend" Jim Jones were persuaded to commit suicide-murder. If so many people, I thought, would follow orders to commit mass suicide, to take their own lives and those of family members and friends, how difficult could it be to motivate people to kill others more distant from them whose racial, religious, sexual, or other characteristics had already been denigrated?

To try to answer these difficult questions for myself, my students, and my children, I began to do research on repression, on injustice, and finally on mass extermination. The subject is not pleasant, and confronting it inevitably effects the manner in which one views oneself and the world. Yet it seemed far more important to me than many of the other subjects to which scholars in the social science disciplines devote their attention.

After a number of years of study, I began to teach classes and to address audiences about genocide. At first, I used to begin my lectures by apologizing for the depressing nature of the material. Eventually I began to wonder: "Why am I apologizing? Did I make up the events? Isn't it important for people to learn and, most important, to remember?" I no longer apologize. Now I explain that we study death to learn about life—about how to live in such a manner as to not cause, and hopefully to learn how to prevent, repetitions of the horrible genocides that have plagued human history in general and our troubled century in particular. Estimates of the toll taken in the twentieth century are astounding; Brzezinski (1993) claims that "167,000,000 to 175,000,000 lives have been deliberately extinguished through politically motivated carnage" (p. 17). How we can make the study of death a life-preserving activity is my topic in this book.

ACKNOWLEDGMENTS

Many of those who have contributed in one or another form to the completion of the present work are people with whom I am not personally acquainted. I am so deeply indebted to all of my teachers, both those who stimulated and moved me in class as well as those from whom I learned by reading their works, that there are no adequate means to repay or even acknowledge the debt.

Primo Levi, Elie Wiesel, Terrence Des Pres, and others who have written about what Levi refers to as "overcoming great troubles" have moved me more than words can describe. Helen Fein, Raul Hilberg, Robert Jay Lifton, Stanley Milgram, Barrington Moore, Jr., George Mosse, George Steiner, and other scholars who have written about life and death helped me to formulate my own ideas. Yet, even for an academic, however much I owe to the authors of what I have read, there is no substitute for human contact. Consequently, my greatest debt is to those who have had the patience to read my ramblings, offer criticism, save me from embarrassment, and provide encouragement.

Leo Kuper, who devoted his life to ending the horror of genocide, has always led by example and by his scholarly work. He was surely one of the kindest, most committed individuals in the academic world. The planet would be an infinitely better place if all of us could approximate even in small ways his example. After this book was written, Leo Kuper passed away. He cannot be replaced, and this work is offered as a partial tribute.

Israel Charny has been an inspiration to many of us in this field. His commitment to stopping genocide and his dedication to discussing the topic are admirable.

Franklin Littell has been a pioneer in the field and, along with Hubert Locke, founded the annual Scholars Conference on the Holocaust and the Church Struggle. Franklin and Hubert have done much to encourage a new generation of scholars, and the annual conferences offer a forum within which they can exchange ideas in an atmosphere of mutual support and admiration marked by an absence of the hostility and jealousy that pervade many other academic gatherings. It is sustaining to know that so many others have interests similar to my own.

As is often the case, the most important acknowledgments are left to the end. My colleague Robert Holsworth is one of the few people who read the entire manuscript, a burden he appeared to undertake cheerfully. My friend and former student Harry O'Hara read this material and offered important insights. Eric Markusen and Roger Smith also read the manuscript and provided me with extensive comments and criticisms. Their academic counsel and friendship mean a great deal. Both are innovative scholars and, more importantly, nice people, and one cannot study the tragedy of mass death without the kind of support they offer.

My longtime friend James Bill has not been directly involved in this project but has been a source of stimulation and friendship for over twenty-five years. Through many personal, academic, and political changes we have managed to remain friends.

My family is a constant source of pleasure and stability. My wife, Gail, is my most astute critic. Her comments on my writing are always helpful and inevitably encourage me to clarify my meaning. She also eats my cooking and supports my interest in genocide, despite the fact that it can occasionally intrude upon one's psychological outlook on life. Whenever that happens, she helps to draw me back to our own reality.

My children, Karen and Mark, are the ultimate reason I wrote this book, and I dedicate it to them. In studying genocide and mass death, I have found that the sense of tragedy surrounding the act of genocide is always heightened when children are involved, and even more so when I think about my own children. My fervent wish is that all children, including my own, never have to experience what I write about in this book.

Finally, none of the above bear any responsibility for errors that may occur in this work; the responsibility is entirely my own.

History does not pass over in silence these scenes of

well nigh un-utterable miseries. It is her duty to give

a true and vivid account of them.

First Sergeant George Hirsch, speech delivered at opening

ceremony of Angrerod Synagogue, Germany, 1945

ONE

Politics, Memory, and Mass Death

In 1945 when the extermination and concentration camps were liberated, unsuspecting people were confronted with scenes of unimaginable horror. The first camp to be liberated by the Western Allies was Buchenwald. Since its construction, it had held about 238,000 persons. Not only Jews, but non-Jewish Poles, Russians, and dissident Germans were incarcerated in this "detention" camp. Buchenwald was not expressly designed for extermination—it was viewed as a "holding" facility. Despite this, 56,000 prisoners died or were murdered there.

On April 11, 1945, forward platoons of American soldiers arrived to find about 20,000 remaining prisoners. The scene they encountered literally made them ill: "Some of the first Americans to enter the camps vomited as their eyes beheld what their minds could not absorb—bodies stacked in obscene anonymity, the barely living whimpering among the corpses, bunks full of shaven-headed emaciated creatures who had wizened into skeletal apparitions. American soldiers put on film the scenes in rooms full of naked, unburied corpses piled ten feet high" (Sachar 1983, p. 4). This was one of many descriptions of what was to be a common experience as the German camps were liberated. The names of these camps have been burned into infamy: concentration camps like Buchenwald included Dachau, Bergen-Belsen, Mauthausen, Ravensbruck, Sachsenhausen, as well as many others. The six camps specifically designed to exterminate human beings were Auschwitz, Treblinka, Sobibor, Majdanek, Belzek, and Chelmno—all in Poland.

The human destruction and brutality seem beyond comprehension—according to the most widely accepted statistic, 5,820,960 Jews died in the Holocaust. Although it is undoubtedly difficult to comprehend the enormity of the numbers, it is perhaps even more difficult to assimilate, and certainly equally depressing to consider, the fact that the Holocaust was neither the first nor the last genocide. Indeed, one observer (Smith 1987, p. 21) has labeled the twentieth century the "Age of Genocide," an observation that is essentially correct based on the fact that the mechanisms and techniques of mass destruction have increased in efficiency throughout this perilous period. The century has moved from the systematic extermination of 1 to 1.5 million Armenians by the Turkish government in 1915–17, to the murder of about 6 million Jews in the Holocaust, and now, with the advent of nuclear and other sophisticated chemical and biological weapons, to the possible extermination of an entire culture or nation.

In fact, as I write these words, many people throughout the world face starvation, some of it induced by the actions of states, such as the tragic events in Rwanda, and active and generally unopposed genocide is occurring in places such as Bosnia. As we consider these somber realities, it is difficult to avoid recognizing the disturbing possibility that the Holocaust and the Armenian genocide were a prologue rather than a conclusion, previews of events that would occur in the late twentieth century.

As one gazes upon this scene of carnage that human beings have designed for themselves, one cannot help but be struck by the apparently unending capacity for cruelty and destruction. Perhaps Nietzsche was accurate when he exclaimed: "What a mad, unhappy animal is man! What strange notions occur to him; what perversities, what paroxysms of nonsense, what bestialities of idea burst from him. . . . Man harbors too much horror; the earth has been a lunatic asylum for too long" (1956, pp. 226–27). How can one read the daily newspaper or watch the television news and not resonate to this reproach?

Since there appears to have been no cessation of the paroxysms or bestialities, one must ask whether the political, social, cultural, religious, and educational institutions of the nineteenth and twentieth centuries have failed in their purported attempts to humanize humanity—that is, to control humans' primal impulses to kill each other in large numbers for reasons of racial, religious, ethnic, or national hatred. It would appear so, for our attempts at international government, at improved education, and at implementing other formulas proposed throughout the long and destructive era have not successfully stopped the massive destruction of human life.

The memory of these primal passions appears to run so deep that they are neither erased, replaced, nor controlled by the attempt to impose a veneer of civilization. People continue to hate and to kill for the same reasons, and the memories of their attachments to ethnic, religious, racial, national, or regional identity continue as prime motivations. We can only hope to ameliorate this condition if we look deeper into the importance of these memories and attempt to understand in greater depth the relationship between memory and politics.

The politics of memory and the psychology of politics are intimately related to each other. Memories, and the myths and hatreds constructed around them, may be manipulated by individuals or groups in positions of leadership to motivate populations to commit genocide or other atrocities. The justification for the acts of violence are generally formulated by invoking some higher or greater "good" such as "purifying the race," "saving democracy," self-defense, or some other overarching ideology. These memories are then passed from generation to generation via the process of socialization, and the cycle of violence may be perpetuated by this continuous reinforcement of the memories of the hatreds that have been passed to succeeding generations. The connection, therefore, between memory and politics may be one key to unlocking the enigma of mass death. This should not be taken to mean that I suggest that socialization and the transmission of hatred through collective memories are the only causes of genocide, war, or atrocity. On the contrary, complex historical events cannot be understood or explained by fastening upon a single antecedent.

Memory, history, politics, and psychology are messy and disorderly processes. Generations pass on their memories, making them part of the historical record, by using language to transmit their particular version of events to the next generation through the process of socialization. These processes contribute to the formation of an individual's identity or sense of self, which may, in turn, influence the decisions a person will make when confronted with a crisis or an order to commit an act that might, in most circumstances, be considered morally questionable—such as an order to march elderly men, women, and children to a ditch and kill them. The individual actor, now the repository of personal and social memory, in turn, becomes the transmitter, the eyewitness through whom history is constructed and interpreted. Narrative accounts and resulting historical interpretations influence the policy of the state, which may be destructive or constructive of human life. The overall goal of this book is to attempt to understand, in greater detail, these connections and, based on this understanding, to propose measures to help present and future generations avoid the continuing horrors of genocide, cruelty, and mass death.

The subject has become unfortunately relevant. Genocide and atrocities of the most horrible kind are once again taking place, this time paraded before the world in plain view on television. Even though no nation can claim ignorance, Serbs, Croats, and Muslims in the former Yugoslavia continue to kill each other without intervention to stop the massacre. Memories are manipulated and myths have been created to motivate genocide and atrocity in Bosnia, a situation that provides a clear introduction to and demonstration of the importance of the politics of memory.

> It is time for the international community to begin
>
> identifying individuals who may have to answer for having
>
> committed crimes against humanity. We have . . . a moral
>
> and historical obligation not to stand back a second time
>
> in this century while a people faces obliteration.
>
> Lawrence Eagleburger, "The Need to Respond to
>
> War Crimes in the Former Yugoslavia" (1992)

1

Memory and Politics in Bosnia

Nearly fifty years after the extermination and concentration camps were liberated, genocide continues unabated, neither punished nor prevented. In what used to be Bosnia, torture, murder, rape, and starvation are everyday occurrences. Approximately 200,000 people have been killed, 750,000 are missing, millions have become refugees, and 30,000 to 60,000 Muslim women have been raped. Although the Serbs are not solely responsible for all atrocities, they are the primary perpetrators. Former secretary of state Lawrence Eagleburger in a statement at the international Conference on the Former Yugoslavia at Geneva, Switzerland, December 16, 1992, outlined the charges against the Serbs. They included:

- The siege of Sarajevo, ongoing since April 1992, with scores of innocent civilians killed nearly every day by artillery shelling

5

- The continuing blockade of humanitarian assistance, which is producing thousands upon thousands of unseen innocent victims
- The destruction of Vukovar in the fall of 1991 and the forced expulsion of the majority of its population
- The terrorizing of Banja Luka's 30,000 Muslims, which has included bombings, beatings, and killings
- The forcible imprisonment, inhumane treatment, and willful killing of civilians at six detention camps, including Banja Luka/Manjaca, Brčko/Luka, Krjina/Prnjavor, Omarska, Prijedor/Keraterm, and Trnopolje/Kozarac
- The August 21, 1992, massacre of more than 200 Muslim men and boys by Bosnian Serb police in the Valsica Mountains near Varjanta
- The May–June 1992 murders of between 2,000 and 3,000 Muslim men, women, and children by Serb irregular forces at a brick factory and a pig farm near Brčko
- The June 1992 mass execution of about 100 Muslim men at Brod
- The May 18, 1992, mass killing of at least 56 Muslim family members by Serb militia men at Grbavicii, near Zvornik
- The continuous and indiscriminate shelling of cities and areas set aside as "safe havens" for the Bosnian Muslims

Perhaps the most horrible atrocity is the planned, systematic use of rape as a political weapon. Although estimates of numbers of rapes vary, they are all outrageously large. The Bosnian government estimates that "as many as 50,000 or even 60,000 women have been raped and claims to have partially documented 13,000 cases of Muslim women violated by Serbs" (Laber 1993, p. 3). A European Commission of Inquiry reported that 20,000 women had been raped, and a Michigan law professor who is representing the Bosnian victims claims that possibly more than 50,000 women have been raped and 100,000 women and children have been killed (Halsell 1993, p. 9). This is an example of depravity unmatched in the twentieth century. Documented cases show that rapes have been committed on children as young as three years of age and on women as old as eighty-four. Halsell, who interviewed Muslim women in Bosnia, recounts examples almost too horrible to repeat. One woman described what she witnessed in a camp for 150 women and children: "I saw Serbs raping children—girls as young as six and eight years old" (p. 8). Another woman, a nurse, described her detention in a "rape camp": "I was one of 1,800 women kept as prisoners in Brocko. There were 600 women in my room. I was given a number—31. When they called your number you had to go. One woman told me she was gang-raped by 50 Serbs" (p. 9).

How did what used to be Yugoslavia, a civilized and sophisticated multiethnic European nation, degenerate into a state of hatred and depravity as extreme as that of any genocide of the twentieth century?

The three groups involved in the conflict, Serbs, Croats, and Muslims, share a common southern Slavic ethnic background. They speak similar languages but are divided by cultural, religious, and political and ideological differences.

Croatia flourished in the tenth to the thirteenth centuries, whereas Serbia prospered in the thirteenth and fourteenth centuries. Croatia became Catholic; Serbia adopted the Eastern Orthodox religion. A third force also arose. From among the contending schools of Christianity, a derivative sect of the Manichaeans called Bogomils took root among the Slavs. They were similar to the Albigenses of southern France, who were in favor of a "purer, simpler monotheism" (Meyer 1993, p. 61). Members of this group were denounced as heretics by both the Orthodox and Catholic churches, and the Bogomils were not regarded as Christians. They were, in fact, sold as slaves and treated harshly.

In 1389, at the battle of Kosovo, the Turks defeated an army of Serbian nobles, and in 1415 the Ottoman Turks "offered the Bogomils military protection, secure titles to their lands and freedom to practice their religion—if they counted themselves as Muslims and did not attack Ottoman forces" (Meyer 1993, p. 61). Many converted to Islam, but hundreds of thousands of Serbs moved to escape Turkish oppression and were welcomed by the Austrians, who used them as a cushion from Turkish invasion.

In 1875 Bosnian Christians, Serbs, and Montenegrins, with the support of Russia, revolted against the Turks, and the Austro-Hungarian army took advantage of the opportunity and invaded the Serbian province of Bosnia. Bosnia and Herzegovina were annexed by Austria-Hungary in 1908, an action that angered Serbia and its Russian ally. As World War I drew to a close, the United States, Great Britain, and France supported the creation of a southern Slavic state, which was named the Kingdom of the Serbs, Croats, and Slovenes. It was renamed Yugoslavia in 1929. The tensions between Serbs and Croats were exploited by the Germans, who set up a Serbian puppet regime in Belgrade and another Croatian regime with the capital at Zagreb (Gutman 1993, pp. xix–xx). The USTASHA party of Ante Pavelić established an independent state of Croatia, which included Bosnia and Herzegovina, under the direct protection of Germany and Italy. This puppet state accepted the Nazi doctrine of a Final Solution for Serbs, Jews, and Gypsies and established the

Jasenovac concentration camp, where thousands were systematically murdered. Estimates of the numbers of victims range from around 70,000 to 100,000 Serbs, Jews, and Gypsies (p. xxi).

The Serbian regime also killed Jews and, along with the Serbian royalists (the Chetniks), was responsible for "cleansing" the state of Bosnian Muslims. With the dissolution of Yugoslavia in the 1990s, they have returned to their genocidal past as each group reawakens and exploits the memory of the old hatred to motivate new atrocities.

GENOCIDE IN MODERN EUROPE

The current conflict is related to the collapse of Communist rule in the former Soviet Union and Eastern Europe. Yugoslavia was composed of six federated peoples' republics and two autonomous provinces in Serbia (Vojvodina and Kosovo), all of which were governed from the Serbian capital of Belgrade. Four of the six republics had non-Serb majorities—Slovenia, Croatia, Macedonia, and Bosnia-Herzegovina—and began to move to gain independence from the Serbian capital once the Communists fell from power. Serbia and Montenegro declared that they would not allow non-Serbs to rule over Serbs, and in 1991 "Serbian troops, wearing the uniforms and supported by the heavy weapons and aircraft of the former Yugoslav army, set out to 'free' Serbian towns and villages in Croatia and Slovenia" (Curtiss 1993, p. 8).

After a year of fighting, 10,000 people were killed and a million Serbs and Croats were driven from their homes. Serbia occupied about a quarter of the territory that had been assigned to Croatia. The cease-fire between Serbs and Croats in January 1992 freed Serbian troops to turn their attention to Bosnia-Herzegovina, and after the European community recognized the Republic of Bosnia on April 6, 1992, followed by the United States the next day, Bosnian Serbs began the siege of Sarajevo. The world began its vigil, watching as the slaughter continued. Neither the United States, the United Nations, the North Atlantic Treaty Organization, the European countries, nor Russia have been willing to take action to stop the genocide.

The Europeans classified the conflict as a civil war, not an international dispute, and openly supported the partitioning of Bosnia, which evolved into the Vance-Owen Plan, all the while ignoring the carnage. Before the war, "4 million Bosnians were divided into 109 municipalities, of which only 32 had an absolute Serb majority" (Cohen 1993, p. 40). Under the European Vance-Owen Plan, the Bosnian Muslims' territory was to be given to the Serbs, but the plan never got off the ground. In its place, a new plan was proposed in June/July 1993 to divide Bosnia into three sections, with the Croatians and the

Serbians gaining the largest amount of territory and the Bosnian Muslims relegated to a series of "safe havens" similar to Native American reservations. In either case, the Muslims would have lost whatever territory they once controlled, and the demise of Bosnia would be a fait accompli.

The United States has talked tough but has done nothing to help end the crisis. As Thomas Friedman noted in the *New York Times* in an astute critique of President Bill Clinton's foreign policy, Clinton has gone from describing Bosnia as a "moral tragedy" (during the 1992 presidential campaign) to talking about it as "a tribal feud no outsider could hope to settle." Not getting involved in Bosnia is now "understandable prudence," not "moral indifference." Unlike the Persian Gulf War, in which the United States took the initiative in forming a coalition to remove Saddam Hussein's forces from Kuwait, U.S. policy toward the Bosnian crisis appears to be: "If the Europeans will not follow, America cannot lead."

The world is left with the apparently accurate perception that genocide and atrocity are legitimate means to attain policy goals. If a leader or group is interested in securing territory, uniting a previously fractious people, or pursuing some other political goal, genocide is a possible means to achieve these ends since the international community is not likely to take action to stop such "crimes against humanity." In fact, the way to motivate people to commit such acts is to manipulate their historical memories by creating myths designed to stimulate racial, ethnic, or national hatreds that feed the violence. Politics is, in this respect, related closely to memory, and until we are able to see and understand the complex connections between the two, the seemingly endless repetitions of mass killing are destined to endure.

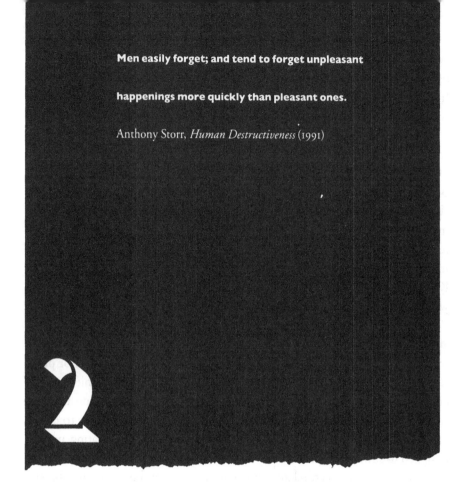

Men easily forget; and tend to forget unpleasant

happenings more quickly than pleasant ones.

Anthony Storr, *Human Destructiveness* (1991)

The Politics of Memory

The fact that many have witnessed human cruelty has not stopped that cruelty, and the fact that many have learned about the destructive actions of the state has not lessened the importance of the state. If the connection between memory and politics is not clarified, the past may be ignored, reconstructed, or manipulated, employed as a mythological justification for the present, leading to passivity or even, perhaps, to despair. How a subject or a historical event or period is studied influences how it is remembered. History is, as Isenberg (1985) notes, "the memory of things said and done" (p. 3). What is said in the present about what was done in the past not only determines how the past is viewed, thus determining what history means in the present, but also probably influences future actions. How we remember past events has a profound impact on what we will do and how we will live. Memory is, therefore, a distinctly political phenomenon and requires analysis as possibly the most important aspect of political understanding. In order to gain even a rudimentary understanding of the politics of genocide, it is necessary to know something about memory, history, and the history of memory.

MEMORY IN HISTORICAL PERSPECTIVE

Humans have always been concerned about their past and have always valued memory. Although the "modern" study of memory dates back to Ribot (1882), Galton (1884), Ebbinghaus ([1885] 1913), Freud and Breuer ([1893] 1974), and Colegrove (1899) in the late 1800s, earlier societies expressed their curiosity about memory by placing the control of memory in the hands of gods and goddesses (Herrmann and Chaffin 1988, p. 6). Thus, as early as 4000 B.C., an Egyptian god was endowed with the responsibility for controlling memory, as was the Greek goddess Mnemosyne, one of Zeus's wives and the mother of the Muses. Memory was placed in the hands of deities because it was thought to defy logical analysis (Herrmann and Chaffin 1988, p. 6).

Sometime around the fifth century B.C., "the first practical writing on how to improve memory appeared," advising that "attentiveness and rehearsal aid learning" (Herrmann and Chaffin 1988, p. 6, citing Yates 1966). During this same time, Heraclitus made the famous observation that "the eyes are more exact witnesses than the ears" (Herrmann and Chaffin 1988, p. 6). As time passed, philosophers continued to display an interest in memory or in some form of the idea of memory—what Rapaport (1971) refers to as the "association of ideas" (p. 4). Some even refer to Plato and Aristotle as perhaps the first "memory theorists" (Herrmann and Chaffin 1988, p. 6). In the Roman period, Cicero, among others, was concerned with improving memory, as were later theorists such as Augustine, who, "like Plato, . . . suggested metaphorical models of memory, likening acquisition to the digestive processes of the stomach and remembering to the exploration of caverns. Additionally, Augustine discussed the relationship between memory and emotions, noting that the knowledge of the emotion held during an experience 'clung to my memory so that I can call it to my mind' " (p. 7).

During the Dark Ages, interest in memory decreased, to be reawakened by Aquinas in the thirteenth century. From the thirteenth to the seventeenth century, studies focused on the practical aspects of how to improve a person's memory. After this time, "the approach to memory scholarship shifted from the practical to the theoretical" (Herrmann and Chaffin 1988, p. 7) as thinkers as diverse as Bacon, Descartes, Hobbes, Hume, Kant, Leibniz, Locke, and Spinoza all considered some aspect of memory.

Finally, the modern period of memory scholarship was introduced in the late 1800s. Some argue that the renewed interest was sparked in 1885 when Ebbinghaus published a monograph documenting his empirical studies of memory. Memory thus became the object of experimental, as well as philosophical, study (Herrmann and Chaffin 1988, p. 7). But Ebbinghaus was primarily interested in examining the act of learning, and among his contemporaries, he was not alone in his interest in memory—in fact he may not have been the first to redirect attention to the topic.

In *Diseases of Memory: An Essay in the Positive Psychology* (1882), Ribot was directly concerned with autobiographical memory. He argued that memory was basically biological and that it was primarily "a vision in time" (Conway 1990, p. 18). Galton (1883) understood memory to be similar to "cumulative ideas" or "generic images," which he thought were "like a composite portrait" (Conway 1990, p. 20). Galton approached memory like a botanist classifying plants; he was "fascinated with variety and sought to describe, quantify, and codify it" (Robinson 1986a, p. 20).

Freud too was interested in memory as a key to understanding and treating psychological problems. Because his prescription for treatment involved the reconstruction of his patient's life history, he focused on biography and, in particular, the early or formative period of a person's life. The interest in biographical memory began to fade in popularity, however, as modern psychology became increasingly "scientific." One author describes the period from 1900 to the early 1970s as a period of great silence since there were so few studies of biographical memory (Conway 1990, p. 16).

Although the biographical tradition never disappeared, it was no longer part of the "mainstream" of psychological research. It does, however, appear to be reemerging as theorists once again recognize the ways in which memory is related to other important phenomenon—including politics and history.

CONTEMPORARY PERSPECTIVES ON MEMORY

Recent memory theorists have spent a great deal of time and energy attempting not only to define memory but also to identify different types of memory. These theorists divide the functions of memory into a number of different categories, explicating each in great detail.[1] For purposes of this

1. Connerton (1989), for example, distinguishes three classes of what he calls "memory claims: personal, cognitive and reproductive." The first, personal memory claims, are "those aspects of remembering that take as their object one's life history. We speak of them as personal memories because they are located in and refer to a personal past" (p. 22). Personal memory claims appear to be the same as what other thinkers label as auto-

discussion of politics and memory, however, our primary interest is in personal or autobiographical memory, a classification which includes, according to a number of theorists, the recollections of eyewitnesses to historical events and may, therefore, act as the basic foundation upon which history is constructed. In other words, personal memory is the cornerstone supporting collective or social memory. Personal memory is so important that it is necessary to examine it in greater detail.

Personal memory involves recalling a particular episode or episodes from one's past. It appears to be a "reliving" of the experience. Brewer (1986) points out that the "contents almost always include reports of visual imagery, with less frequent occurrences of other forms of imagery. . . . Personal memories are experienced as occurring at specific times and locations. This does not mean that the individual can assign an absolute date, just that the memory is experienced as having occurred at a unique time" (p. 34).

For example, my early memory of experiencing anti-Semitism is visual—I can see in my mind the image of the individual cursing Jews—but I cannot recall the exact date or time. The fact that I "know" it occurred even though I cannot describe all the details demonstrates that a personal memory is accompanied by the belief that it occurred in the past. Since I "know" it happened, I also believe it is "true," raising the question of whether or not personal mem-

---

biographical memory. Brewer (1986) argues that there are six "major forms of naturally occurring memory": personal memory, semantic memory, generic perceptual memory, motor skill, cognitive skill, and rote linguistic skill (p. 28). He defines autobiographical memory as "memory for information relating to the self, where memory for the self is given more complete definition by the structural account of memory" (p. 33). According to Brewer, autobiographical memory cannot be meaningful unless it includes a concept of identity or self. Consequently, he discusses this connection, dividing the self into three aspects: "an experiencing ego, a self-schema, and an associated set of personal memories and autobiographical facts" (p. 27). The ego is the "conscious experiencing entity that is the focus of our phenomenal experience. . . . It is the memory for the ego's moment-to-moment experience that we call personal memories." The self-schema "is the cognitive structure that contains generic knowledge about the self." Just as individuals have knowledge about things outside themselves, they also have knowledge about themselves. The self "is the complex mental structure that includes the ego, the self-schema and portions of long-term memory related to the ego-self (e.g. personal memories, generic personal memories, and autobiographical facts)." The individual is "the larger entity that includes the self, the depersonalized (nonself) aspects of the mind, and the body. Thus, it is the individual who has depersonalized knowledge about biology . . . and who possesses cognitive skills . . . , motor skills . . . , and rote skills."

ory is always, or even sometimes, a "veridical record of the originally experienced episode" (Brewer 1986, p. 35). It is important to recognize that even though an individual memory of an event may not be "factual," however that may be determined, the person involved most likely believes his or her memory is reliable. The strength of that conviction may lead to problems when another person's account of the same event is different. In other words, observers of events, whether contemporary or historical, may in reality perceive them differently because they may have experienced them differently. How an event is experienced is affected by the emotions and sensations a person feels (Rapaport 1971, pp. 113–14) and by the social groups he or she belongs to, feels part of, or identifies with at the time. Rapaport refers to these factors as "selective force[s]" because they select or influence the final product of memory. One cannot, therefore, talk about memory apart from these forces because individual memory is filtered through emotions and through group experience. Religious, class, and family affiliations all help construct the manner in which a memory will be interpreted. Memory, in short, is a social phenomenon that does not occur in a vacuum.

In fact, what we are discussing is socialization, the process by which an individual acquires his or her identity and view of the world and by which the memories of one generation are passed on to the succeeding generation. I will discuss the process of socialization in more detail in chapters 10, 11, 12, and 13, when I examine the formation of identity and, in particular, the motivation to participate in genocidal massacres. For the moment, however, I will explore how and why certain memories are recalled clearly whereas others remain obscure.

Brewer (1986) has observed some "moderate agreement about the characteristics of the events that lead to well-recalled personal memories" (p. 44). These characteristics include the uniqueness of the event, its importance or "consequentiality," its "unexpectedness," and its emotional content or the degree to which it was "emotion-provoking." Conversely, events that are recalled dimly or not at all are trivial, non-emotion-provoking, not unique, and expected. One often-cited example of the former is the assassination of President John Kennedy. It has become a cliché for people to claim the ability to remember precisely where they were, who they were with, and what they were doing when they first heard about the killing. Other momentous events stimulate similar responses. One could argue, consequently, that the testimony of observers of unusually violent or traumatic events, while perhaps not completely veridical or accurate, must be etched quite clearly in their own minds. However, individuals may differ significantly in what they consider a momentous event, and, therefore, different people will remember different events more clearly than others.

Personal memory is obviously a highly complex and complicated subject. Omitted in this brief description are additional complexities such as the role of chemicals in the functioning of the brain and, therefore, in stimulating or hindering memory. Even from this relatively brief analysis it is possible to conclude that there is a close relationship between personal and historical memory. Also, even if it is not possible to be more precise and even if one cannot ascertain the accuracy of personal memory, it is certainly the case that history is partially constructed from the accounts of witnesses and from primary documents that reveal the memories of those involved in events. Of course, as with personal memory, there are always problems concerning accuracy.

Brewer (1986) proposes, therefore, what he calls a "partially reconstructive view" (p. 44). This perspective suggests that even if personal memories retain a relatively large amount of specific information about the original event, such as time and location, the events are, over time, reconstructed to "produce a new nonveridical personal memory that retains most of the phenomenal characteristics of other personal memories," such as strong visual imagery and beliefs, but that may not be completely, or even partially, accurate.[2]

In other words, personal memory is not an orderly phenomenon, and, since history is often based on personal memory, history is not as clear-cut and orderly as some interpreters would like us to believe. History is, from this perspective, a form of reconstructed memory, but it is memory reconstructed after historians have attempted to corroborate the memories and recollections by using documents and gathering other testimony. This is what historians do to attempt to distinguish history from legend or folklore (Robinson 1986a, p. 19). However valiant the attempts of historians to present a verified account, history remains tied to memory and is profoundly influenced by the paradigms, ideologies, and perspectives of those who write it. These factors, in turn, are influenced by the historian's overall view of time. History, in spite of the academic conventions, remains memory.

2. Conway (1990) argues that autobiographical memory is not necessarily a veridical account of an event but an interpretation that contains information about the location of the event and about the date or time of occurrence. Even if autobiographical memories are not necessarily factual, they may contain relevant information about actors, actions, and locations (pp. 11–12). The information is generally transmitted in the form of images that are organized according to temporal sequences. Recent memories, for example, are more likely to be accurately recalled than later memories (pp. 29–35).

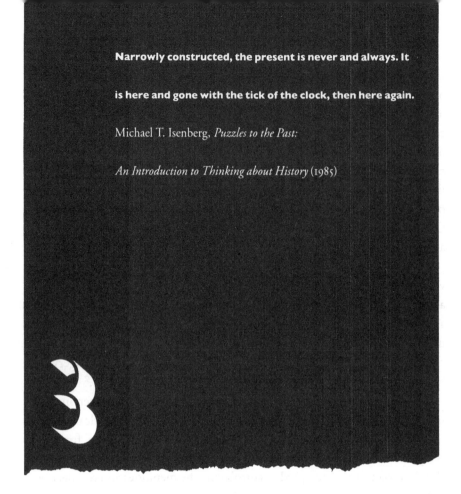

Narrowly constructed, the present is never and always. It

is here and gone with the tick of the clock, then here again.

Michael T. Isenberg, *Puzzles to the Past:*

An Introduction to Thinking about History (1985)

History as Memory

The Influence of Time and Paradigm

Soviet artist Mikhail Savitsky, who had been a non-Jewish prisoner in several concentration camps, provided an interviewer with this explanation for why he continued to paint scenes from the Holocaust: "I can never forget what I saw there, and what you see [in the paintings] is what I remember" (quoted in Miller 1990, p. 209). In the same way, the writings and memoirs of survivors and witnesses, which become the material of historians, are accounts of what people remember. Each person has a unique history, and his or her memory of that history is influenced by how the person has lived, what the person has learned, and how and in what context that learning occurred. Neither individual nor historical memory are, as we saw in the previous chapter, orderly phenomenon.

In attempting to reconstruct our own history from what Langer (1991) calls the "ruins of memory," we should be aware of the fact that what we come up with is composed partially of remembered experiences, partially of events we have heard about that may be part of the family or group mythology, partially of images that we have perhaps created from a series of faintly remembered events. The picture we arrive at is, as Hampshire (1989) notes, "confused, overlaid by accretions, often emotionally toned" (p. 122).

Nevertheless, historians and philosophers agree that personal recollections are used to formulate both the individual and collective past (Robinson 1986a, p. 19; Isenberg 1985, pp. 131–32). This belief in an "archival function of memory" is based on the assumption that life memories are "time capsules," records of an unrepeatable past. When historians write history, they are both utilizing and creating memory—constructing a past, a sense of a previous time. As a record of humanity, history is an attempt to chronicle human events remembered by human beings, therefore time is an important concept or framework because how it is viewed affects how one views history. In fact, the past, memory, or history—whatever we call the idea of what came before the immediate moment of being—rests on a fundamental concept of time.

MEMORY AND TIME

Apart from simply living into the next moment, historical inquiry is the only time-travel there is.
—Louis O. Mink, *Historical Understanding* (1987)

Just as historians create memory as they write history, as I write about memory, I am constructing a way to think about memory and history and am consequently creating a paradigm—a way of thinking used to analyze and interpret some phenomenon.[1] Since history is often equated with time, how we view time may very well affect how memory is created.

Time is a puzzling, ubiquitous, and fascinating concept. Brilliant minds from Albert Einstein to Stephen Hawking have attempted to explicate and understand it. For me, time is simply remarkable. Steiner (1977) captures the amazing incongruities of time by pointing out that at this very moment, somewhere on earth, repression, cruelty, or perhaps genocide is in process or being planned (p. 157). As it occurs, you and I remain sheltered and relatively secure—although not immune—living, as he puts it, "as if on another planet."

---

1. The *Random House College Dictionary* (1988) defines "paradigm" as follows: "An example; pattern or model, mold, ideal, standard, paragon."

Yet, as he goes on to note, at any moment our personal situation might change and we may "drop out of humanity." Any writing or thinking about genocide and mass murder should serve to make us all aware of how tenuous our lives are and how complex are the riddles of time and place.

Along with Steiner and the survivors of events such as the Holocaust, we may ask, "Why me?" Why am I able, at this moment, for example, to be sitting comfortably at my word processor while in Bosnia-Herzegovina Serbs, Croats, and Muslims are massacring each other? How is it that I am fortunate enough to have just finished lunch when millions of people are starving on the African continent? Such dilemmas suggest that history is actually chaos and that events have always been out of control, rendering our individual fates merely accidental. What does my life mean to the dying in Bosnia and the starving in Africa, and, concomitantly, what do their lives mean to me? If we answer honestly, very little. We all simply try to live our lives day-to-day. Perhaps we pause to contemplate whether the events affect our everyday lives or experience sadness at the death and destruction, but our lasting effect on each other is minimal. Given these intricacies of time and distance, how does one communicate about the history and memory of mass death?

Some historians claim that historical study has three dimensions: chrono-logical, geographical, and topical (Isenberg 1985, p. 48). In addition, they argue that history is moved by a series of social forces, including economics, religion, and institutions, mainly political, technological, ideological, and military (p. 143). Although undoubtedly true, this view fails to acknowledge the complexity outlined in the discussion above. Namely, it ignores the fact that multiple events transpire at the same time; even as I write this sentence, numerous other people are experiencing other things throughout the world. My understanding is severely limited by my own experience and also by my perceptions of time and history.

Isenberg (1985) notes that the historian Frederick Lewis Allen once sug-gested that if the historian could find some way to write several stories of simultaneous events and "construct them in parallel columns so some special human brain could follow all of the threads in the stories at the same time, then he might have a chance to help the reader sense the multiplicity, hetero-geneity, and simultaneity of events" (p. 51). We are, therefore, caught in a dilemma. It is virtually impossible to communicate the multitude of events occurring at any single moment in time, giving rise to the view that perhaps the world is chaotic and unruly and that the course of events follows no pattern. As Isenberg points out, "If we deny *all* pattern to history, we endorse chaos. If we insist *all* history is pattern, we deny humanity. Our position is somewhere in the infinite middle ground, where people struggle to make sense of their past and to widen the possibilities for their future" (p. 78). If history is studied as pattern—that is, if it is seen as an unfolding plan guided either by God or by some type of "strong" leadership—a kind of false order is imposed upon events. Events appear to be more predictable and controllable than they actually are, which leads historians and nonhistorians alike to perceive some kind of order in the past, the present, and the future. In particular, events seem more logical in hindsight than when the observer is caught in the middle of the confusion.

Of course, the world is both changing and consistent. Presidential administrations change, people holding power change, and wars take place, while at the same time, an individual experiences periods of consistency and change. People, even those caught in the midst of traumatic events, develop a more or less consistent pattern of daily life. Sometimes changes are not obvious until years later. Interpretations of what occurred or is occurring depend upon one's perspective. One person might see change, another conservation; one observer might see order, another randomness. History, as a record of humanity, is an attempt to chronicle all of this activity.

Since history is the record of human events remembered by human beings, time is simply a concept, not an actor—it cannot do anything. But our concept of time influences our view of history. White (1973) argues that the "very claim to have distinguished a past from a present world of social thought and praxis, and to have determined the formal coherence of that past world, *implies* a conception of the form that knowledge of the present world also must take, insofar as it is *continuous* with that past world" (p. 21). He proceeds to argue that "commitment to a particular form of knowledge predetermines the *kind* of generalizations one can make about the present world, the kinds of knowledge one can have of it, and hence the kinds of projects one can legitimately conceive for changing that present or for maintaining it in its present form indefinitely." The same is true for a particular view of time. Many historians believe that history and time are synonymous. Isenberg (1985), however, differentiates between time and historical time. For him, historical time is the "kind of time that gives the past dimension in relation to the present. Historical time is relatively brief. The time scale of recorded human activity pales alongside the span of geological time" (pp. 41–42). But time is not absolute any more than history is unchanging. Even the scales used to measure time differ from culture to culture. For example, the Chinese measured time according to the ruling dynasty, not in years, decades, or centuries. However time is conceived, it provides a unifying and organizing principle, a means of imposing order and providing a pattern that supports a sense of past and future. Since all cultures do not conceive of time as linear, as moving from past through present to future, time is not a universal concept, and historians often focus on different configurations of time and use different time periods to conceptualize or frame their subjects of analysis.

A historian might examine a period of hundreds of years, a presidential administration, a person's life, one year, or a day, for instance. Historians also study periods considered "important" or "critical," a determination that is, of course, highly subjective. This means, obviously, that what is studied is human activity within a chosen time frame. History is studied as action, and time is an organizing principle by which actions thought to be significant are arranged. Usually the activity studied is supposed to have had a major impact upon a state, group, or culture—such as a war, election, or assassination. Memory is thus structured around action and a conceptualization of time. We remember most clearly actions that have a profound, imprinting impact. This impact may very well be the result of the frequent retelling of events, such as the continuous reinforcement in U.S. public schools of the belief that Columbus "discovered America" or the glorification of leaders in times of war. The focus is often on violent, traumatic, or emotionally satisfying actions because of the intensity of emotions involved. Tennis players, for example, can recall significant matches, even points, and replay them clearly in their minds. History as memory is probably reconstructed on the same temporal basis.

Memory, therefore, is connected to the historian's view or conceptualization of time, that is, to the paradigm used to frame and interpret historical actions. Historians may sometimes adopt nonhistorical paradigms within which to frame their study of history. Kemp (1991), in fact, argues that the way history is viewed is shaped by the culture and that a culture that views the past as a burden, believes in the inevitable "goodness" of progress, and adopts science as a new, religionlike belief will view history as "supersessive" rather than "successive" (p. 150). Such cultures, he argues, have a "model of time" that is "one of epistemological supersession, of new forms of knowledge superseding and making irrelevant the old." This perspective celebrates the present as more rational and progressive and views not only its own past but also that of other cultures as inferior. The belief in the triumph of science, for example, over religion or mythology is such a view. It does not perceive a relationship between the two; it does not acknowledge that one might grow out of the other, that science, for example, might be another mechanism for constructing an understanding of the world not so different in effect from myth. If, consequently, as Kemp argues, history is supersessive, then all that has happened "in the past is insubstantial. History is a history of illusions superseding one another, a science of nothing, not even of anything as substantial as memory, but of forgetting," because supersession implies a forgetting of the past (p. 166). The present is not built from the past but springs to life as a result of some spontaneous revolutionary event, hence the penchant among historians for specifying particular events or dates as monumental or important, such as assigning the origin of the nation-state to the year 1648 when the Peace of Westphalia was signed.

This paradigmatic view of history as supersessive does not conceive of memory as connecting human activity in the present with that in the past. The supersessive paradigm manifests a kind of contempt for the past and has "an almost infinite tolerance for the new, for successive waves of revolution. Also because it builds no system other than the supersession of systems, it is almost impervious to destruction" (Kemp 1991, p. 177). In other words, supersessive history destroys memory because it views the present as a departure from the past. It denies interconnectedness and tends toward viewing events as unique. The perspectives of scientific history and scientific social science are the primary contemporary manifestations of a supersessive paradigm. These perspectives are often ahistorical and lead to a very obvious dehumanization of history and, consequently, a denigration of memory. This topic will be explored further in section 2, where I examine the ways memories of genocide may be constructed. For now, it is important to point out that history is not simply a supersessive series of events; rather, it is constructed in memory and texts and is framed by our conception of time.

If our paradigm of time is supersessive, we attempt to find the empirical or scientific reason for the revolution that led to the abandonment of the past. But as Kemp (1991) notes, "The past is, by its very pastness, removed from the instruments of empirical observation. When dealing with the past, we cannot escape the question . . . : Where is this thing that we call past time?" (p. 175). Kemp continues to argue that the answer cannot be "given materialistically" because "Constantine's dust is not Constantine." Hence, for him the "past exists in memory and in communal memory expressed in literary texts. It will not do to deconstruct these texts . . . in the hope of finding something 'real' or 'actual' behind them, for this can only be a figment of imagination. . . . The objects that occupy the historical field of vision are precisely texts, histories, literary accounts of the past imposed and superimposed upon one another" (pp. 175–76).

If one accepts the argument that history is not supersessive and is essentially literary, then, according to Kemp (1991), one must draw certain conclusions. First, systems of history are "responses to problems of earthly time and duration" that are peculiar to a culture (p. 176). Second, a change of historical system is preceded by a change of ideology. History is invented, although not consciously, to justify ideology. "As an inverse correlative to this, a historical system will fail when it can no longer contain the phenomenal or conceptual world of its culture." Third, although history is "invented," at least partially, by ideology, it exerts great force on ideology. History becomes social memory and may "force a culture that holds it to follow its logical consequences to their limits." Fourth, supersessive history is deconstructive and fosters skepticism as it relativizes and temporalizes all ideologies. Supersessive history "builds no system other than the supersession of systems" and is, therefore, destructive rather than constructive (p. 177).

As a result, viewing history from the supersessive paradigm gives rise to the perception of history as a "succession of petty ages, each in ideological conflict with all of the others" (Kemp 1991, p. 178). The consequence is a "tone of historical scholarship" characterized as "*dismissive contempt.*" Historical events are seen as in "conflict rather than in continuum, in schism rather than in syncretism, with the past." The problem with the supersessive paradigm is that history cannot be supersessive, memory cannot be erased, the connectedness between human memory and traditions cannot be denied. The present is always fashioned from materials of the past. Only the writing of history can be supersessive, and it is in this manner that paradigms of time influence the construction of memory. But paradigms of time are not the only influence upon the construction of memory; history is also written to serve other, more earthly ends. Memory is also manipulated to serve political power, and the ability to manipulate memory is, in itself, a measure of that power. Memory is tied to politics as well as to the more abstract concept of time.

There is no set of maxims more important for an historian

than this: that the actual causes of a thing's origin and its

eventual uses, the manner of incorporation into a system

of purposes, are worlds apart; that everything that exists,

no matter what its origin, is periodically reinterpreted by

those in power in terms of fresh intentions.

Friedrich Nietzsche, *The Birth of Tragedy*

and the Genealogy of Morals (1956)

The Manipulation of Memory
and Political Power

As noted in the previous chapters, individual memory is analogous to, and one of the building blocks of, historical memory. The record of any group or state is as intricate and susceptible to manipulation as that of an individual. The past is always constructed out of materials as perceived in the present, and memory may be viewed as related to politics in the sense that "images of the past commonly legitimate a present social order" (Connerton 1989, p. 3) and are used to justify present policy (White 1973, p. 332; Nietzsche 1957, p. 209). It is in this manner that the control of memory is a type of political power. Persons in a position to manipulate memory, and with it the valued symbols of a society or group, hold, by my definition, political power.

Memory, therefore, is very much a sociopolitical phenomenon since it is related to power and to the position—be it subordinate or dominant—in which an individual or group is placed or places itself. The past is often constructed or reconstructed out of a culture's accumulated myths, which are used as the basis of writing or rewriting history.

MYTH AND MEMORY

Replacing history by myth is a procedure that would hardly be dangerous if there were an absolute criterion allowing one to distinguish at first sight between the two.
—Pierre Vidal-Naquet, *Assassins of Memory:*
Essays on the Denial of the Holocaust (1992)

Just as individual memory may vary in accuracy and quality for many different reasons, nation-states or individuals seeking or holding power often act on the basis of their own particular interpretation of historical memory. The writing of history, therefore, is not as straightforward a process as most believe. Philosophers, historians, and other thinkers have puzzled over and debated the connection between memory and history and the proper, best, or most objective way to conduct historical investigation.

The eminent historian C. Vann Woodward (1989) points out that it is difficult for historians to keep the present in "reasonable touch with the past" because, as he notes, "the passage of time is forever putting distance between past and present and increasing the obscurity of the past. Another thing complicating this task of the historian is the eagerness of so many volunteers who would not only assist him but perhaps take over entirely. These include writers of fiction and drama and the makers of film and television programs. It is from them more than from historians that the public mainly receives whatever conceptions, impression, fantasies and delusions it may entertain about the past" (p. vii). History is, according to this notion, not exclusively the domain of historians. In fact, the general public is more likely to remember events as they are portrayed in film or on television than as they are presented in historical texts. Even though historians may think, very often correctly, that this reliance on film and television results in oversimplification of history, most people are not historians. Their memories are usually in the form of stories or narrative sequences and are often enhanced by combinations of other sources, such as personal experiences, stories told to them by others, events they think they remember, and myths (Brown, Shevell, and Rips 1986, p. 138).

Myths, as Robertson (1980) explains, are "part of all individual human experience, and of all collective human experience" (p. 346). They are the "self-justifying" carriers of social ideals and are not, in themselves, good or evil. They are the way people weave rational and irrational elements into an acceptable explanation for some event or set of events or into some justification for their own or their group's or state's behavior. Robertson suggests that history may be described as the memory or memories of the lives, actions, and beliefs of the human beings who lived in particular spaces and that memory is contained or found in things such as the names of people, places, events, and institutions (p. 3). It is embodied in stories, poems, histories, speeches, films, jokes, rituals, games, and social groupings and in political, economic, and religious institutions. These are the conduits and holders of memory, and they are the concretization of the stories, whether true or not, that have been remembered and transmitted. Even if they are myths, these myths "create the social illusion of understanding" (p. 5) and may very well be the basis of behavior. It is possible that the persistence of racial, ethnic, and national hatreds is closely associated with the persistence of myths that are transmitted from generation to generation.

McNeill (1986) has, in fact, suggested that "myth and history are close kin in as much as both explain how things got to be the way they are by telling some sort of story" (p. 3). People use myths to organize and explain the world. As Robertson (1980) notes, "Everybody likes a good story; most people admire someone heroic; myths are often couched in good stories, very often told of heroes and heroines" (p. xv). Myths are good stories. They represent "the way things are as people in a particular society believe them to be; and they are the models people refer to when they try to understand their world and its behavior. Myths are the patterns—of behavior, of belief, and of perception— which people have in common." This sometimes mythical and at least partially reconstructed past is used to create a pattern of identity that shapes behavior and maps the future. Kammen (1991) writes that the renowned anthropologist, Bronisław Malinowski, described myth as "a story about the past which has the function of justifying the present" (p. 17).

For many people, however, the notion of myth implies falsity, while the notion of history implies veracity. If we wish to reject someone's argument, we call it "mythical." Yet, as McNeill (1986) notes, "What seems true to one historian will seem false to another, so one historian's truth becomes another's myth, even at the moment of utterance" (p. 3). What ultimately becomes history—that is, the memories that are written into the accepted texts—consequently, may be a combination of eyewitness accounts believed to be true and myths that are true, believed to be true, or not even remotely true.

Whereas memory or history used to be tied to religion or to family, in modern times it has become linked to the nation-state. Memory that is transformed into history may play both positive and negative roles in a society. It may well serve as the basis of social cohesion in a heterogeneous nation. On the other hand, it is, as Kammen (1991) recognizes, commonly relied upon by those who possess power to create an illusion of social consensus (pp. 4–5). Such people invoke the legitimacy of an artificially constructed past "in order to buttress presentist assumptions and the authority of a regime." C. Vann Woodward (1989) offers a telling chronicle of the uses to which the manipulation of history may be directed (p. viii). According to his comprehensive formulation, historical mythology may be manipulated to "improve, sanitize, gentrify, idealize, or sanctify the past; or, on the other hand, to discredit, defame, denigrate, or even to blot out portions of it." Other motives might involve "desires to enhance lineage, pedigree, national pride, or status . . . or to teach 'lessons' to the present, shame modern evil-doers, provide a heritage to live up to, or furnish solace for shortcomings. Denigration of the past, on the other hand, can serve to expunge or dismiss a shameful heritage, discredit an opponent or rival, or stress the depravity of ruling or subordinate classes."

This depressing yet commanding chronicle illustrates quite well how myths are created by a state or by individuals and then used to justify certain actions. Nation-states in particular use, create, or respond to myths about themselves that they wish to perpetuate, and, in turn, the myths are used to justify or rationalize policies that the leadership of the state wishes to pursue. National self-image is enhanced by memory—in particular, memory about how the state responded to a crisis situation. These myths allow the nation to avoid confronting reality and to forget or suppress certain memories. All states engage in these activities, and it is not difficult to find examples.

For instance, the former Soviet Union rewrote the history of Stalin's state-induced famine and the purges (Conquest 1986; Mace 1988). France has done the same thing with the Dreyfus affair and Klaus Barbie's crimes and collaboration with the Nazis. Austria has hesitated to examine Kurt Waldheim's actual war record, and the United States has avoided outright discussions of the events that transpired at Wounded Knee and My Lai. As we shall see, one event, the Holocaust, is prototypical of the ways in which mythology is developed to avoid confronting the reality of the events that occurred and the role each state played.

Countries have, for example, dealt with the memory of the Holocaust in very different ways. Not only have they constructed their own versions of the history and meaning of that event, but they have even assigned different names to it. This is important because naming something influences how it is perceived and how it will be written about and thought about by the general public.

For example, in what used to be the Soviet Union, the period of World War II is referred to as the "Patriotic War" (Young 1988, p. 87). In the Soviet Union, memory of the Holocaust is submerged in the memory of the gallant struggle of the Soviet people to achieve victory over fascism. Atrocities committed by the Soviet army are obscured and memory is reconstructed. As Soviet historian Roy Medvedev has observed: "History in my country changes with each change in Soviet leadership. So instead of history there is Soviet mythology, alleged history, which serves as the main instrument of ideology, of state legitimation" (quoted in Miller 1990, p. 198). The Soviet Union is not, however, alone. All states present their own unique versions of historical events. Some revise history more blatantly than others and, as we shall see, engage in outright revisionism. Others, as in the case above, use more subtle, less overt, means.

Germans, for example, prior to unification, were reluctant to refer to "World War II" or the "Holocaust" but instead called this period "Hitler time" (Young 1988, p. 87). As Miller (1990) notes, the former West German Republic went through several stages in facing its Nazi past. In the late 1940s and 1950s, the extermination of the Jews was not examined, and "Nazism was portrayed as a kind of accident, whose sources could be traced only to 1933" (p. 33). The second phase began toward the end of the 1950s. New generations of German historians began to "explore in depth major aspects of Nazi ideology and policies, including the regime's anti-Jewish laws and regulations." In the 1970s, additional topics, including the involvement of the army in implementing Hitler's policies, were studied. It was not until 1983, however, that international historians met in Germany to discuss the Nazi extermination of the Jews. Other German historians began to look at life in the Third Reich as a kind of normal and efficient mode of living, giving rise to historical revisionism that culminated in the 1980s in what became known as the "historians' debate," to be discussed below under the topic of denial.

Even though the former West Germany has at various times genuinely attempted to acknowledge its past through vehicles of memory such as commemorations, war crime trials, and judicial proceedings and public education, Germany continues to define its problems, present and past, as the fault of others. Thus, Germans have perceived a Jewish problem, a Polish problem, and now an asylum problem but never a German problem (Breslau 1992, p. 27). Such phrasing allows a country to avoid confronting the uglier aspects of its behavior and to deflect responsibility onto the problem, a practice known in some circles as blaming the victim (Ryan 1976) or, as in the case of denial, as the outlook that "it never happened and besides they deserved it" (Opton 1971, pp. 49–70).

Most nations attempt to avoid honest self-recognition, especially when their past behavior may be viewed as less than morally justifiable. Germany and the Soviet Union are not alone. Austria, for example, has never confronted its Nazi past. Its program of de-Nazification was even less effective than Germany's, and Miller (1990) provides four critical examples (p. 88). First, out of 123,000 Austrians tried for war crimes between 1945 and 1955, only 13,600 were convicted. Second, "the head of the Vienna Gestapo, the chief of the Nazi Euthanasia program and the Gauleiter of Tyrol were all living quietly in Austria in April 1988" (p. 69). Third, history textbooks are inaccurate, and the state has made no attempt at reeducation. Fourth, Waldheim's election as president of Austria in 1987 brought anti-Semitism to the surface. "A Gallup survey in July 1986 showed that the percentage of Austrians who thought Jews had an aversion to hard work had risen from 32 percent in 1980 to 39 percent after Waldheim's election. The proportion of those who thought that Jews had too much economic and political influence rose from 33 percent in 1980 to 48 percent in 1986. Sixteen percent of those polled in 1986 said they believed it would be better for Austria to have no Jews; 38 percent said they believed Jews were partly responsible for their own frequent persecution in the past" (p. 88).

France also manipulates the memory of the period of the Holocaust through the use of language—in this case, to obscure its collaboration with the Nazis and to create a more heroic image of resistance. In France, for example, victims of the Holocaust are referred to as "déportés." Language is used to obfuscate the fact that the French helped to round up and ship the Jews to death camps.

In the United States, the period is known as "World War II." Very often the Holocaust is treated as a secondary event and is sublimated to use in the romanticization of a just war against the brutal Nazis. Memory of the Holocaust in the United States is turned to political purposes, such as tying it to political campaigns or efforts to increase support for the state of Israel (Miller 1990, p. 224).

The politics of memory is very evident in the case of the President's Commission on the Holocaust, created on November 1, 1978, by President Jimmy Carter. The commission's final report contained four recommendations:

First, . . . that a museum be built rather than an abstract statue or monument similar to the Vietnam War Memorial. Second, it was agreed that the national Holocaust museum should be built with private donations on federal land in the nation's capital. Third, the report recommended that the

President implement a resolution approved by Congress designating national days of Remembrance of Victims of the Holocaust. Fourth, the group urged that a Committee on Conscience of prominent citizens be established to sound an alarm wherever and whenever human rights are violated. (Miller 1990, p. 227)

The only recommendation not implemented was the fourth, because, as Miller notes, "the State Department and the White House vigorously opposed it. Neither favored the establishment of an officially sanctioned, private group of human-rights busybodies who might offer competing assessments of various international human-rights crises and the efficacy of the U.S. Government's efforts to resolve them." As one committee member commented: "Our proposals were fine as long as they did not ask the government to extend the lessons of the Holocaust to our current foreign and national security policies" (pp. 227–28).

What these examples have in common is the obvious fact that language is used to create a different version of events that serves a distinctly political purpose. The version of events that is accepted and transmitted into the texts reflects the "national mythologies and ideologies" of a culture. These generally function to prevent confrontation with the past, allowing the state to avoid self-reflection and self-criticism and, consequently, to avoid understanding what happened.

The creation of national myths is, however, not the only mechanism employed to avoid self-reflection. Miller (1990) identifies four others (p. 280). She argues that societies repress memory in similar ways, attempting to change or suppress that which they would like to forget. Even though the events may be different, the mechanisms of repression are the same. As Miller states, "Cultures tend to employ the same vehicles to suppress pain and unpleasant memories as individuals: denial, the shifting of blame, rationalization, and relativization."

Shifting blame is a technique that exonerates the perpetrator by blaming others, thus making the perpetrator a victim. For example, Russians commonly blame the Nazis for the suffering Stalin inflicted upon them, arguing that it was thus necessary to fight the Germans. France, in its national mythology, did not resist the Germans because it was overwhelmed so quickly by them. According to the German viewpoint, the Germans were actually victims of Stalin's plot to conquer the world and were providing a service by resisting the Bolshevist-Communist aggression. Most of the Jews who died were in Soviet territory and were "subversives, partisans, spies, and criminals" (Vidal-Naquet 1992, p. 20).

Rationalization involves finding logical reasons to explain behavior that might cause embarrassment. The United States, for example, insists it did not do more to help the Jews during the Nazi period because the main priority was on winning the war and helping Jews was not a prime military objective. Rationalization is a form of justification. Germany was defending itself against Communist aggression, and, since Jews were often Communists, its behavior was defensive.

Relativization seeks to explain away the horror of an event such as the Holocaust by comparing it to other actions. Miller (1990) illustrates this mechanism: "Yes, six million Jews were killed by the Germans, but the United States also committed mass murder. . . . Yes, the Germans slaughtered Jews, but was Hitler not a response to Stalin? Yes, the Germans massacred Jews, but did the Soviet Union not kill more than a million Germans on the eastern front? Yes, the Jewish genocide in Europe was horrific, but was not Pol Pot's slaughter of his own people . . . equally horrible?" (p. 281).

Denial is the most straightforward, yet in many ways the most insidious, form of memory manipulation. Denying that genocide occurred requires the almost total reconstruction of historical events and a revision of memory. In fact, all the mechanisms of memory revisionism come together in the technique of denial. Vidal-Naquet (1992) cites as an example of denial or "revisionism" "the doctrine according to which the genocide practiced by Nazi Germany against Jews and Gypsies did not exist but is to be regarded as a myth, as fable, or a hoax" (p. 79). The case for the deniers is based on several more or less shared beliefs.

1. The genocide did not happen, and the gas chambers did not exist.
2. The Jews were not killed but were expatriated from the East.
3. The number of Jews killed is much smaller than has been claimed. The total casualties are no more than 200,000, many of which were the result of Allied bombing.
4. The Jews, not Germany, were primarily responsible for World War II.
5. The major threat to humanity during the 1930s and 1940s was not Germany but Stalin's Soviet Union. The Germans were simply defending themselves against the threat of Bolshevism-communism, and since Jews were Communists, they were killed.
6. Allied propaganda invented the genocide as part of a Zionist plot. (pp. 18–19)

These beliefs are drawn from different ideological strands, including "German nationalism, neo-Nazism, anticommunism, anti-zionism, [and] anti-Semitism" (p. 20).

Since the basic argument is clearly fabricated and ideological, it should be easy to refute. However, the purveyors of denial present details as valid information, and therefore refutation requires counterintelligence. Moreover, since people have a tendency to believe what they want to believe, actual historical evidence does not always triumph over fabrication, oversimplification, or outright lying. Thus, while denial may appear easy to refute, it is much more widespread and difficult to expose than it seems because it appears to serve both individual and collective needs and is often vigorously embraced.

For example, Holocaust denial publications have a fairly wide distribution among what appears to be an international network of "revisionists" dedicated to denying that the Holocaust occurred. Since the so-called facts of the denial are often presented as data in what appear to be academic journals, the deniers create the facade of academic acceptance. The deniers, in short, have succeeded in raising questions concerning the existence of the Holocaust or, as Vidal-Naquet notes, in creating the "appearance of 'reasonable doubt'" (1992, p. xiii).

The revisionists', or deniers', activities are most clearly demonstrated by the actions of the "American Institute for Historical Review (IHR), founded in 1978. Leading European, American and Arab 'Historical Revisionists,' as they prefer to be known, have attended IHR conferences and contributed to its *Journal of Historical Review*" (Eatwell 1991, p. 121). Two of the most active revisionists were Arthur Butz and Robert Faurisson. Butz was "Associate Professor of Electrical Engineering and Computer Science at Northwestern University and is known for his book, *The Hoax of the Twentieth Century*, first published by the Historical Review Press (Brighton)." Faurisson was a senior lecturer in literary criticism at the University of Lyon who noted in an interview that "the alleged Hitlerian gas chambers and the so-called genocide of the Jews form a single historical lie whose principal beneficiaries are the State of Israel and international Zionism [and] whose principal victims are the German people, but not its leaders, and the Palestinian people in its entirety" (quoted in Vidal-Naquet 1992, p. xiii).

It is, therefore, immediately obvious that the major function of this type of literature is not academic debate, as the title of the journal and the name of the institute might suggest, but political manipulation and ultimately the manipulation of memory. The facade of the academy is used to give denial a veneer of respectability and to disguise the pernicious repercussions of this form of rewriting history. The deniers appear to have gained some modicum of success since their writings are quite widely distributed.

In fact, Smith (1992a) argues that "denial of genocide is the universal strategy of perpetrators. Those who initiate, or otherwise participate in genocide typically deny the events took place, that they bear any responsibility for the destruction, or that the term 'genocide' is applicable to what occurred. Denial, unchecked, turns politically imposed death into a 'non-event': in the place of words of recognition, indignation, and compassion, there is, with time, only silence" (p. 8).

In the long run, all of these tactics have the same goal—the suppression or manipulation of memory, resulting in the reconstruction of history. The outcome is that the event is rewritten, revised, or perhaps, as Young (1988) notes, "unwritten" (p. 23). Very clearly, these mechanisms are intended to have an impact on the behavior of both individuals and states. Memory is reconstructed to influence the way a state acts in national and international politics.

The shifting sands of politics and power are the foundations upon which the collective memory is constructed or reconstructed. That memory is, as we have seen, elusive because of its insecure base, which moves every time the winds of politics blow in a different direction. These variable winds of politics influence the interpretation of history because the particular version that gains acceptance is used to justify present policy and future action that formerly may have been dismissed. Maintaining memory in the face of the repeated onslaught aimed at reconstruction and revision is not an easy task. It is also one that imposes stiff moral obligations and burdens to be carried into the future. If memory can be facilely rewritten and new myths created, does memory or history mean anything at all? Who, after all, really cares?

MEMORY AND PURPOSE

If an event is not constantly in the news, who will care if memory is revised and history reconstructed? As Smith (1992a) notes, if there is no state support or spokesperson for the victims of genocide, they will not be "heard across the barriers of a preoccupied and indifferent world" (p. 3). Indeed, as he maintains, "Memory . . . requires renewal. There have to be 'reminders' that call attention to the past: public commemorations, a literature or art that can summon the past into the present, the incorporation of historical accounts into the school curriculum." These mechanisms of renewed memory may help to fight against revision and denial, but memory, however it is constructed, is not necessarily its own reward.

Remembrance of the past should not function to imprison contemporaries within a cell of constricted behavior as they worry whether the past will be repeated. On the other hand, it is bound to be repeated as long as human beings remain caught in the recurring cycles of constricted memory. Consider contemporary Israel as an example.

Because of its unique past, Israel is dominated by memory more than any other nation in the world. Kammen (1991) argues that Israel has developed a "veritable memory industry" (p. 3), with at lest ten public institutions such as museums and research centers specifically devoted to the Holocaust. We have just seen in the examples of Germany, Austria, France, and the United States how the state can manipulate memory to avoid confronting a past it wishes to forget. Now the argument turns and we find an example of a state whose present behavior is, as Friedman (1990) argues, trapped in a memory—in this case, of the Holocaust (p. 279).

Friedman (1990) asserts that this was not always the circumstance and that Israel was founded upon a vision of hope for the future. This hopeful posture, Friedman claims, has been replaced by a perspective that views the hostility of the Arabs as another example of anti-Semitism following the same pattern that brought about the Holocaust. Friedman writes: "Israel's motto changed from Herzl's 'if you will it, then it is no dream' to . . . 'That is how things are, what can we do?' In other words, the future is fixed: a permanent struggle for survival against a hostile world" (p. 278). Many Israelis therefore see themselves as another generation of Jews on the brink of a great massacre, and they come to identify with the preceding generation of Holocaust victims and survivors. This viewpoint, Young (1988) suggests, creates a situation in which Israelis perceive themselves as victims and precludes positive action other than reflexive violence to forestall the second great massacre (pp. 136–37).

In this instance, memory has become a yoke. Instead of building a future on the basis of past memories, the past has been held up as the model for the future; the dream is in danger of evaporating and "the Holocaust is well on its way to becoming the defining feature of Israeli society" (Friedman 1990, p. 281). This leads Israelis to see themselves as "weak victims" who cannot see their strength and remain unaware of, or unwilling to consider, alternative options (p. 283). Instead of realizing that they have the strength to compromise, instead of looking to the future, Friedman asserts, Israelis are caught in the past. He warns: "A country that sees itself living on the lip of a volcano, or inside the eerie hallways of Yad Vashem, doesn't plan for the future and doesn't think about bold initiatives. It only holds on for dear life."

In fact, the danger of memory is that we may begin to view past and present events as the same. Every large-scale mass destruction of human life may appear to be like the Holocaust. Every dictator, at least those one does not like, is another Hitler. If, however, an enemy is a Hitler, then compromise is out of the question—how do you negotiate with the person who engineered the killing of 6 million people? Furthermore, the comparison with Hitler is quite selective. If the leaders of a state wish to create the perception that another leader is an enemy, then they label that leader as Hitler-like. If, however, they wish to promote a more positive image, they use other comparisons. This tactic was perhaps most clearly seen in 1991 during the Persian Gulf War when President George Bush compared Iraqi leader Saddam Hussein to Hitler. Once such a comparison is made, one's policy initiatives are severely limited, and if the comparison is accepted, it is likely that the only politically viable option is to engage in military action designed to destroy the Hitler-like dictator. The problem, of course, is that events are not the same; it is by recognizing both the similarities and the differences that we might begin to see patterns that allow us to understand and hopefully prevent similar future miscalculations.

MEMORY AND THE "LESSONS" OF HISTORY

As we have seen in this section, memory and history are closely tied to politics. History is reconstructed memory, and states and individuals use and manipulate it to serve sometimes less than noble ends. The importance of memory and history, as Liddell Hart (1971) has argued, is as a "*warning* sign" (p. 115). In other words, "History can show us what to *avoid*, even if it does not teach us what to do—by showing the most common mistakes that mankind is apt to make and to repeat." History is a "universal experience—infinitely longer, wider, and more varied than any individual's experience" (p. 15). The idea that history teaches lessons is, however, misleading. History cannot teach—people learn or they do not. If they examine the collective record of historical memory and try to understand what happened and why, perhaps they will begin to see connections, or perhaps not; perhaps they avoid seeing connections to protect themselves from knowledge that might cause them to reevaluate much of their present surroundings. According to Isenberg (1985), the "ultimate importance of history, then, must lie in its immediate, personal relationship to the single, questing, human mind" (pp. 210–11).

The preservation of memory and the writing and studying of history are halting steps. If people build the present and the future on the basis of past memories, they must be careful not to construct that present and future in such a fashion as to guarantee that the past will be repeated and that in fact nothing is learned. The past is always being turned into moral lessons by groups interested in using it to legitimize their agenda or justify their actions. If, on the other hand, memory serves as the basis for, and ultimately gives way to, hope—to positive attempts to resolve disputes and solve critical problems—then perhaps human beings may begin to undo the vast amount of destruction they have visited upon each other over the centuries. Obligations that look backward as opposed to forward do not help in this task. Thus, while the preservation of the past is important, the utilitarian obligation is to the future. This movement toward a better future is often impeded by fixating on the past and, in particular, by creating a romanticized past.

The admonition to "never forget" has become a repetitious theme, but it has become clear to me over time that not forgetting is not in itself the solution. Although simply remembering may be necessary as a start, memory must serve as a foundation upon which to build a humane, just, and peaceful future.

The mythological reconstruction of the past involves a retrospective falsification of the real past that leads to a form of disappointment or disillusionment with the present and lack of hope for the future. Everyday life is seemingly threatened by past evils, and one must continually look to the past to learn how to thwart those evils. Both nations and individuals "renew their strength and their sense of identity by returning to the myth of the noble ambitions associated with their foundation" (Hampshire 1989, p. 151). Memory, then, is associated with the formation of individual and political or national identity, and the policies individuals or nations follow may be destructive or constructive. Nietzsche, in fact, divided people according to their outlook on history into life-denying or life-affirming types and argued that there were as "many different versions of history as there were projects for winning a sense of self in individual human beings" (White 1973, p. 332). Since memory is so susceptible to manipulation, and since individuals may simply have different recollections of the same or similar events, history written on the basis of memory or observation cannot function as a safeguard against war and fanaticism. Hampshire (1989) argues that such safeguards "must be found outside the historical process and the teleologies that are imputed to it" (p. 137). In other words, the idea of history as some inexorable process moving toward the perfection of the human species and an era of justice and tranquillity is another of those figments of the human imagination wholly without precedent.

In fact, events such as the Holocaust demonstrate that throughout history most religious and political ideologies "have had, as part of their creed, the belief that they are destined in the long run to triumph over the infidels. The slaughter-house of history will be finally redeemed when one true morality— Christian, Jacobin, Communist—reigns everywhere and all heresies and deviations are suppressed" (Hampshire 1989, p. 136). This perspective appears throughout history as all ideologies claim truth, and we must turn to the question posed earlier: Are we destined to play out succeeding scenarios of memory and destruction? In short, why is there no change if we have so many memories of so many destructive acts?

In order to reach some understanding of this question, it is necessary to turn our attention to some of the ways memory has been constructed—the kinds of texts in which memory of genocide and political atrocity in general, and the Holocaust in particular, are located. The examination of several different types of texts, or forms of writing about these topics, will provide some insight into how memory is constructed and transmitted. It is important to study how we have studied death.

TWO

Studying Death

1

Constructing Memory

SURVIVORS AND THEORISTS

Many different ways exist to study a topic such as genocide or a particular genocide such as the Holocaust. Among the possibilities are some of the major tools used to construct the memory of an event, including eyewitness testimony and memoirs; fiction; film; history texts, although, as we have seen above, they are influenced by images of time and paradigm; political science and/or sociology; psychology and psychiatry; philosophy, including religion and ethics; and museums. Many books summarizing some of these techniques and examining different genocides have been written. The best recent works include Chalk and Jonassohn (1990), which also includes a brief review of the literature, Charny (1982), Fein (1979; 1992), Kuper (1982), Lerner (1992), Lifton (1986), Lifton and Markusen (1990), and Staub (1989).

In this section, I examine the construction, explanation, and transmission of memory. Construction will be explored through the explication of two very different accounts of surviving incarceration in a Nazi camp. Explanation will be viewed via a critique of positivist social science and an examination of an alternative form of analysis, that of Robert Jay Lifton. I analyze transmission by deciphering how individuals develop the motivation to kill, how created memories are transmitted into the minds of individual human beings, how they become part of the collective memory of a group, society, culture, or nation, and what influence this has on a person's behavior.

As I argued in section 1, when people write history—when eyewitnesses or survivors write their memoirs and record what they believe they have been able to drag from the depths of their souls or when a social scientist analyzes data and draws conclusions—they are constructing, reconstructing, or trying to explain memory, and at the same time, they are affecting the future. How the past is portrayed influences how we think. Therefore, adopting one or another technique of constructing, explaining, and transmitting memory can have very different implications.

Since, as I have argued previously, personal memory is such an integral part of historical memory, and since eyewitness and survivor memoirs are among the basic building blocks of history, I first examine, in detail, two examples of eyewitness testimony. I then contrast the study of such accounts with the method used in modern, positivistic social science. My basic argument is that social science, based on the model of physics or other positivist assumptions, dehumanizes human memory, while the testimony of witnesses and survivors adds a human dimension to tedious facts and obscure variables. Only this human dimension has the possibility of establishing in the audience an empathetic identification that might lead to a determination to prevent such horrible events from reoccurring.

In short, one way of making the study of death a life-preserving activity is to inspire empathy for the survivor in those who are the inheritors of the memory. I have found that when I teach my course on "The Politics of Genocide," my students are moved not by definitions and sociological accounts, although these are covered, but by the writings of survivors such as Primo Levi and Elie Wiesel and by films such as *The Warsaw Ghetto* and *Shoah*. The goals of reaching an audience, enhancing public understanding, and stimulating respect for memory may be obstructed by esoteric variables and incomprehensible definitions.

Fortunately, it is not necessary for scholars interested in studying genocide and human rights issues to forsake humanity for method. Social scientific rationality may be usefully contrasted with a focus on human beings. People—

perpetrators, victims, and the people of the future, the children, who must understand and feel the torment of the victim and the injustice of oppression and violence—must be the central focus.

My own view is that we learn much more about life from the memory of those who have survived mass death than from any social science text. People who have struggled to survive and bear witness to evil are heroes and prophets. Survivors preserve life by testifying, and perhaps suffering, often speaking, in the manner of the Just Man in the tale recounted by Elie Wiesel, to unhearing ears.

> One of the Just Men came to Sodom, determined to save its inhabitants from sin and punishment. Night and day he walked the streets and markets preaching against greed and theft, falsehood and indifference. In the beginning, people listened and smiled ironically. Then they stopped listening: he no longer even amused them. The killers went on killing, the wise kept silent, as if there were no Just Man in their midst.
>
> One day a child, moved by compassion for the unfortunate preacher, approached him with these words: "Poor stranger. You shout, you expend yourself body and soul; don't you see that it is hopeless?"
>
> "Yes, I see," answered the Just Man.
>
> "Then why do you go on?"
>
> "I'll tell you why. In the beginning, I thought I could change man. Today, I know I cannot. If I still shout today, if I still scream, it is to prevent man from ultimately changing me." (Wiesel 1978, pp. 94–95)

In short, survivors function as prophets, warning a seemingly unconscious humanity of what it does not wish to hear and forcing confrontation with what it may not wish to see. Survivors are those who have "encountered, been exposed to or witnessed death" and have remained alive. Very often they are witnesses to grotesque inhumanity who transmit memory of a qualitatively different experience. Their memory and the history written from it are among our only weapons in "the struggle of memory against forgetting" (Kundera 1981, p. 3), and we must listen to them.

Listen, for example, as Elie Wiesel describes, in *Night*, the punishment of a young boy suspected of participating in blowing up a power station at one of the industrial plants at Auschwitz. The boy is sentenced to death and is to be hung in front of the entire camp:

> The three victims mounted together onto the chairs. The three necks were placed at the same moment within the nooses.
>
> "Long live liberty!" cried the two adults.
>
> But the child was silent.

"Where is God? Where is He?" someone behind me asked.

At a sign from the head of the camp, the three chairs tipped over.

Total silence throughout the camp. On the horizon the sun was setting.

"Bare your heads!" yelled the head of the camp. His voice was raucous. We were weeping.

"Cover your heads!"

Then the march past began. The two adults were no longer alive. Their tongues hung swollen, blue-tinged. But the third rope was still moving; being so light, the child was still alive. . . .

For more than half an hour he stayed there, struggling between life and death, dying in slow agony under our eyes. And we had to look him full in the face. He was still alive when I passed in front of him. His tongue was still red, his eyes were not yet glazed.

Behind me, I heard the same man asking:

"Where is God now?"

And I heard a voice within me answer him:

"Where is He? Here He is—He is hanging here on this gallows. . . ."

That night the soup tasted of corpses. (Wiesel 1960, pp. 61–62)

Listen to Primo Levi relate how he survived and what he thinks his survival means as we examine the construction of memory through the firsthand narrative of a writer who survived incarceration at Auschwitz.

5

Primo Levi

Recording Memory and Teaching Humanity

Primo Levi, who survived Auschwitz, was a writer of great humanity and sensitivity whose life was devoted to bearing witness to the past and continuing horrors of the twentieth century. By his very existence, Levi forces any observer of the continuing crisis of genocide and mass murder to pause to ask the question: Is it possible for great humanity and sensitive intelligence to survive the recurring memory of inhumanity and massive destruction of human life, both actual and potential, which appear to dominate the twentieth century?[1]

1. Indeed, Roger Smith portrays the twentieth century as "an age of politically sanctioned mass murder, of collective, premeditated death intended to serve the ends of the

Primo Levi's life and writings cast a harsh but moving and compassionate light on our troubled and troubling epoch. One of the tragic heroes of this century, Levi does not fulfill the traditional image of the hero as a person who gains martyrdom through death (Des Pres 1977, p. 3). Rather, Levi's life validates the persuasive arguments put forth by Des Pres and Lifton (1987), who note that the successful struggle to survive and transmit the memory of evil is an act of heroism. The survivor preserves life in order to help shape the historical memory—in short, to tell unconscious humanity what it does not wish to hear and to live a life, and in Levi's case to write words, that might force confrontation with the guilt of indifference and might compel historians to incorporate the survivor's memory and vision into contemporary human chronology.

LIFE AND WORK

Primo Levi was a writer of immense humanity whose powerful evocation of human character in inhuman settings establishes him as a true teacher, one of the just from whom we are able to learn much about the human spirit. The details of Levi's life are examined in Howe (1986), Levi (1984), and Hughes (1983).

Born in Turin, Italy, in 1919, Levi was raised in a middle-class assimilated Jewish family. As a young man, he studied to be a chemist, receiving his doctorate in 1941. Following the Fascist takeover of Italy, Levi joined a group of partisans in September 1943. He was arrested in December and was deported to Auschwitz in 1944. His stories of his year in Auschwitz and his adventures in returning home form the core of his literary achievement. Their particular power derives from Levi's ability to evoke and describe human character and from, in the words of Irving Howe, his "special gift for the vignette" (1986, p. 12). This gift is apparent throughout his work, but never more so than when Levi reflects on how he came to write about his experiences.

In the Afterword to the 1986 combined edition of his first two works, *Survival in Auschwitz* and *The Reawakening,* Levi discusses his first book (1986c, pp. 375–97). He writes that *Survival in Auschwitz* has a destiny, a distant "birth certificate," in the words, "I write what I would never dare tell anyone" (p. 375). Auschwitz gave Levi the need to tell his story, a need "so strong" that he began describing his experience in the camp, "in that German

---

state. It is an age of genocide in which . . . men, women, and children . . . have had their lives taken because the state thought this desirable" (1987, p. 21).

laboratory laden with freezing cold, the war, and vigilant eyes; and yet I knew that I would not be able under any circumstances to hold on to those haphazardly scribbled notes, and that I must throw them away immediately because if they were found they would be considered an act of espionage and would cost me my life." The memories, however, "burned so intensely" that within a few months of his return to Italy, he wrote *Survival in Auschwitz*. Levi's experience of a unique, consequential, and emotion-provoking event caused his memory to remain clearly etched in his psyche.

The story of the book's publication is itself dramatic: "The manuscript was turned down by a number of important publishers; it was accepted in 1947 by a small publisher who printed only 2,500 copies and then folded. So this first book of mine fell into oblivion for many years: perhaps also because in all of Europe those were difficult times of mourning and reconstruction and the public did not want to return in memory to the painful years of the war that had just ended" (1986c, p. 375). It was not until 1958 that a large publisher, Einaudi, republished *Survival in Auschwitz*. Since then, the book has achieved public and critical acclaim and has been translated into eight languages and adapted for radio and theater. It is an amazingly humane account of inhumanity.

Captured on December 13, 1943, at the age of twenty-four, Primo Levi describes himself at that time as "with little wisdom, no experience, and a decided tendency—encouraged by the life of segregation forced on me for the previous four years of the racial laws—to live in an unrealistic world of my own, a world in-habited by civilized Cartesian phantoms" (1986c, p. 9). At Auschwitz he was confronted with another experience, out of which he emerged with wisdom. That he would retain his humanity despite having, in his own words, "reached the bottom," is a tribute to this great writer.

> Then for the first time we became aware that our language lacks words to express this offense, the demolition of a man. In a moment, with almost prophetic intuition, the reality was revealed to us: we had reached the bottom. It is not possible to sink lower than this; no human condition is more miserable than this, nor could it conceivably be so. Nothing belongs to us anymore; they have taken away our clothes, our shoes, even our hair; if we speak, they will not listen to us, and if they listen, they will not understand. They will even take away our name; and if we want to keep it, we will have to find in ourselves the strength to do so, to manage somehow so that behind the name something of us, of us as we were, still remains. (p. 22)

Thus Levi began his experience of the ultimate dehumanization. It was the most complete example in history of a program designed by human beings to dehumanize other human beings, to eradicate their being and the memory of their being, and to prepare for their ultimate extermination.

In order to understand this process, it is important to hear Levi's description. He continues:

> Imagine now a man who is deprived of everyone he loves, and at the same time of his house, his habits, his clothes; in short, of everything he possesses: he will be a hollow man, reduced to suffering and needs, forgetful of dignity and restraint, for he who loses all often easily loses himself. He will be a man whose life or death can be lightly decided with no sense of human affinity, in the most fortunate of cases, on the basis of a pure judgement of utility. It is in this way that one can understand the double sense of the term "extermination camp," and it is now clear what we seek to express with the phrase: "to lie on the bottom." (1986c, p. 23)

So Primo Levi descended to hell and began adjusting for survival. Even in this hell, people, Levi notes, "gain a certain equilibrium after a few weeks" (1986c, p. 51). Such an equilibrium relies on humanity's ability to adjust to the most horrible and degrading circumstances, and it is an equilibrium punctuated by tantalizing dreams:

> One can hear the sleepers breathing and snoring; some groan and speak. Many lick their lips and move their jaws. They are dreaming of eating; this is also a collective dream. It is a pitiless dream which the creator of the Tantalus myth must have known. You not only see the food, you feel it in your hands, distinct and concrete, you are aware of its rich and striking smell: someone in the dream even holds it up to your lips, but every time a different circumstance intervenes to prevent the consummation of the act. Then the dream dissolves and breaks up into its elements, but it reforms itself immediately after and begins again, similar, yet changed; and this without pause, for all of us, every night and for the whole of our sleep. (p. 55)

Levi goes on to describe the continuing nightmare of the days of useless and grueling work; the cruelty and inhumanity of the Nazis and the guards; the chemistry examination that ultimately allowed him to work as a chemist, in a warm laboratory, and helped him survive; and, finally, the liberation, or more precisely, the German desertion of the camp. Through it all, he sketches a series of marvelously human characters. For example, he writes of his "friendship" with Lorenzo:

> The story of my relationship with Lorenzo is both long and short, quiet and enigmatic; it is the story of a time and condition now effaced from

every present reality, and so I do not think it can be understood except in the manner in which we nowadays understand events of legends or of the remotest history.

In concrete terms it amounts to little: an Italian civilian worker brought me a piece of bread and the remainder of his ration every day for six months; he gave me a vest of his, full of patches; he wrote a postcard on my behalf to Italy and brought me the reply. For all this he neither asked nor accepted any reward, because he was good and simple and did not think that one did good for a reward. (1986c, p. 109)

Imagine in Auschwitz a "good and simple" person who did not operate on the principles of selfishness so routinely institutionalized in contemporary society and so necessary for survival in extraordinary circumstances. Levi believes that "it was really due to Lorenzo that I am alive today; and not so much for his material aid, as for his having constantly reminded me by his presence, by his natural and plain manner of being good, that there still existed a just world outside our own, something and someone still pure and whole, not corrupt, not savage, extraneous to hatred and terror; something difficult to define, a remote possibility of good, but for which it was worth surviving" (1986c, p. 111).

Lorenzo appears again in Levi's moving book, *Moments of Reprieve: A Memoir of Auschwitz* (1987). Here Levi paints a more complete portrait and adds to the earlier story. The soup Lorenzo brought Levi and his friends provided additional calories that allowed them to survive. It was "weird soup. In it we found plum nuts, salami peels, once even the wing of a sparrow with all its feathers; another time a scrap of Italian newspaper" (1987, p. 155).

Both Lorenzo and Levi returned to their homes in Italy after the war, and Levi went to Lorenzo's town "to see him again and bring him a woolen sweater for the winter" (1987, p. 159). Levi found a man who was "mortally tired, a weariness without remedy. Lorenzo no longer worked as a mason but went from farm to farm with a small cart buying and selling scrap iron. He wanted no more rules or bosses or schedules. The little he earned he spent at the tavern; he did not drink as a vice but to get away from the world. He had seen the world, he didn't like it, he felt it was going to ruin. To live no longer interested him."

Levi attempted to help Lorenzo by finding him a mason's job, but Lorenzo refused. Finally he told Levi "something which in Auschwitz I hadn't suspected." "Down there he helped not only me. He had other proteges, Italian and not, but he thought it right not to tell me about it: we are in this world to do good, not to boast about it. In 'Suiss' he had been a rich man, at least compared to us, and had been able to help us, but now it was over; he had no more opportunities" (1987, pp. 159–60). Having lived through Auschwitz, Lorenzo was adrift. He became ill, and after Levi took him to a hospital, he ran away. "He was assured and coherent in his rejection of life. He was found nearly dead a few days later, and died in the hospital alone. He, who was not a survivor, had died of the survivor's disease" (p. 160).

Neither a military hero nor a political leader, Lorenzo was actually much more—he was among those moral men whose lives enhance ours by their simple existence. Lorenzo and Levi also demonstrate the unique power of memory, the ways in which an event such as incarceration in Auschwitz can be so powerful that memory of it never fades and, in fact, influences our actions from the time it occurs. Lorenzo's memory may have killed him, and Levi's memory and his realization that the world had changed very little may have eventually led to his death as well. It is the power of these memories that moved Levi to write about his experiences. Without Levi's sense of humanity expressed through his power of description, we would have never become acquainted with Lorenzo or with the other rich characters who populate Levi's writing and would, therefore, have been deprived of this powerful building block of history.

Surviving by luck, chance, perseverance, and intelligence, as well as with the help of Lorenzo, Levi began his extraordinary journey back to humanity and back to Italy. The return to humanity started in the deserted camp. Abandoned by the Nazis and confined to the infectious disease ward, where they were waiting for the Russian troops, Levi and two companions repair a broken window and secure and light a stove; as the

> stove began to spread its heat, something seemed to relax in everyone, and at that moment Towarowski (a Franco-Pole of twenty-three, typhus) proposed to the others that each of them offer a slice of bread to us three who had been working. And so it was agreed.
>
> Only a day before a similar event would have been inconceivable. The law of the Lager [concentration camp] said: "eat your own bread, and if you can, that of your neighbor," and left no room for gratitude. It really meant that the Lager was dead.
>
> It was the first human gesture that occurred among us. I believe that moment can be dated as the beginning of the change by which we who had not died slowly changed from Haftlinge [inmates or prisoners] to men again. (1986c, p. 145)

The success of *Survival in Auschwitz* encouraged Levi to write *The Reawakening*. Levi had traveled directly to Auschwitz aboard a train; his journey back to his home in Turin, chronicled in *The Reawakening*, was much less direct. Often tragic, sometimes comic, it took Levi through Eastern Europe, to the Soviet Union, and then back through Eastern Europe to Italy. Once again, he fills his story with remarkable and seemingly improbable characters and events.

The vignettes in the book can be prophetic and moving, such as the scene in which Levi and his companions happen upon a group of twelve German soldiers in the Soviet Union, dressed in rags, without their military hierarchy:

> They saw us, and some of them moved towards us with the uncertain steps of automata. They asked for bread; not in their own language, but in Russian. We refused, because our bread was precious. But Daniele did not refuse; Daniele, whose strong wife, whose brother, parents and not less than thirty relatives had been killed by the Germans; Daniele, who was the sole survivor of the raid on the Venice ghetto, and who from the day of the liberation had fed on grief, took out a piece of bread, showed it to these phantoms and placed it on the ground. But he insisted that they come to get it on all fours; which they did, docilely. (1986c, p. 286)

Many of the people characterized in *The Reawakening* exude great strength as they find mechanisms to adapt to their liberation. They appear, disappear, and reappear. They enter Levi's life, influence his vision of the world, and then depart, never to be seen again. Through it all, Levi maintains a sense of humor, relating some events as almost comical.

In one such incident, Levi and his companion, Cesare, arrive in rags late at night in a small Russian village of about thirty houses. They wish to exchange with the Russian peasants six plates for a chicken. The peasants speak no Italian and Levi and Cesare speak no Russian. Cesare, unable to accept the fact that not everyone speaks Italian, becomes increasingly angry as he attempts to negotiate with the Russian peasants:

> Was it possible that it was so difficult to understand what a chicken is, and that we wanted it in exchange for six plates? A chicken, one of those beasts that go around pecking, scratching and saying "coccode-e-eh"; and rather half-heartedly, glowering and sullen, he put on a very second rate imitation of the habits of the chicken, crouching on the ground, scraping first with one foot and then with the other and pecking here and there with his hands shaped like a wedge. Between one oath and the other, he also cried "coccode-e-eh." . . .
>
> Hopping mad by now, Cesare even tried to lay an egg, pouring far-fetched insults on them all the while, so rendering the meaning of his performance even more obscure. (1986c, pp. 299–300)

Finally, after twenty months, after Auschwitz, after an extremely difficult journey, Levi and his companions cross the border into Italy. Levi describes the moment: "Our less tired companions celebrated with a cheerful uproar; Leonardo and I remained lost in a silence crowded with memories. Of 650, our number when we had left, three of us were returning. And how much had we lost in those twenty months? What should we find at home? How much of ourselves had been eroded, extinguished?" (1986c, p. 372).

Unlike most other survivors, when Levi arrived at his home on October 19, 1945, he found his house still standing and all of his family alive. He appeared

swollen, bearded and in rags, and had difficulty in making myself recognized. I found my friends full of life, the warmth of secure meals, the solidity of daily work, the liberating joy of recounting my story. I found a large clean bed, which in the evening (a moment of terror) yielded softly under my weight. But only after many months did I lose the habit of walking with my glance fixed to the ground, as if searching for something to eat or to pocket hastily or to sell for bread; and a dream full of horror has still not ceased to visit me, at sometimes frequent, sometimes longer, intervals. (1986c, p. 373)

People respond to horrific experiences in many different ways. Some withdraw into silence as they attempt to block out all memory. Others become bitter and vengeful. Levi's response was to continue to try to untangle the puzzles of life and to devote the remainder of his life to communicating his memories and ideas to the rest of us. His struggles with his past and with the events of the late twentieth century are detailed in his most recent books. He struggled not only to continue to survive but also to maintain his humane perspective. His memory of the experience of the concentration camp structured his perception of life in the late twentieth century, a fact that is evident in his novel, *If Not Now, When?* (1986).

A story of the Jewish resistance in Eastern Europe, the book chronicles the adventures of Jewish partisans who made their way from Russia to Italy to Palestine. Levi calls upon his own journey from Auschwitz to the Soviet Union and back to Italy in creating characters and describing places in the novel. He portrays the partisans as

ghostly bands, cloudlike bands: here today, blowing up the railroad track, and forty kilometers away tomorrow, looting the silos of Kolkhoz. And the faces were never the same. Russian faces, Ukrainian, Polish; Mongols, who had come from no telling where; Jews, too, yes, some; and women, and a kaleidoscope of uniforms: Soviets dressed as Germans, in police uniforms;

Soviets in tatters, still with their Red Army tunics; even some German deserters. . . . How many? Who knows? Fifty here, three hundred there, groups that formed and broke up: alliances, quarrels, sometimes even shooting. (1986a, p. 39)

It is the people—seemingly improbable yet believable—who give to Levi's tale its power and who sustain the narrative. *If Not Now, When?* is a hesitantly hopeful book. Its characters fight to exert their humanity and not only survive but also create, in the end, new life. At the conclusion of the book, a baby is born, but Levi wonders what sort of world the child will face. After one of the most horrible periods in human history, the new life emerges into an even more threatening world. On the day of birth, "the newspaper, consisting of a single sheet, bore a very big headline, whose meaning he couldn't understand. That newspaper bore the date of Tuesday 7 August 1945 and carried the news of the first atomic bomb, dropped on Hiroshima" (1986a, p. 346).

To a survivor of Auschwitz, nuclear weapons must have come as a horrible shock of recognition. People who every day had faced the possibility of extinction by gas and fire were now "liberated" into a world in which all people were confronted by that possibility. Faced with this realization, what does a survivor, or any person, do? How does one cope with the horrible possibility that, after surviving one Holocaust, another awaits? Can memory serve as a warning? Can it function as an inoculation against further destruction? Even in the face of repeated mass death, we all cling, perhaps naively, to the hope that this will be the last incident, that this warning will be heeded. Levi certainly hoped, as he continued to dig into his past, to reconstruct a memorable cast of characters to bear witness to the seemingly perpetual crisis of the twentieth century. Levi's sense of character, his pleasure, his wit and joy of living come together in his collection of stories, *The Periodic Table* (1984).

The Periodic Table is filled with the poetry of memory brought to life via the analogy of Dmitry Mendeleyev's periodic table. For Levi, the elements of the periodic table serve as metaphors for people and experiences or play an important role in actual events in his life. The book contains incisive personality profiles, demonstrating Levi's ability to describe with great depth in a few words. Yet, as with all of his work, *The Periodic Table* is more than a book of individual profiles. In Levi's deft hands, chemistry becomes a metaphor for life and an avenue for philosophical rumination. For example, zinc is not, according to Levi, "an element which says much to the imagination, it is gray and its salts are colorless, it is not toxic, nor does it produce striking chromatic reactions; in short, it is a boring metal" (1984, p. 33). Yet its reaction to acid, especially in a pure state, prompts Levi to consider "two conflicting philosophical conclusions: the praise of purity which protects from evil like a coat of mail; the praise of impurity, which gives rise to changes, in other words, to life" (p. 34). After dismissing the first philosophical conclusion as "disgustingly moralistic," Levi lingers on the second, which he finds more "congenial." "In order for the wheel to turn, for life to be lived, impurities are needed, and the impurities of impurities in the soil, too, as is known, if it is to be fertile. Dissension, diversity, the grain of salt and mustard are needed. Fascism does not want them, forbids them, and that's why you're not a Fascist; it wants everybody to be the same and you are not" (p. 34).

Vivid personalities and philosophical speculations leap from these pages and are placed within the context of important historical events. The rise of Fascist states, the ascent to power of Hitler and Mussolini, the accompanying anti-Semitism and ultimate attempt to destroy the European Jews, are all part of Levi's story. Finally, he brings events full circle.

In the next to the last section of *The Periodic Table*, "Vanadium," Levi recounts an incident that occurred while he was working as a chemist for a varnish company. After the company received an apparently defective shipment of the element vanadium from a German company, Levi contacted one of the company's chemists. He began to suspect that this man might be the same person who was his superior in Auschwitz and who, when Levi arrived for his assignment in one of the camp's labs, gave him a pair of shoes. Levi eventually learned that his suspicions were correct.

The German chemist maintained that he did not know that Jews were being killed at Auschwitz, when, in fact, over 1 million were exterminated. He did not ask questions, utilizing, as Levi states, the "common technique" of trying to know as little as possible. He "had not demanded explanations from anyone, not even from himself, although on clear days the flames of the crematorium were visible" (1984, p. 221). He was, as were most people, "neither infamous nor a hero; after filtering off the rhetoric and the lies in good or bad faith there remained a typically gray human specimen, one of the not so few one-eyed men in the kingdom of the blind" (pp. 221–22). The chemist asked to meet Levi, perhaps hoping for forgiveness or for salvation. Eight days after Levi agreed to see him, but before the meeting occurred, "Doktor Lothar Muller" died unexpectedly at age sixty. Levi describes him as "honest and unarmed." "A world in which everyone would be like him, that is, honest and unarmed would be tolerable, but this is an unreal world. In the real world the armed exist, they build Auschwitz, and the honest and unarmed clear the road for them; therefore every German must answer for Auschwitz, indeed every man, and after Auschwitz it is no longer permissible to be unarmed" (p. 223).

Despite the repeated warnings of Primo Levi and other survivors, much of the world appears to remain unarmed, unhearing, and uncaring. So, forty-two years after surviving Auschwitz, Primo Levi threw himself down the stairwell of his apartment building in Turin. Having devoted his life to the preservation of memory and the fight against evil, Levi could not help but despair as he watched the events of the late twentieth century. Robert J. Lifton (1987, pp. 5, 224) has, in fact, written that suicide in the twentieth century, with its massive destructive forces, may well be a "quest for the future," a search for meaning born of despair. According to Lifton: "In despair, one feels unable to maintain or envision any larger human connections of significance—any ongoing link in the great chain of being" (p. 224). Despair is fed by "radically negative expectations of the future," and the person experiencing despair may perceive that the only way to create a future is by taking his or her own life (p. 225).

As I noted earlier, Levi began to signal his increasingly negative expectations in the moving conclusion to *If Not Now, When?* That he was haunted by the past and anguished by negative expectations for the future is most clearly revealed in *The Drowned and the Saved* (1988). Levi's goal, as he states it, is "to answer the most urgent question, the question which torments all those who have happened to read our accounts: 'How much of the concentration camp world is dead and will not return, like slavery and the dueling code? How much is back or is coming back? What can each of us do so that in this world pregnant with threats at least this threat will be nullified?'" (1988, p. 21). When he casts his gaze upon the technology and efficiency of destruction massed in the hands of the modern nation-state, his vision is bleak because he sees that the "pressure that a modern totalitarian state can exercise over the individual is frightful" (p. 29). Given this reality, Levi asks how secure we, at this moment, may be when "we have been told, and there's no reason to doubt it, that for every human being on the planet a quantity of nuclear explosives is stored equal to three or four tons of TNT. If even only 1 percent of it were used there would immediately be tens of millions dead, and frightening genetic damage to the entire human species, indeed to all life on earth, with the exception perhaps of the insects" (pp. 165–66).

Confronted with this terrifying possibility, face-to-face with the suggestion that, as the physicist Isidor Rabi put it, "the nations are now lined up like people before the ovens of Auschwitz, while we are trying to make the ovens more efficient" (quoted in Herken 1987, p. 346), how could a survivor of the original Auschwitz not despair for the future? What, Levi asks, are any of us doing to prevent the horrible repetition? "So then? Are today's fears more or less founded than the fears of that time? When it comes to the future, we are just as blind as our fathers. Swiss and Swedes have their anti-nuclear shelters, but what will they find when the come out into the open? There are Polynesia, New Zealand, Tierra del Fuego, the Antarctic: perhaps they will remain unharmed. Obtaining a passport and entry visa is much easier than it was then, so why aren't we going? Why aren't we leaving our country? Why aren't we fleeing 'before'?" (1988, p. 166).

How fitting to turn back on *all* of us the questions so often asked of the Jews: "Why did you stay in Germany?" "Why did you not fight back or resist?" "Why did you not die as a martyr instead of living to write words we do not wish to hear?" And so Primo Levi died because, as he wrote, "If we had to and were able to suffer the sufferings of everyone, we could not live" (1988, p. 56). He nevertheless left behind a chronicle of memory, a landscape peopled with remarkable characters. Levi introduces us to these people and invites us into their lives and into his life. He provides an example, leaving us with a vision of kindliness and compassion, of humanity, and a warning to be considered seriously: "Few countries can be considered immune to a future tide of violence generated by intolerance, lust for power, economic difficulties, religious or political fanaticism, and racialist attritions. It is therefore necessary to sharpen our senses, distrust the prophets, the enchanters, those who speak and write 'beautiful words' unsupported by intelligent reasons" (p. 200).

As I once again read Levi's words and find myself transmitted into his memory, I cannot escape the lingering doubt that such powerful emotional expressions of experience can be communicated by the methods of modern social science. As I think about Primo Levi, I find myself growing ever sadder—sad because I will never again be introduced to new people in his mind; sad because I can no longer look forward to more words of wisdom and humanity; sad because he is dead. Even though I never met Primo Levi, I was comforted that his humanity improbably survived the most dehumanizing experiences. Now, I wonder, how? How could such a person survive Auschwitz? How could he "cope" with life after Auschwitz—with the continuing destructive evil of this century? How could he write so humanely about his fellows? What else was deep in his memory? Did he really exist, or did we create him to represent the exception that enables us to grasp at straws of hope? Was he our Lorenzo? Although I miss him, I know I will never forget the words he has written, especially the last paragraph in *Moments of Reprieve*, which is repeated in *The Drowned and the Saved*: "Like Rumkowski, we too are so dazzled by power and money as to forget our essential fragility, forget that all of us are in the ghetto, that the ghetto is fenced in, that beyond the fence stand the lords of death, and not far away the train is waiting" (1987, p. 172; 1988, p. 69).

Testimony or memory like that left to us by Primo Levi is, as Langer (1991) notes, a "narrative which makes possible the birth of history for succeeding generations" (p. 108). It is not an itemized past, but it presents a "continuity of consciousness" within which an individual may recognize himself or herself "as a continuing identity," possibly leading to self-awareness (Oakeshott 1983, p. 15). The memory transmitted by Primo Levi may provide ensuing generations with more than simply a version of history. As Smith (1992a) eloquently asserts:

> Recognition and remembrance involve more than regard for truth: they express compassion for those who have suffered, respect for their dignity as persons, and revolt against the injustice done to them. In the deepest sense, recognition and remembrance are related not only to what happened, but to questions of who *we* are, what *society* is, and how life and community can be protected against visions that would destroy both. To remember those who have come before us is an expression of ourselves—our care, our capacity to join in a community, our respect for other human beings. And through our capacities for memory and foresight, a community comes to include those who are living, those who have died, and those yet to be born. (p. 14)

Yet all memory is not constructed with the same "compassion for those who have suffered." In fact, when the experience of the survivor is filtered through some forms of theory, which can function as an ideological screen separating the survivor's experience from the survivor's humanity, a great deal of the compassion and humanity are removed. The memory that is thus constructed is harsh and condemning and not likely to lead to empathy and understanding. The work of Bruno Bettelheim clearly demonstrates this process.

> People still free must decide how much their "freedom" is
>
> worth: how many lies they will live by, how far they will
>
> acquiesce while their neighbors are destroyed. The choice
>
> is always there.
>
> Terrence Des Pres, *The Survivor: An Anatomy of*
>
> *Life in the Death Camps* (1976)

6

Memory and Survival

A Reconsideration of the Bettelheim–Des Pres Debate

The Bruno Bettelheim–Terrence Des Pres controversy over the meaning of surviving is important because history is often constructed on the basis of the testimony of survivors.[1] The way in which the narrative left by these survivors is viewed cannot help but influence what is written and re-membered about the event.

1. This chapter owes a great debt to the fine article by Helen Fein (1980) that covers much of the same territory. Also, unless otherwise specified, all page numbers cited in this chapter for Bettelheim are from the collection of his work, *Surviving and Other Essays* (1980), and references to Des Pres are from *The Survivor: An Anatomy of Life in the Death Camps* (1976).

Bettelheim and Des Pres differ over what it means to survive what Primo Levi refers to as "troubles." For Bettelheim, the survivor is not an example or a teacher. He condemns survivors as childlike, regressive, and passive. For Des Pres, on the other hand, the survivor is "not a metaphor, not an emblem, but an example" (p. 208). The debate between the two sheds light on the meaning of memory. In this chapter, I briefly summarize the perspectives of Bettelheim and Des Pres and conclude by pointing out how their politics influenced their interpretations.

SURVIVING AND MEMORY

As memory fades and witnesses die, history is often reconstructed and actual events recede into the background. Survivors are the eyewitnesses to historical tragedy. They speak, as Primo Levi has noted, not because they are heroes or villains but "because they know they are witnesses in a trial of planetary and epochal dimensions. They speak because (as a Yiddish saying goes) 'troubles overcome are good to tell'" (1988, p. 149).

As an eyewitness helps to establish guilt and innocence in a criminal trial, so the accounts of those who have experienced suffering help to convey the actual events, as well as the memory and meaning of them, to future generations. Without an eyewitness, there may not even be a trial, and certainly no assurance of guilt or innocence, and without the survivor, there can be no communication of the experience, no establishment in one human being of identification with those who have overcome great "troubles." Without this identification, memory is not served because the focus is abstracted. The debate over the meaning of surviving must be put back into perspective. Survivors are neither heroes nor villains—they are more like messengers, or perhaps prophets, and they have important stories to tell and warnings to issue to future generations.

Within this context, the Bettelheim–Des Pres controversy is important because, for many people, Bettelheim, who has little positive to say about survivors, remains one of the primary witnesses and interpreters of the events we collectively know as the Holocaust. According to his views, the "best" died; those who survived did so because they were selfish or because they controlled the "cruder demands" of the body; survivors identified with the aggressor or cooperated with the SS; and survivors regressed to childlike behavior and were passive. These interpretations are obviously influenced by the psychoanalytic, partially Freudian, perspective through which Bettelheim views events. Earlier I argued that the paradigm adopted by a historian influences his or her interpretations. Bettelheim is an excellent example of the fact that this is also true for a witness and for those adopting a less historical, more psychological approach.

PSYCHOANALYTIC THEORY AND BETTELHEIM'S VIEW OF THE SURVIVOR

Bettelheim accepts Freud's notion of a "death drive" and argues that Hitler "created a death mania" (p. 100). Like many others whose view of history is based on such assumptions, Bettelheim believes this drive dominates all others. As these can never be more than assumptions, they must be made explicit since they become the foundations upon which historical events are reconstructed. They reveal perceptions concerning the nature of human beings, and they fall into two categories: humans are either bad or good—they have either a dominant death drive or a dominant life drive. But psychoanalytic theory, as Des Pres notes, is intended for use in "normal" circumstances. Moreover, as Helen Fein (1980) points out, "As a psychoanalyst," Bettelheim "is best at firsthand observations of individuals, simplistic on inferring causes of collective behavior, and least reliable on historical facts and generalizations" (p. 51). The primary criticism of the psychoanalytic interpretation of the concentration camp experience is that it ignores the context.

In short, it is not valid to base observations of behavior in the camps upon "a theory of culture and man in the civilized state" (Des Pres 1976b, p. 182). Although this approach might yield insights when examining behavior in everyday society, behavior in extremely threatening situations is oriented toward different goals—toward keeping alive—and survival becomes all. Psychoanalytic theory looks for meaning hidden in the unconscious. Survivors, however, are not acting out their unconscious impulses but act as they do "because they must—the issue is always life or death—and at every moment the meaning and purpose is fully known" (p. 184).

Psychoanalytic studies often argue that prisoners in the camps regressed to an infantile stage of development because they were preoccupied with food and excretory functions. As Des Pres notes, "The fact that the survivor's situation was itself abnormal is simply ignored. That the preoccupation with food was caused by literal starvation does not count; and the fact that camp inmates were forced to live in filth is likewise overlooked" (p. 61). Bettelheim, Des Pres points out,

> does not distinguish between behavior in extremity and civilized behavior; for of course, if in civilized circumstances an adult worries about the state of his bowels, or sees the trip to the toilet as some sort of ordeal, then neurosis is evident. But in the concentration camps behavior was governed

by the immediate death-threat; action was not the index of infantile wishes but of response to hideous necessity. . . .

The fact is that prisoners were *systematically* subjected to filth. They were the deliberate target of excremental assault. (pp. 62–63)

"Excremental assault" functioned as a tactic to divide persons from each other. If morale was maintained at the "lowest possible level," at what Primo Levi referred to as "the bottom," then it was difficult for the victims to respect each other and develop solidarity. "The prisoner was made to feel subhuman, to see his self-image only in the dirt and stink of his neighbor" (Des Pres 1976b, p. 67). The SS, by contrast, were elegant and superior, and the degraded appearance of their victims made their jobs easier. It is, after all, easier to kill nonhuman-looking prisoners covered with shit and stinking; as Des Pres notes, "They looked inferior." Survival was a constant struggle to "remain visibly human" (p. 71), and the behavior exhibited by survivors was not, therefore, childlike but a "rapacious battle in one's best self-interest" (p. 178). Bettelheim, moreover, is not content to argue that the survivors were childlike. He proceeds to note that their childlike behavior led to passivity and identification with the aggressor.

PASSIVITY AND IDENTIFICATION WITH THE AGGRESSOR

In further attempting to fit his narrative into a preconceived framework, Bettelheim claims that the Jews were passive and that this passivity was due to the fact that they permitted "death tendencies to engulf them" (p. 256). One problem with his analysis is that he never examines his idea of "passivity" and never considers the psychological, political, social, and cultural forces that determine how a person responds to an extreme situation. Instead, his analysis results in the oversimplified dichotomy that persons either "had a grip on life" and resisted or submitted to the death drive and were passive (p. 256).

In condemning what he defines as passivity, Bettelheim poses as a champion of action—as a political activist guarding against any recurrence of the Holocaust. He argues that one must be prepared to face changing realities and take a firm stand, but he never confronts the complexity of what he is attempting to argue. The question of how one recognizes changing reality is paramount. Social and political events are difficult to predict, even for those who study them in detail. For example, few were able to predict the changing realities of Eastern Europe and the Soviet Union in 1989–90. Human behavior is complex and baffling and all the more so because of the complexity and vagary of memory; it is not at all as simple as Bettelheim seems to suggest.

Realities may change quickly or over long stretches of time. The Nazis built upon historic patterns of anti-Semitism, using this as the basis for their particular break with tradition. In place of the usual policy of periodic pogroms, they launched a systematic program aimed at complete annihilation. In doing so, they changed tactics in a pattern of succession, not supersession, since the Jews historically had been subjected to discrimination. What troubles Bettelheim is the fact that the seeming respite from violence when the pogroms ended, as the Jews were somewhat assimilated into German society, clouded their consciousness of the approaching dangers. Bettelheim argues that one must be able to recognize the potential hazards but identifies no warning signs.

Not only does Bettelheim believe that the intended victims failed to recognize change and were passive, but he also argues that they cooperated with the SS. Specifically, he states: "That the SS state could not have functioned without the cooperation of the victims, I can testify to from my own camp experience. The SS would have been unable to run the concentration camps without the cooperation of many of the prisoners—usually willing, in some cases reluctant, but all too often eager cooperation" (p. 269).

Lack of resistance is not necessarily cooperation and certainly not "eager cooperation." Most survivor accounts make no mention of cooperation, and Des Pres points out that what can be mistaken as cooperation was merely survival. When human beings are stripped of their humanity, of their connection with the world and with alternative views of it, they are unlikely to initiate any action at all, let alone active resistance. As Des Pres states: "To pass from civilization to extremity means to be shorn of the elaborate system of relationships—to job, class, tradition and family, to groups and institutions of every kind—which for us provides perhaps ninety percent of what we think we are" (p. 214).

The destruction of a person's self-esteem limits political behavior as he or she concentrates solely on questions of survival and reconstruction of the self. A new or different self may appear as a survival mechanism—a "concentration camp self." This process is not restricted to the concentration camps; any radical alteration in a person's normal existence, especially changes involving incarceration, may give rise to similar reactions. Cooperation, in short, is not the correct term for what happened; destruction of the previous self and severe control of behavior in forming a new self-image, as Des Pres demonstrates, are more accurate descriptions.

In addition, Bettelheim's argument that the SS state could not have functioned without the cooperation of the victims ignores the reality that total institutions and regimes often function without cooperation of inmates. Prisons, prison camps, and all sorts of mechanisms of repression and murder function very well without the cooperation of the victims. The use of force is an effective method, at least for a short time, of control. Terror works, and the first action engaged in by any total state is to eliminate potential opposition.

Consequently, while there can be little disagreement with Bettelheim's call for resistance, one must remember that the Jews were completely outgunned and outnumbered and received little assistance or support from non-Jews. Even if one agrees with his stated intent, Bettelheim's conclusion becomes a condemnation when he writes: "In retrospect, it is quite clear that only utter non-cooperation on the part of the Jews could have offered a small chance of forcing a different solution on Hitler. This conclusion is not an indictment of Jews living or dead, but an empirical finding of history. To deny or ignore it may open the door to the genocide of other races or minority groups. Active resistance arouses admiration, watching violent subjugation of the victim evokes revulsion; while passive compliance permits us to put it all out of our minds fairly soon" (p. 269).

Despite Bettelheim's denial, of course this is a condemnation. Active resistance may arouse either admiration or resentment, depending on the previous views of the resisters and which side the observer takes. Thus, when Israel in its early period was viewed as protecting itself, the use of force against the Arabs was almost universally applauded. After Israel was identified as the superior military power in the Middle East and was seen as repressing the Palestinians, however, the outlook changed so that Israel was perceived as the tyrant and oppressor. Whatever the merits of each case, these examples demonstrate that resistance does not always evoke admiration. Sometimes it evokes greater violence or an excuse to use violence, sometimes assistance, sometimes nothing. The politics of the situation is ignored by Bettelheim as he pursues a hidden agenda. His objective was not to understand or elucidate the survivor experience but to compare the "survivor's experience with the predicament of modern man in 'mass society,' in order to arrive at a critique of the latter" (p. 190). The comparison is, however, not valid because, as Des Pres notes, "no matter how disconcerting conditions become for us, they do not hinge at every moment on the issue of life and death; pain is not constant, options abound, the rule of terror and necessity is far from total. Life for us does not depend on collective action—not directly, that is; nor is death the price of visibility. Bettelheim wishes to rouse us from our sense of victimhood; but by claiming that pressure reduces men and women to children, and by praising a heroism based on death, he tends instead to support what he fears."

For Bettelheim, survival that is "not dedicated to something *else*" is "viewed with contempt" (p. 192). Meaning in life does not come from the struggle to survive but from some ideology, religion, or other metaphysical system, or, as

Des Pres states, from "any *higher* cause or goal which defines life in terms other than its own and thereby justifies existence. Survivors are suspect because they are forced to do openly, without a shred of style or fine language to cover themselves, what the rest of us do by remote control. The bias against 'mere survival' runs deep and derives its force from the fact that all of us think and act in terms of survival, but at a crucial remove and with all the masks and stratagems which cultivated men and women learn to use" (p. 193). Although Bettelheim's views on survivors appear quite unambiguous, he altered them when he turned his attention to responding to Des Pres's critique.

BETTELHEIM'S VIEW OF DES PRES

Bettelheim accuses Des Pres of misconstruing the history of the concentration camps in order to "propagate a questionable message: survival is all, it does not matter how, why, what for. This questionable approach also implies that it is both wrong and silly to feel guilty about anything one may have done to survive such an experience" (pp. 284–85). According to Bettelheim, Des Pres's conclusion is that "the main lesson of survivorship is: all that matters, the only thing that is really important, is life in its crudest, merely biological form" (p. 285). This, Bettelheim argues, is a distortion that presents only a small segment of truth. "If," he says, "presentation of what is involved in survival is to have any meaning, it cannot restrict itself to stating simply that unless one remains alive one does not survive. It must tell what is needed: what one must be, do, feel; what attitudes, what conditions are required for achieving survival under concentration camp conditions." According to Bettelheim, those most likely to survive were prisoners who tried to help one another and exercised "some small moral restraint over the body's cruder demands" (p. 286). Yet, after arguing that the prisoners' actions influenced their survival, he states that "survival has little to do with what the prisoner does or does not do: For the overwhelming majority of victims, survival depends on being set free either by the powers who rule the camps or—what is much more reliable and desirable—by outside forces that destroy the concentration camp world by defeating those who rule it" (pp. 287–88). At this point, it is not clear precisely what Bettelheim is saying about how survivors behaved and how inmates survived. Did it make any difference how the prisoners behaved? Levi and others have demonstrated that mutual support was integral to survival, whereas Bettelheim argues that whatever the prisoners did was of no consequence because survival depended on chance or outside forces over which the inmates had no control. Bettelheim generalizes from his experience in the early days of the camps when people were freed because of whim, money, or intervention, to the later periods when this was no longer the case. Survival did indeed depend on mutual support and actions. Those who gave up died.

Survival is clearly a complex process that may be attributable to many factors, including chance or accident, how the prisoners behaved and helped each other, the often capricious and random behavior on the part of camp personnel, and finally liberation. Bettelheim's perspective leaves little room for the survivor as an acting human being. In fact, he makes this explicit when he states that whatever the prisoner does is "insignificant compared to the need to defeat politically or militarily those who maintain the camps—something the prisoners, of course, cannot do" (p. 289).

But how does one survive until liberation? Clearly, not by doing nothing. Bettelheim asserts that Des Pres's view that the prisoners survived on their own is merely "what people wish to believe thirty years later about the German camps" because "it can permit us to forget about Russian and other concentration camps of today" (p. 289). Bettelheim does not explain who these unspecified "people" happen to be and why they wish to believe this, and he further accuses Des Pres of portraying the survivor as hero in order to avoid recognition of contemporary abuses of human rights.

Bettelheim next attempts to extricate himself from some of the more unfortunate statements he made in earlier writings. At one point, he states that "in reality, even while seemingly standing passively at attention, prisoners, to survive, had to engage in protective behavior. Those endless roll calls were physically and morally so destructive that one could survive them only by responding with determination to their destructive impact, through action when this was possible and, when it was not, then at least in one's mind—and this was true for practically everything else that made up the prisoners' lives" (p. 292). Bettelheim thus suggests here that not all prisoners regressed to childlike behavior or were passive. Some, and Bettelheim clearly includes himself in this group, resisted, if only in their minds. Even though they did not fight, or die, or become martyrs, their survival, as Des Pres argues, could be construed as heroic—although Bettelheim never goes that far. Even so, in order to survive, it was not necessary, according to Bettelheim's argument, to identify with the aggressor, but "one had to want to survive for a purpose" (p. 293). For Bettelheim, the purpose is revenge. Other "purposes" include staying alive to bear witness and staying alive for those one loves. These, he thought, required an active mind, and only "active thought could prevent a prisoner from becoming one of the walking dead (Muselmanner)" whom he saw all around him—one of those who were doomed because they had "given up thought and hope." After all, it appears that Bettelheim believed there was some action the prisoners could take.

Bettelheim then accuses Des Pres of comparing the prisoners to "monsters" and states that he mistakenly glorifies the resistance at Treblinka, Sobibor, Auschwitz, and Buchenwald. In fact, Des Pres does not call the prisoners "monsters" but states that the notions that "survivors suffered regression to infantile stages, *and* that they were amoral monsters, were very widespread" (p. 178). Now Bettelheim, who argued earlier that the prisoners were passive and should have resisted, dismisses resistance as irrelevant because it creates the impression that the "prisoners, all by themselves, were able to assure their survival" (p. 293). Des Pres does not make this assertion, however. In fact, he merely attempts to demonstrate that passivity was not all-encompassing, that resistance occurred, and that people survived in various ways.

Eventually, Bettelheim accuses Des Pres of bearing "witness to the opposite of the truth" (p. 313). The survivor experience, according to Bettelheim,

> did not teach us that life is meaningless, that the world of the living is a whorehouse, that one ought to live by the body's crude claims, disregarding the compulsions of culture. It taught us that miserable though the world in which we live may be, the difference between it and the world of the concentration camps is as great as that between night and day, hell and salvation, death and life, difficult though that meaning may be to fathom— a much deeper meaning than we had thought possible before we became survivors. And our feeling of guilt for having been so lucky as to survive the hell of the concentration camp is a most significant part of this meaning— testimony to a humanity that not even the abomination of the concentration camp can destroy. (p. 314)

This is a conclusion that Des Pres conceivably might have drawn, but it is not a conclusion that follows logically from Bettelheim's analysis. In fact, Bettelheim's arguments glorify the traditional mythical conceptualization of the Western hero who straps on the gunbelt, mounts the white horse, charges into the conflict to fight against great odds, and sacrifices his life for the cause. Bettelheim celebrates martyrdom and ultimately death, while Des Pres celebrates life and humane resistance to oppression.

WHAT DID DES PRES REALLY SAY?

Terrence Des Pres approaches survival from a humanistic, literary perspective. He defines survival as "the capacity of men and women to live beneath the pressure of protracted crisis, to sustain terrible damage in mind and body and yet to be there, sane, alive, still human" (p. v). For Des Pres, "The survivor is the figure who emerges from all those who fought for life in the concentration camps, and the most significant fact about their struggle is that it depended on fixed activities: on forms of social bonding and interchange, on collective resistance, on keeping dignity and moral sense together" (p. vii). Des Pres, in short, is concerned with life, with how one survives and lives, not with how one dies or becomes a martyr to some cause. Des Pres's essential argument is that although most human activity involves simply living day-to-day life, "we reserve our reverence and highest praise for action which culminates in death" (p. 3). Although he refers specifically to the image of the hero in Western religion and literature, his argument also applies to written history in general, which concentrates on wars, generals, and the "heroic" sacrifice of life. The heroes are the warriors, and everyday life is relegated to a secondary, less-exalted, and less-exciting niche. Hence, Des Pres challenges the Western literary and historical tradition, in which death and war are glorified, because he believes that it draws its heroes from death: "Those who for centuries have commanded love and imitation—Christ, Socrates, the martyrs; the tragic hero always; the warrior from Achilles to the Unknown Soldier—all are sacrificial victims, all resolve conflict by dying and through death ensure that the spirit they spoke or fought for shall not perish. The pattern is so honored and familiar that a connection between heroism and death seems natural."

The result of this emphasis on the hero as a sacrificial figure whose death commands respect is that survival is viewed as suspect. We speak, Des Pres notes, of " 'merely' surviving, as if in itself life were not worth much; as if we felt that life is justified only by things which negate it" (p. 3). Culture creates symbolic systems that mask the harsh realities and, through the hero, provides an illusion of grace or redemption—thus, it is through the heroic sacrifice of one's life that one will reach the kingdom of heaven. The problem, Des Pres argues, is that symbolic manipulations of consciousness no longer work. Death and terror are too much with us. Not only do they linger in our individual and collective memories, but they have become an integral part of our daily diet of overwhelming information. Television and daily newspapers inundate the mind with information—most of it concerning death, tragedy, or war. Des Pres sums up the modern condition in a telling phrase when he notes that the "the 'final solution' has become a usual solution, and the world is not what it was" (p. 4). "Within a landscape of disaster, places like Auschwitz, Hiroshima or the obliterated earth of Indochina, where people die in thousands, where machines reduce courage to stupidity and dying to complicity with aggression, it makes no sense to speak of death's dignity or of its communal blessing." Death is not to be wished for in most circumstances, and in a "world of mass murder," the tragic, dying hero is no model for contemporary life. "When men and women must live against terrible odds, when mere existence becomes miraculous, to die is in no way a triumph" (pp. 4–5). The age of the traditional hero, according to Des Pres, is gone, not only because death at the hands of the state is so commonplace but also because we know too much about ourselves to allow the mythic hero to survive. In addition, in the "century of mass murder" we have succeeded in rendering life so precarious and the instruments of destruction so efficient that there are no bystanders—we are all now willing or unwilling participants, and survival is an end to be achieved. But simple survival is not Des Pres's only concern. He also sees the need for "a move beyond despair and self-pity to that fierce determination which survivors call up in themselves. To come through; to keep a living soul in a living body" (p. 6).

Survivors persist and struggle against and within conditions of extremity from which there is no escape, "no place to go except the grave" (p. 6). The situation does not have a beginning and an end—the end is indeterminate or determined by forces outside the survivor's control. There is no single battle to be fought, no model of heroism to follow. To survive in such a situation requires a strong sense of one's self as something more than a victim. The survivor fights as best as he or she can and does not accept the logic imposed on the situation. All previous conditions of life are altered and even time disappears as the anchors provided by the seasons, work, cultural rituals are all lost. One has no idea how long the ordeal will last. The situation appears endless, days are the same, years pass by, and time is truly destroyed (pp. 11–12). With that destruction comes the destruction of the concept of self and the necessity to rebuild one's self. Despite the limitations and destruction, choices must be made; choice, of course, is what life is about. As the murderers make choices, the victims have more limited choices. They did not choose to become victims, but having been placed in that role, they must then choose how to behave. The essential "distinction is between those who live at any price, and those who suffer whatever they must in order to live humanly" (p. 19). Through this struggle, Des Pres believes, comes a "fundamental knowledge of good and evil, and the will to stand by this knowledge, on which all else depends" (p. 22).

Although survival is certainly a very special experience, it does not insure that survivors will not in turn commit acts of violence or deny dignity to others. Choice does not stop when one is liberated or escapes. Survivors should, from the terrible perspective of their experience, cry out against injustice. Survival and bearing witness are, as Des Pres notes, collective acts rooted in compassion and care exposing the illusion of separateness (p. 40). Through the survivor as witness, events are verified and reality becomes all too clear. "The survivor-as-witness, therefore, embodies a socio-historical process founded not upon the desire for justice (what can justice mean when genocide is the issue?), but upon the involvement of all human beings in the common care for life and the future" (p. 51). The survivor brings conscience through knowledge of previous behavior—in other words, memory. In reality, the survivor is an educator, teaching humanity lessons based on past events it might wish to forget—confronting the species with hard doses of reality, forcing confrontation with evil.

Finally, while both Des Pres and Bettelheim have different conceptualizations of the act of survival, it is in the political content and the politics of their analyses that they reveal the basic reasons for their respective views.

THE POLITICS OF BETTELHEIM AND DES PRES

Both Bettelheim and Des Pres are concerned about the ascendancy of the state in contemporary life. Bettelheim places great emphasis on technology, arguing that the modern technologically based state has a "tendency to transcend the human dimension—to manipulate the individual for the purpose of the state, rather than have the state serve the individual" (p. 258). His actual politics is revealed when he proceeds with an interpretation of the student revolt of the 1960s. What emerges is a distinctly individualistic defense of authority based on a psychoanalytic perspective generally concerned with an individual's unconscious and ignoring political, social, and cultural factors. For Bettelheim, there are no politics and, one is tempted to add, no enduring social or political structures.

Although Bettelheim appears to argue for human action against forces of destructive authority, he is actually troubled by individuals defying authority. At one point, he argues that the students who defied authority did so because of the "adolescent itch to confront for the sake of confrontation. Such individuals are convinced that they are struggling actively for personal autonomy, but they are in fact destroying it as radically as those who withdraw into solipsistic isolation" (p. 353). Bettelheim even equates the student radicals of the 1960s with Hitler youth, overlooking the distinction that the latter supported an oppressive state while the former had the courage to oppose what they perceived as the unjust and immoral actions of a state. He argues that the students were not really concerned about Vietnam but were disturbed by their feeling that "youth has no future" because modern technology had made them obsolete—that they had become socially irrelevant and, as persons, insignificant. Their future appeared bleak to them, not because of the prospect of nuclear holocaust or death in the jungles of Vietnam but because of their fear that technology had made them irrelevant and society could do nicely without them (p. 355).

Bettelheim attributes motives to the students, as he does to the survivors. As with the survivors, he does not grant the students of the 1960s any positive motives. He disparages the motives of those whose actions he does not approve. The students' revolt was against technology—even though they were not aware of that fact—not against war or injustice. This suggests that the students were not engaged in a quest to bring about a more humane world but that their revolt was a cruder and unconscious rebellion against "automation and computerization" (p. 355). These students, according to Bettelheim, were the modern equivalent of the "nineteenth-century Luddites." Instead of being in school, they should have been working. Bettelheim's analysis of the 1960s students reveals his distinctly proauthority political bias.

Des Pres, on the other hand, reveals his politics through an analysis of poetry. He sees the relation of poetry and politics as humane and fluid, expressed in the telling of stories and by confronting authority through language. Politics is admitted as a central theme in Des Pres's schema. In his last book, he attempts to outline what politics is and how it relates to everyday life. For Des Pres, politics has come to be "less a means than an end in itself—a condition, in fact, that the human spirit and therefore poetry must take into account" (1988, p. xvi). Politics is defined as the "play of impersonal force disrupting personal life" and is, therefore, a "primary ground of misfortune." It involves "acts and decisions that are not ours but which nonetheless determine how we live; events and situations brought about by brute force or manipulation of power; whole peoples ruined by the dictates of government, of the military, of the big multinationals. Politics, then, as the conditions we find ourselves in when, without consent, we become the means to others ends—politics as endured by the victims, as seen by the witnesses, as beheld by the poet" (1981b, p. 73).

Politics turns to violence when those in power close off choice for those not in power, and it is here, according to Des Pres, that "the fatality of politics resides" (1988, p. 5). For Des Pres, politics is victimization, but he neglects to point out that it can also have positive outcomes. Without politics, there would be no positive change, such as the end of racial segregation in the United States resulting from the political activity of the civil rights movement. Although Des Pres rightly deplores the destructive violence often associated with politics, he is unable to resolve the classic dilemma. Politics may indeed turn destructive, but without political action there is no change and no opposition to violence. People cannot remain passive victims when they are faced with political violence.

Like Bettelheim, Des Pres is concerned about the rise of the state, but his discussion does not degenerate into a criticism of those who oppose state power. Des Pres points out that after 1789 the "basic metaphor of politics shifted from 'the body politic' to 'the ship of state.'" Events speeded up, and "political turmoil has become an expected part of the environment" (1988, p. 13). Nothing is local and politics now intrudes on all aspects of life. Governments have taken control, and Des Pres asks: "Who among us has not known men and women broken or destroyed for refusing to follow their government's will? Ordinary people, burdened with the ordinary problems of birth and love and death, suddenly find private responsibility blocked by public decree. . . . Antigone's fate can be anyone's or everyone's at once. Innocence counts for nothing, if only because terrorism and police states both require random victims. That is the terrorist's terror, the state's proof of power—and the real threat of nuclear deterrence" (p. 14). There are, in short, no bystanders; the personal has been transformed into the political and "the logic of apocalypse asserts itself" (p. 16).

Des Pres believes that the preservation of memory, transmitted through language, helps human beings confront the disintegration of the boundary between the personal and the political that has left them face-to-face with the omnipotent state. Poetry, literature, memory help, "in hard moments, with our private struggles to keep whole" (1988, p. 228). It is the task of imagination, according to Des Pres, to "help us repossess our humanity," and by pushing back against external pressure, it "makes space for liberty of spirit." A formidable problem, however, brings us back to Des Pres's criticism of Bettelheim. Death casts a long shadow, and "even to be firmly on the side of life is no guarantee. The problem with facing death in order to defend life is that death begins to cast its shadow everywhere. A sort of vertigo sets in, as if the hysteria of the world were infectious, which it is" (p. 229). In short, the mythic hero who sacrifices life for a cause remains a potent symbol, and we are brought ultimately back to Bettelheim's *Surviving* and Des Pres's *The Survivor*. For what is most important is how the experience is communicated, how memory is preserved and passed from generation to generation. For Des Pres, poetry and fiction—words—are weapons against oppression. For Bettelheim, only martyrdom will overcome oppression—a fate not likely to be embraced by many of us who wish to survive, and a fate very much related to visions of Armageddon.

In the end, Des Pres's vision is more humane. He speaks for the survivor, for the victims, and in pursuit of liberating the human spirit. In this pursuit, language is a weapon; even though a memoir or a poem will not change the violent world, Des Pres asserts, "a poem can make something happen. It allows me to know what I fear, to understand (by standing under) the burden of my humanness. It also makes possible the essential decency of compassion, of suffering with—a symbolic action, to be sure, but one without which the spirit withers, the self shuts down" (1988, p. 23).

Memory is also a weapon against oppression, as Des Pres eloquently argues in *The Survivor*, and language is the vehicle. The way in which one talks about a past event, or writes about it, or makes movies about it, determines to a very large extent how it is remembered, as we have previously seen. Events enter history as they are reconstructed. If that reconstruction centers on the view that survivors' behavior was the result of infantile regression, identification with the aggressor, and passivity, it is not only historically incorrect but it creates a memory that celebrates death as the only means of heroic liberation. Des Pres's vision is life affirming. Human beings, he argues, "cannot dispense with memory. Wisdom depends on knowledge and it comes at a terrible price. It comes from consciousness of, and then response to, the deeds and events through which men have already passed. Conscience, as Schopenhauer put it, 'is man's knowledge concerning what he has done' " (p. 52). The task facing modern humanity is made more difficult by the "most pressing spiritual dilemma today: how to bear the burden of historical consciousness without despair. Morally, we must say No to life as it is, because terror and injustice are everywhere apparent and no one is immune or exempt. But just as much, we must say Yes to life as it is, because we cannot live without some affirmation of our own existence" (Des Pres 1978, p. 742).

We are, as ever, confronted with choices to either affirm or deny existence. Life-affirming choices are not always easy to recognize, but they may be illuminated by the accurate memory of past horrors, which helps to light our precarious path out of the darkness of the seemingly persistent "logic of apocalypse."

The memory reconstructed by Bettelheim is, as we have seen, not always life affirming. The experience of survivors such as Primo Levi is tempered when run through the filter of Bettelheim's version of psychoanalytic theory. It is further removed from human empathy and understanding when modern, positivist social science turns its attention to explaining memory.

Explaining Memory

POSITIVIST AND INTERPRETIVE

SOCIAL SCIENCE

Telford Taylor, U.S. chief counsel at Nuremberg, concludes his book, *Nuremberg and Vietnam: An American Tragedy* (1970), by stating that "we failed to learn the lessons we undertook to teach at Nuremberg, and that failure is today's American tragedy" (p. 207). As we gaze upon the late twentieth century, it becomes apparent that Taylor was depressingly accurate. We have, indeed, failed to learn lessons taught by the history of human destructiveness, and the continued repetition remains our human tragedy. One has only to examine the daily newspaper to read accounts of "ethnic cleansing" in Bosnia, famine in Somalia, war and ethnic hatred in numerous other portions of the globe. While all this occurs, contemporary, "scientific" social science focuses on less complex issues. Blinded by their concern with methodology and their hesitation to confront controversial and depressing subjects, modern social scientists have either abandoned the study of genocide to scholars emerging from older traditions or constructed pleas for the study of genocide to become more scientific and rigorous. In the contemporary disciplines of the social sciences, dominated as they are by positivist paradigms, a primary assertion has been that the best way to study mass death is through rigorous social scientific analysis using the most technical methodology and developing rigid typologies to categorize the phenomenon under study. These social scientists believe that the study of genocide, in order to be scientific and rigorous, should concentrate on defining genocide and counting the number of genocides that have occurred.

Science is no panacea, however. Indeed, as I argue in chapter 7, at the same time that they pursue, in the name of science, a rigorous method and an all-encompassing paradigm, certain types of social science research lack theory and are not particularly useful for enhancing our understanding of genocide. They often appear to manifest an almost unlimited ability to trivialize the most cherished and significant aspects of human experience. Love is reduced to cost-benefit analysis, nuclear war is conceptualized as a series of games, and economic injustice is analyzed by calculating marginal utilities. Missing from most social scientific analysis is what one observer calls "a feel for people and an ability to think in time" (Sanders 1988, p. 83).

Fortunately, alternative models of social science that are based on a concern for humanity exist. Robert Jay Lifton is a prime example of a scholar who follows this alternative tradition. He seeks to identify actions that might be undertaken to prevent human violence and to create a more peaceful and just world. In chapter 8, I explore Lifton's eloquent argument that scholars must listen to and learn from survivors and cease blinding themselves to the plagues of human destructiveness. My purpose in studying Lifton is to explore the alternatives to the main paradigms of social science, which, I argue, are atheoretical and potentially dehumanizing.

> Who can say that the history of human events obeys rigorous logic, patterns. One cannot say that each turn follows from a single why: simplifications are proper only for textbooks; the whys can be many, entangled with one another or unknowable, if not actually nonexistent. No historian or epistemologist has yet proven that human history is a deterministic process.
>
> Primo Levi, *The Drowned and the Saved* (1988)

7

Trivializing Human Memory

Social Science Methods and Genocide Scholarship

As noted in chapter 5, Primo Levi was anguished by the apparent unwillingness of the contemporary world to confront the legacy of the Holocaust. In one of his last testaments, he contemplated the possibility of repetition: "How much of the concentration camp world is dead and will not return? . . . How much is back or is coming back? What can each of us do so that in this world pregnant with threats, at least this threat will be nullified?" (1988, pp. 20–21). This plea from a survivor of Auschwitz who devoted his life to bearing witness, to keeping alive the memory of cruelty and inhumanity, is very different from the perspective of contemporary social science, which, in the words of one observer, has become "obsessed with the rigors of paradigm-building and methodology" (Sanders 1988, p. 19). Advocates of this "scientific rationality" have now begun to move into the area of Holocaust and genocide studies and propose that scholars studying genocide follow the path of such disciplines as political science, sociology, and economics, which have, in their uncritical pursuit of the chimera of science, lost their substantive souls.

A conspicuous manifestation of this plea for science may be found in one study that counts the number of human disasters resulting in mass death. This genre of research is basically descriptive, lacking interpretative theory, and sometimes addresses questions such as: "How many people have to be killed for an event to be labeled genocide?" or "What is the scientific or best definition of genocide?" The practice of counting the dead sometimes results in creating new concepts, such as "politicide," to fill the gap between genocide and individual or lesser crimes of violence. Advocates of this approach have argued that increasing the "scientific rigor" of genocide studies will enhance our understanding of genocide and gain acceptance from the social science disciplines. For example, the study mentioned above argues:

> We believe that a more systematized approach to an emotion-laden subject matter will both advance knowledge and help to overcome the preconceptions of a social scientific community which heretofore has largely ignored one of the most challenging issues in the study of conflict. We urge scholars and activists concerned with genocides not to dismiss empirical approaches as too restrictive. Studies of genocide and mass political murder need to be part of the subject-matter of a variety of disciplines which are committed to scientific rigor and accept new topics only if work on them meets well-established standards of systematic inquiry. (Harff and Gurr 1987)

Indeed, the objective of convincing social science disciplines to turn their attention to issues of life and death is not arguable. Nor can one dispute the need for various disciplines to include genocide and human rights issues among their concerns. The problem involves the use of terminology such as "emotion-laden" contrasted with other terms such as "scientific rigor" and "systematic." The implication is that "emotion-laden" subjects will be rendered acceptable to social science disciplines only when they are studied "systematically"—that is, empirically. Any proposal that suggests that it is necessary to render an emotion-laden subject neutral or nonemotional through the application of social science methodology is nonhuman, perhaps sick. What is actually intended, it appears, is recasting a disturbing and troubling topic into a trivial and nonthreatening format by focusing on method instead of substance.

In a recent essay, Yehuda Bauer made some significant comments on the modern insistence on systematic inquiry, which is similar to positivist notions of "objectivity." Bauer writes that he starts his research from the standpoint of "denying the possibility of an 'objective' stance" (1987, p. 209). He argues, in fact, that "the very decision to deal with some facts rather than others is itself subjective." In Bauer's opinion, the scholar must make his or her bias obvious, for to do otherwise is to engage in amoral posturing. Thus, studies of genocide and other human atrocities cannot be objective unless the scholar is willing to posit that morality is not, in Bauer's phrase, "an absolute value—that is, absolute as long as one posits the existence of the human race as a desired condition" (p. 210). Scientific rigor cannot, therefore, be the defining characteristic of a body of literature contemplating some of the greatest crimes against humanity that have ever been committed. Nor can the person engaged in such inquiry be concerned about acceptance, or the lack thereof, on the part of the "established" social science disciplines. If social science disciplines only accept new topics "if work on them meets well-established standards of systematic inquiry," something is amiss at the very core of these disciplines. In fact, social scientists do not appear to understand or acknowledge the historical background or significance of genocide studies. Genocide is certainly not a new topic needing acceptance from the social sciences; it is as old as humanity and hardly an idiosyncratic occurrence in human history.

The Holocaust has probably been studied in greater detail than most of the subject matter under investigation by positivist social science. One recent summary of the literature points out that the topic is examined in "nearly 2,000 books and a far greater number of other publications—over 10,000 entries on Auschwitz alone" (Isaacs 1988, p. 11). Moreover, genocides are connected. Although the Holocaust is the most studied genocide, it was preceded by the extermination of the Armenian people in 1915–17, which served Hitler not only as a model for the processes of extermination but also as an indication of the world's lack of concern (Hovannisian 1987). As Smith (1992a) notes, "Would-be perpetrators of genocide have seen what has happened with the Armenians: they know that they can commit genocide and get away with it, and through denial eventually erase any recollection of their crime. And by ignoring the Armenian Genocide, knowledge important to prevention of genocide was, for too long, lost" (p. 13). Memory is, therefore, constructed and manipulated by the topic chosen for investigation, and it is hardly legitimate to argue that social science disciplines have ignored the topic of genocide because it is new. Rather, genocide is a controversial topic that may very well pit the researcher against the state. If the nation-state has been the major perpetrator of genocide in the twentieth century, and if most nation-states have committed genocide or some other form of atrocity, then any researcher investigating this topic must begin to ask critical questions about the nature of the state in general and his or her state in particular. Social scientists are sometimes reluctant to raise such critical questions because serious contemplation of them may force the "scientists" to evaluate or reevaluate their principles or their connection to their government. It is not, then, the case that social scientists have been unwilling to investigate genocide because it is not empirical. True, it does not generally fit the paradigmatic definitions accepted in modern, positivist social science, but, as a matter of fact, research on genocide is empirical and factually based.

Generally speaking, two broad classifications of genocide scholarship exist. One is composed of witnesses' accounts or memoirs, such as those discussed in the previous chapters, while the second involves "the modes of discourse, the scholarly techniques, and the kinds of analyses used for all other historical issues" (Isaacs 1988, p. 11). But the advocates of scientific rigor do not consider historical research sufficiently empirical. They call for "systematic" description, disregarding the thousands of books on the Holocaust because they are not rigorous and scientific. "Rigor" and "science" are defined as the attaching of mathematical symbols to the categories of analysis; although much can be learned from exercises of this type if they are grounded in theory and based on historical understanding, very often the method becomes an end in itself and results in trivialization in the name of science. Method replaces content as the primary concern, and human emotions and feelings, concepts of good and evil, are all reduced to techniques of measurement.

To be sure, method and measurement have a place, but they must not be allowed to replace the human being as the primary focus because the pursuit of science does not generally result in greater understanding or enhanced memory dedicated to preventing atrocity. In fact, social science disciplines have been engaged in various forms of empirical, rigorous, or scientific analysis for decades but have not succeeded in providing solutions to the problems studied. Economists have econometric studies of economic systems, but they have not been able to prevent, or even predict, stock market crashes, huge deficits, or other seemingly unpredictable manifestations of human economic behavior. Political scientists have game-theorized nuclear war and other types of conflict but have not yet discovered a mechanism to lessen the tensions of the late twentieth century. Other social scientists have studied poverty and injustice, but they have not successfully prevented an increase in the number of human beings living in misery. Empirical study by itself is no solution. It may, in fact, contribute to misunderstanding, and it certainly does little to build memory that will resonate to other human beings and establish empathic identification. A subject may be empirically analyzed until nothing remains but numbers, but interpretations may still be wrong and policy prescriptions may be based on invalid deductions.

A very prominent example of the misuse of empirical evidence is presented in Stanley Karnow's 1983 history of Vietnam, in which he points out that despite the existence of many empirical studies on the Vietnam War, the United States consistently engaged in wrongheaded policies.

> No conflict in history was studied in such detail as it was being waged. Military and civilian officials from nearly every Washington agency would sooner or later conduct surveys in Vietnam along with specialists from dozens of private think tanks, like the RAND Corporation and the Stanford Research Institute. They included weapons technicians, economists, sociologists, political scientists, anthropologists, agronomists, biologists, chemists, and public opinion pollsters. They investigated the effects of defoliants, the impact of bombs, the efficiency of cannon. They scoured villages and interviewed peasants. They interrogated enemy defectors and prisoners. They pored over captured Communist documents and scrutinized Hanoi statements—and they produced voluminous graphs, charts, pamphlets, brochures, and books. But the statistics somehow failed to convey an accurate picture of the problem, much less offer solutions.
>
> For the missing element in the "quantitative measurement" that guided McNamara and other U.S. policy makers was the qualitative dimension that could not easily be recorded. There was no way to calibrate the motivation of Vietcong guerrillas. Nor could computers be programmed to describe the hopes and fears of Vietnamese peasants. (p. 254)

Missing from the rigorous quantitative approach to studying the Vietnam War was the qualitative element of understanding the people, their culture, and their motivations. Missing from most rigorous social scientific analysis is what one observer calls "a feel for people and an ability to think in time" (Sanders 1988, p. 19).

Fortunately, it is not necessary for scholars interested in genocide and human rights to forsake humanity for method. The approach of positivistic, social scientific rationality may be usefully contrasted with several alternatives. Among them are interpretive social science, survivor and eyewitness accounts, the "narrative ethics" of Philip Hallie (1984/85), and the "advocacy research" of Robert Jay Lifton (1987).

Interpretive social science attempts to preserve the human aspects of the subject of its inquiry by seeking understanding instead of prediction. Although this approach has many advocates, it is far from dominant in the social science disciplines. In fact, it is often relegated to the periphery as the dominant paradigms in disciplines such as political science remain modeled after those used in physics or economics. Most of the works cited in this book are part of the tradition of interpretive social science. In addition, many interpretive social scientists utilize an approach known as oral history (Miller and Miller 1993), which is generally not considered "scientific." In other words, it is possible for social science to be conducted in ways that do not dehumanize victims or lead practitioners to passivity, but these alternative models are far from dominant and are often not even accepted in many disciplines as "real" or "scientific" social science.

A second alternative is the study of eyewitness accounts. Primo Levi, as noted previously, remains one of the most eloquent and humane witnesses of grotesque inhumanity. In addressing the question, "Why do [survivors] speak of such seemingly inexplicable horror?," Levi replied: "They speak because they know they are witnesses in a trial of planetary and epochal dimensions. They speak because (as a Yiddish saying goes) 'troubles overcome are good to tell'" (1988, p. 149). Levi wanted, in his own words, to communicate the "experience of others, which is all the more pronounced the more distant these experiences are from ours in time, space, or quality. We are prone to assimilate them to 'related' ones, as if the hunger in Auschwitz were the same as that of someone who has skipped a meal. . . . It is the task of the historian to bridge this gap, which widens as we get farther away from the events under examination" (p. 158). Levi, in short, was very interested in memory—in communicating and transmitting to the next generation the hopes, fears, and atrocities of the previous generation. This important task is not necessarily facilitated by method and rigor, which are questionable approaches to communicating experience and are probably not capable of establishing in one human being an identification with another who has overcome "troubles." In fact, the focus on method abstracts the experience of each individual to the point that people are no longer recognizable in the analysis.

Levi is part of the tradition of narrative because, as Philip Hallie (1984/85) notes and as I explain in earlier chapters, history is personal memory, often based on stories. For this reason, Hallie proposes an alternative to empiricism—actually empiricism is the alternative since the telling of stories has been around much longer—what he calls "narrative ethics," which "concerns little moral forces that work from individual to individual" (p. 48). Hallie argues that we must recognize that the Holocaust, or any genocide, is composed of "many stories" of "plain fact" that must not be lost if memory is to be preserved. It is possible for these stories to be told and the witnesses to be heard while at the same time the scholarship is "systematic" and "rigorous" but not abstracted and uninvolved. The overall concern must be people, not variables.

My view is that this concern can be communicated through emotional identification, empathy, which is found in narrative, memory, and an accurate reconstruction of events. People are moved not by definitions and sociological accounts, although these are valuable, but by the writings of survivors and witnesses. Scientific method and rigorous analysis may be able to count bodies, but they cannot communicate the experience, cannot establish in one human being an identification with another. Listen, for example, as Mary, an Armenian woman, writes to her brother in Boston of a horrible attack she has experienced:

My dear Brother—

I hope that you are well; as to me, thank God I am in a condition to write to you, and sorrowfully inform you what misfortunes and horrible times have befallen us during a few months. My dear brother, we were in our country place when a crowd of Turks and Kurds suddenly fell upon us, shooting and striking right and left. One of the bullets lodged in my foot and I was almost senseless. I at once grabbed my three-months-old baby and ran through the bushes, over rocks and hills to a valley. After running a short distance, in a condition which I hope no one witnessed, I was unable to run further from the bullet in my foot. I . . . hid myself behind a rock. . . . All this time the thought of my three children whom I had left behind among those human tigers made me forget my condition.

After three hours I took my baby in my arms and started toward the house. When I reached the house everything was gone and the house was burned down and four beautiful trees in front of the house were cut down. I was almost insane at the sight, and not finding my loved ones I began to hunt around the vineyard, and suddenly I found Anna (six years) lying in a ditch, stabbed in the side of the stomach, covered with blood, and her internal organs pressing out. I took her up and laid her in a more comfortable place and began to hunt for the other two. I found them after some wandering. Ephraim (thirteen years) under a tree a short distance back of the house, lying down with two wounds, one in the arm, another in the head, and his little sister sitting beside him. (Burnham 1938, pp. 104–5)

After being helped by an old Turkish farmer, Mary arrives at Marash, where she notes "three massacres" have occurred. She continues:

We bolted our doors day and night. In the massacres some of our ablest and best young men have been killed by stones, hatchets, bayonets and bullets and hundreds of beautiful young widows and orphans are left utterly destitute. The fear and horrible fright we have had I cannot describe to you. . . .

We have nothing left to live on. . . . We hope you will not come while things are in such an awful condition, and I only beg to know if you cannot find some way of taking us away from this hell.

Thanks be to God, my children, and my wounds, are better now, and I only pray, dear brother, that you may never witness such an awful drama. (p. 105)

Scientific analysis cannot communicate the sheer human tragedy expressed in this letter, nor can it accomplish the goals of enhancing understanding and of prevention. Consequently, even though at first glance it may seem desirable for the social sciences to pay more attention to genocide, it is doubtful that the simple application of social science methodology to the study of genocide will have the impact desired by survivors such as Primo Levi.

In reality, it may well be that scientific rationality, as Lifton aptly demonstrates in *The Nazi Doctors* (1986), has "been ideologized in lethal directions, again in the name of science" (pp. 490–91). Indeed, the complex issues yet to be understood will not be unraveled by scientific approaches that abstract and oversimplify complicated human dramas. Only interpretive social science, narrative memory, and oral history and involvement are capable of communicating the necessary human identification. Fortunately, all of these elements come together in the approach used by Robert Jay Lifton. His studies of memory and mass murder are based on a model that provides essential insight into the behavior of human beings, both victims and perpetrators, without dwelling on questions of method. His analyses are informed by theory and make extensive use of the historical method as well as in-depth interviews. As such, his work is "empirical," "systematic," historical, and theoretical and still retains the essential humanity of the people involved. It manifests the best of interpretive social science, which allows the investigator to relate to the experiences of the witnesses or survivors and helps to overcome the "tendency to negate or minimize survivors' experiences, largely in response to our own psychic numbing" (Lifton 1987, p. 232).

In other words, scholars investigating genocide must declare their own involvement and take care not to allow themselves to grow so distant from their subjects that they become psychically numb, unable to feel the horror about which they are writing. Psychic numbing results in constructing memory or history that is essentially removed from the stories of the human beings upon which it is based. Lifton believes that psychic numbing is a "second scandal of our time, the scandal of our failure to be scandalized by man-made holocausts, by mass murder" (1987, p. 236).

For the most part, the social sciences have helped to perpetuate this scandal by contributing to the phenomenon of distancing and abstraction. The reality of death and suffering is abstracted by the focus on method, and investigators are able to distance themselves since they are simply counting. Lifton provides a telling alternative based upon his own extensive work, which, he argues, "convinced me of the immorality of claiming professional neutrality in the face of ultimate forms of destruction. . . . We need a model of the professional that balances technique with carefully thought-out ethical principles" (1987, p. 243).

Such a model does not emerge from the proposals of the advocates of increasing the "rigor" and "systematic" nature of Holocaust and genocide research. Instead, these proposals articulate a technicist's view of the world and attempt to induce those of us engaged in such research to follow the tired models of positivistic social science, which, as I argue above, have not only been barren and unproductive of human concern but have failed to enable concerned people to understand or prevent human cruelty and suffering. All of our empirical investigations of war, peace, poverty, injustice, racism, sexism, and good and evil will not move us any closer to a world in which we can all live in peace and satisfy our basic needs. Only by understanding the experience of the survivor and the motivation of the perpetrator can we move toward such a goal. As Lifton argues, "Only by understanding more of what happens to victims and survivors, and of what motivates victimizers, can we begin to imagine the future holocausts that threaten us, and thereby take steps to avoid them" (1987, p. 243).

In conclusion, it is unfortunate that Holocaust and genocide studies, which are interdisciplinary, are being pressured into a phase of social scientific rationality. I have watched for many years as the social science disciplines traveled that muddy road only to become bogged down in the pursuit of the elusive variable and definition, as everyday life has been almost entirely eliminated from their concern. As a result, positivistic social science has become an increasingly irrelevant undertaking in which the practitioners of the arcane sciences communicate with each other but with no one else—neither policymakers nor the public understand much of what passes for "scientific" analysis. It would therefore be a very profound error for Holocaust and genocide studies to move in that same direction. Rather, it seems much more desirable for the social sciences to adopt the interdisciplinary, historical, human-oriented approach of genocide studies. The problems we must confront and the questions to which we seek answers are not problems and questions of method, they are problems concerning the use of state power to murder human beings and how we construct and communicate the memory of these events; they are questions concerning why people are willing to follow orders to commit atrocities; they are questions concerning why genocide appears to be so difficult to stop. Our efforts must be devoted to understanding how and why people in every historical epoch appear to be so willing to kill each other and to finding mechanisms to prevent future atrocity, however it is defined or measured.

If modern social science is unable to construct or communicate memory that is accurate or that induces empathy, we must turn to other alternatives that may be more successful. Although the testimony and memory of survivors and eyewitnesses may be useful in creating memory, it is still necessary to find some mechanism to theoretically aid understanding of what happened and why people were willing to participate in what would normally be considered immoral acts of large-scale human destructiveness. The next chapter examines one of the widest-ranging and most stimulating attempts to develop theories to explain and understand genocide—that of Robert Jay Lifton.

Robert Jay Lifton

Memory and Mass Death

Robert Lifton is no stranger to the memory of some of the most abhorrent acts of human destruction in the twentieth century. He has, in fact, devoted his career to pursuing the fundamental questions of life and death—in particular, to wrestling with the troubling repetition of human violence. Due to the range of his interests and the complexity of his thoughts, I will not attempt to examine the entire scope of his work but will focus only on those areas most closely related to genocide and memory.

In his overall perspective, Lifton is similar to Levi and Des Pres. For Lifton, "hope" is central to human connectedness and is necessary for survival.

Central to all of Lifton's work is the question of "hope." He offers the best explanation when he notes that the title of his book, *The Future of Immortality* (1987), is his "way of speaking of our efforts to maintain ourselves as part of the great chain of being" (p. 3). Indeed, in this book, Lifton points out that his work contains two fundamental components, "holocaust and transformation," which are ever present. He traces his concern with these themes back to 1962, when he interviewed survivors of Hiroshima and found

> in talking to these survivors that after this experience of extraordinary devastation they sought not only to re-establish their lives in their families, in their work, in the immediate world around them, but also to recover something else they had lost—something on the order of trust or faith in human existence. Trust or faith in the flow of generations, in the expressions of the human spirit. That quest for a sense of immortality was, as I thought more about it, by no means unique to Hiroshima survivors, but was rendered especially palpable, almost visible, among them and to me by the sea of death and the sense of human end to which they had been exposed in that city. (p. 12)

The connection, in short, between present reality and any sense of hope, any sense of the future possibilities of existence for the person or his or her children, is broken by confrontation with the devastation of mass death. *The Broken Connection* (1979), another of Lifton's major works, contains numerous examples of such "broken connections," including the continued imagery of extinction that, at least until the recent breakup of the Soviet Union, surrounded the threat of nuclear war. The imagery of extinction leads to fear and futurelessness and is fed by the increasingly sophisticated technology of destruction, which is supported by "the pseudoreligious phenomenon" Lifton calls "nuclearism" (1987, p. 22). Nuclearism is quite simply the worship of technology, in this case nuclear bombs, which present a threat to the future, to immortality systems. But the worship of technology, as Lifton notes, is not restricted to nuclear weapons. Nerve gas, bombs, airplanes, ships, computer-guided weapons systems, all form a part of this syndrome. Lifton believes that "this ultimate form of idolatry—worshipping a technological object as a god—creates its own immortality system, so that the very objects that could destroy human civilization and the human species are embraced as a basis for symbolizing the endless continuity—the immortality—of that species" (p. 25). The danger, of course, is that replacing traditional immortality systems with those based on the technological fix of nuclearism—a process Lifton might call "technologicalism"—does not "contribute to maintaining the planet"

(p. 26). Rather, it is a destructive substitution, and its dangers must be recognized if there is to be any future at all: "Above all, the future of immortality, if it and we are to have a future, exists within us now, here—at this moment and this place" (p. 27). The future is, according to Lifton, in our hands, and what we do with it is essential to the continued survival of the species. Thus, two additional themes emerge: first, the questions of how and whether we heed the warnings of survivors of previous atrocity, and, second, how the professional and academic community reacts to the continuing crisis of destructive evil.

Lifton echoes Des Pres in his argument that the successful struggle to survive and bear witness to evil is an act of heroism. Survivors preserve life in order to testify to and warn a seemingly unconscious humanity of what it does not wish to hear and force confrontation with what it may not wish to see. Whether they are survivors of the Holocaust, Hiroshima, or Vietnam, they appear in many forms and, according to Lifton, confront us with the "imagery of extinction of the human species versus the creation of a human future" (1987, p. 112).

As defined by Lifton, "A survivor is one who has encountered, been exposed to, or witnessed death and has himself or herself remained alive" (1987, p. 235). Very often the response to a survivor's memory is what Lifton refers to as "numbing." Numbing is one of the key concepts Lifton introduces to explain the repeated destruction of human life. It is, he argues, "a second scandal of our time, the scandal of our failure to be scandalized by man-made holocausts, by mass murder" (p. 236). To Lifton, numbing "suggests the cessation of what I call the formative process, the *impairment* of the human being's essential mental function of symbolization. The term refers to an incapacity to feel or to confront certain kinds of experience, due either to the blocking or to the absence of prior imagery that would enable one to connect with such experience. Thus there is an essential separation of image and associated feeling. This I take to be more the problem of our present age of numbing" (p. 240).

Although numbing appears to be widespread throughout the species, it is, according to Lifton, particularly prominent among professionals. This is so because, as Lifton points out, "the professions have a dismal record in relationship to holocaust. More often than not they have lent themselves to a denial of its brutalizing effects" (1987, p. 243). Blinded by the myths of objectivity and the mask of scientific methodology, professionals are able to distance themselves, in the name of scientific rigor, from emotional confrontation with mass death. Lifton, while rigorous, avoids the trap of scientism. His essays are informed by theory, and he uses historical method as well as lengthy in-depth interviews. As such, his work is "empirical," "systematic," historical, and theoretical and still retains the essential humanity of the investigator and the participants. Lifton views his work as "both political and psychological," calling his approach "advocacy research" (p. 64). By this term, he means that his work "draws upon and extends earlier principles of participant observation and disciplined subjectivity to suggest an investigative equilibrium between the detachment required for intellectual rigor and the passions of social commitment. While the ethical-political dimension in this experience was especially compelling, I believe that open acknowledgement of advocacies in all investigative work can strengthen, rather than diminish, one's scientific enterprise."

Lifton contrasts his approach with what he calls "technicism." The concept of the professions, he argues, was originally derived from the notion of professing

> one's spiritual commitment. Gradually, as it became secularized, the emphasis shifted more and more to professional skills and techniques. The premodern image of profession as advocacy based on faith gave way to the modern image of technique devoid of advocacy. What we need is a post modern model of professions that would include both knowledge and skill on the one hand and specific advocacies and ethical commitments on the other. This would mean divesting ourselves not of technique but of *technicisms*, the claim of moral neutrality on the model of the machine. (1987, p. 66)

Lifton's model encourages historians and others engaged in explaining memory to understand and feel the anguish and pain of those exposed to mass violence and helps to overcome the "tendency to negate or minimize survivor's experiences, largely in response to our own psychic numbing" (p. 232). In short, according to Lifton, historians must declare their personal involvement and take care not to allow themselves to become so distanced that they grow psychically numb, unable to feel the horror about which they teach and write.

Lifton argues that it is immoral to claim "professional neutrality in the face of ultimate forms of destruction. . . . We need a model of the professional that balances technique with carefully thought-out ethical principles" (1987, p. 243). Lifton makes an eloquent and telling plea for ethics—for the inclusion of ethics in the writing and transmitting of memory—in other words, he is an advocate of the old idea of learning lessons from history. Only by understanding the experience of the survivor and the motivation of the perpetrator are we able to "imagine the future holocausts that threaten us, and thereby take steps to avoid them."

Lifton's work contains material of particular relevance to the politics of memory. If the experience of survivors, if the motivations of executioners, if the pain of death and suffering, are not communicated to future generations, then memory will have been eradicated, and only memory can insure the existence of justice and prevent repetition. This, then, is Lifton's general approach, which is more specifically elaborated in *The Nazi Doctors* (1986) and *The Genocidal Mentality: Nazi Holocaust and Nuclear Threat* (1990), co-authored with Eric Markusen.

HOLOCAUST, NUCLEAR WAR, AND MEMORY

Lifton's latest work, *The Genocidal Mentality*, is an interesting but problematic attempt to derive from an examination of the Holocaust lessons that apply to the nuclear capability for world destruction. The spirit that informs this book is that a consideration of the psychological and moral dimensions of atrocities such as the Holocaust and the nuclear threat will allow human beings to become aware of how precarious their planetary existence is and will lead to the development of what Lifton and Markusen call a "species mentality." This journey from the "genocidal mentality" of the Holocaust and nuclear weapons strategists to a "species mentality" is worth the price of a ticket even if the tracks are littered with barriers and the rails in less than prime condition.

In the preface, Lifton points out that after completion of his monumental work, *The Nazi Doctors*, he "was convinced that certain forms of behavior in German society during the Nazi period had relevance for American and Soviet behavior in connection with nuclear weapons" (1990, p. xi). The comparisons and differences, he hoped, would illuminate the contemporary crisis and "help open the way to alternative possibilities in the direction of human realization" (p. xiii). Lifton and Markusen begin the resulting book by quoting Elie Wiesel: "Once upon a time it happened to my people, and now it happens to all people. And suddenly I said to myself, maybe the whole world has turned Jewish. Everybody lives now facing the unknown" (p. 1). The extermination of the Jews of Europe, Wiesel suggests, was a prologue rather than a conclusion. The Holocaust signified the crossing of the abyss, and so, as Terrence Des Pres correctly notes, "the Final solution has become a usual solution" (1976b, p. 4). Governments are now all too aware that genocidal extermination is a viable policy option when dealing with opposition or minority groups; the recent extermination of the Kurds by Iraqi poison gas and the continued murder of the Bosnian Muslims by the Serbs are two examples. Lifton and Markusen extend this notion to include human extermination as a policy option when nations confront each other in the sphere of international politics. Previous genocides, in particular the Holocaust, they argue, should force human beings to face the awful possibility that genocide in the contemporary world, with its thousands of more efficient and more destructive weapons, might have become "omnicide" (Beres 1984).

Although some of this analysis now appears to be dated, the perspective on weapons of destruction, as noted above, remains the same. It is, consequently, important to identify the connections between these attitudes toward destructive technology and the persistence of destructive behavior.

Lifton and Markusen argue that what they call "nuclearism" is best exemplified by a primary strategy that was in place for conducting nuclear war—"deterrence." Deterrence, they claim, was an absurd strategy whereby the United States and the Soviet Union, together, prepared their own extinctions. Deterrence is less a strategy, according to Lifton and Markusen, than an "overall constellation of men, weapons, and war-fighting plans which, if implemented, could end human life on the planet within days or even hours" (1990, p. 3). Since deterrence as a strategy depended on each side believing that the other side was actually willing to use the weapons, "deterrence policy gives rise not only to a genocidal system but to a 'genocidal mentality,' which can be defined as a mind-set that includes individual and collective willingness to produce, deploy, and, according to certain standards of necessity, use weapons known to destroy entire human populations. . . . And that genocidal mentality can become bound up with the institutional arrangements necessary for the genocidal act."

This "nuclearism" is said to contain "certain parallels" and similar "casts of mind" to the type of thinking manifested by the Nazis as they orchestrated and played out the Final Solution. We should, therefore, be able to examine the Holocaust and learn something relevant to our time.

Lifton and Markusen assert that there are "common patterns in Nazi genocide and potential nuclear genocide" (1990, p. 12). One similarity is that both adopted a "genocidal ideology." The Nazis' genocidal ideology was found in their "biomedical vision" of racism, or

> the idea that a cure for the sickness of the Nordic race lies in destroying the infecting agent—namely Jews . . . ; and in the case of the weapons, the ideology of nuclearism, the exaggerated embrace of the weapons, and dependency on them for security, peace, and something close to salvation. Both ideologies were embraced as a resolution or "cure" for a severe historical trauma: the humiliating defeat in the First World War in the case of the Nazis; and the appearance of atomic weapons and their use in Hiroshima and Nagasaki in the nuclear case. (p. 12)

Both ideologies, according to Lifton and Markusen, also had relatively large-scale followings among professionals—in the Nazi case, physicians and biologists, and in the nuclear case, physicists and strategists. A third parallel involves the psychological mechanisms that protected "individual people from inwardly experiencing the harmful effects . . . of their own actions on others" (p. 13). Lifton and Markusen identify several of these mechanisms, all of which function to "blunt human feelings." They include "dissociation or splitting, psychic numbing, brutalization, and doubling."

Dissociation or splitting is "the separation of a portion of the mind from the whole, so that each portion may act in some degree separately from the other" (1990, p. 13). " 'Psychic numbing' is a form of dissociation characterized by the diminished capacity or inclination to feel, and usually includes the separation of thought from feeling. 'Doubling' carries the dissociative process still further with the formation of a functional second self, related to but more or less autonomous from the prior self." Finally, numbing or doubling may enable a person, "with little psychological cost, to engage in sustained actions that cause harm to others," that is, brutalization.

As an example of doubling, Lifton and Markusen focus on the Nazi doctors at Auschwitz who participated in the "selections" and killings and yet were able to carry on "normal" relationships with their families. Although the notion of doubling is theoretically appealing, it is possible that the behavior the authors call doubling is actually the ability to take on different, even conflicting, roles. In contemporary society, for example, police officers who spend their time dealing with some of the most horrendous aspects of society must develop mechanisms to adapt to their nonpolice roles. Do they "double," or do they simply learn to discriminate between situations? What Lifton and Markusen refer to as doubling may be a survival technique employed by anyone who is asked to perform functions he or she might find upsetting or distasteful. In addition, "numbing" can occur only if one assumes that human beings are not rewarded for performing such tasks. If, on the other hand, a reward structure provides positive enticements to kill Jews or develop nuclear weapons—enticements such as prestige, money, or access to the corridors of power—then perhaps the perpetrators have merely learned to play the roles that society has designed in order to gather the rewards of status and privilege. Although important insights can be derived from the concept of psychic numbing, the assumptions upon which it is based are plainly individualistic; it is also necessary to examine the culture, society, politics, and economics of such complex situations. One of the major problems with Lifton and Markusen's analysis, therefore, is that it essentially ignores the complexity of the human environment, placing undue emphasis on individual psychology and, consequently, oversimplifying a complex set of problems into a much too tidy set of answers. The "issue of how men and women can be apparently normal and yet killers" (1990, p. 14) must be examined within a context broader than the individual psyche.

In fact, this very issue has received attention from some of the best minds of the late twentieth century. Hannah Arendt, mentioned only in passing by Lifton and Markusen (1990, p. 232), examined what she referred to as "the banality of evil" (Arendt 1965). For Arendt, doubling or dissociation does not exist. Furthermore, congruent with the arguments put forth by Stanley Milgram (1974), Arendt points out that evil is most likely committed by "normal" people performing their everyday jobs—following the orders of authority and obeying without question. A job that involves manufacturing, targeting, or firing nuclear weapons or releasing Zyklon B into gas chambers will not have any different dynamic from that of a bureaucratic functionary. In any case, according to Milgram, people learn to perform their jobs without asking questions about the moral or ethical outcomes, a topic we will discuss further in chapters 10 and 11. They are numb because they have been trained to be numb and because the reward structure of the society reinforces numbness.

Despite their limitations, Lifton and Markusen have interesting things to say about the historical parallels between the Holocaust and nuclearism. Using interviews with weapons strategists and Lifton's earlier interviews with Nazi doctors, they describe the evolution of the genocidal mentality with frightening clarity. The historical precedents, including the strategic bombing during World War II, the role of technology, the development of atomic and hydrogen bombs, and the allure of nuclearism, are all described as leading to the development of the doctrine of deterrence and ultimately to the strategy of fighting wars with nuclear weapons as part of the strategic arsenal.

After demonstrating how psychological mechanisms operated to protect the Nazis and proponents of nuclearism, Lifton and Markusen focus on deterrence. They explain that the logic of deterrence was that if each superpower built up gigantic stores of nuclear weapons and had the readiness to use them, the threat of mutual annihilation would deter either of them from attempting to launch a first strike. It was based on the notion of "mutually assured destruction," or the idea that if either of the superpowers launched a first strike, the other would have sufficient second-strike capacity left to destroy the civilian population and industrial capacity of the aggressor. Neither country, consequently, would use the weapons because each knew the other could destroy it. Although nuclear weapons are clearly genocidal or omnicidal, deterrence is easier to criticize in the abstract than in the real world. What policy short of mutual disarmament or wiping out the memory of how to build nuclear weapons could have been pursued? Whether deterrence in fact kept the world from nuclear disaster can only be speculated, but the two superpowers, as a result of the horrible specter of nuclear disaster, did refrain from direct confrontation. Instead, they fought proxy wars in places like Korea, Vietnam, and Afghanistan. Whether they were engaged in dissociation or not, so-called conventional forces were used in place of nuclear weapons. In 1980, when Presidential Directive 58 was signed, the United States shifted its policy from deterrence to war fighting. At this time, the situation became much more clearly one in which preparations for genocide were operative, for war fighting implies not deterring the use of nuclear weapons but a willingness to use them in a first strike to cripple the enemy's nuclear capability and consequently gain an advantage—as though there can be any "advantage" after launching a nuclear strike. Strategy evolved from an essentially defensive to an essentially offensive posture, and the genocidal mentality was given free rein. Consequently, the doctrine of deterrence does not involve dissociation so much as a rather limited analysis of the options available in the real world. The political reality of a situation must always be considered when policy is examined since that reality is often less clear at the time than it is in retrospect.

Deterrence then, according to Lifton and Markusen, is part of what they refer to as "the dissociative field," which is based on the assumption that "we must be prepared to kill hundreds of millions of people in order to prevent large-scale killing, to cure the world of genocide" (1990, p. 226). The contradiction lies in the suggestion that killing can be the cure for large-scale killing, but does this require dissociation? Can people be motivated to kill without dissociating? Suppose, in fact, that all people have within themselves the contradictory impulses for both helping and killing, which are expressed or not depending upon the cues emanating from one's society and culture, as I argued earlier in referring to Arendt's theses on the "banality of evil." Suppose that these impulses are not the result of dissociating or numbing and that, in fact, "normal" human beings operate this way in the pursuit of their daily lives. The same person who helps a child who has fallen off her or his bicycle may very well tells ethnic jokes, condemn minorities, or, when ordered to do so, commit violence. In short, suppose the Nazis supported Hitler because they did not like Jews or because they would benefit from their destruction— why should they like them, after all, after thousands of years of anti-Semitic propaganda? Suppose those who make weapons do know how the blast and heat will tear apart human bodies? Probably humans are neither wholly good nor wholly evil but influenced by political and social conditions and the expressions of their leaders. It is, therefore, possible for the same person to help a hurt child and to shoot a Vietnamese child in the village of Son My, hamlet of My Lai. This viewpoint implies that creating the conditions to tap the better side of our nature becomes the single most important task and that the types of behavior labeled as dissociation or doubling are symptoms of or are caused by social conditions. Therefore, the type of society, polity, and economy, the language of the leaders, and the cultural traditions that are socialized and passed on to future generations are all more important since they shape the psyche. Lifton and Markusen, although they have a great deal to say, do not grasp this complexity. Their book, which is very well intentioned in its criticism of destructive impulses and calls for the development of a species mentality, neglects these factors and consequently fails to offer suggestions as to how one travels from the genocidal mentality to the species mentality.

"Species mentality," according to Lifton and Markusen, is a "moral equivalent" to "genocidal mentality: an alternative that serves similar psychological needs in ways that are life enhancing" (1990, p. 255). A person with a species mentality, when confronted with a situation in which he or she is ordered to commit an act of human destruction, will say, "No, I won't do it!" (p. 257). Other than calling for the replacement of deference to authority and encouraging human beings to become "conscious of ourselves as members of the human species" (p. 258), however, Lifton and Markusen do not clarify how humanity will move from a genocidal to a species mentality. Of course, developing an ethical core for the professions is essential, but how can it be accomplished? And how do we escape from the "Cartesian sickness" of scientism and technicism when they dominate our views of the contemporary world? Lifton and Markusen, along with many other recent analysts (for example, Hirsch and Hirsch 1990), argue for the formation of a global consciousness, but, once again, fail to propose methods of attaining it. They describe global consciousness as the view that all human beings share the fragile planet and that we must act to preserve rather than destroy it. And they conclude with an eloquent call for each of us to "join in a vast project—political, ethical, psychological—on behalf of perpetuating and nurturing our humanity" (p. 279).

Lifton and Markusen's study, while inspiring and important, neglects to confront the hard question of how we get from where we are to where we wish to be. In fact, the major problem with Lifton's work, as well as that of others, is that he often ignores political, cultural, and economic factors.[1] Despite this

1. Lifton and Markusen's work is also marred by factual errors. For example, Thomas K. Jones, who stated that Americans could survive nuclear war if they had "enough shovels," was not a "Defense Department official concerned with the Federal Emergency Manage-

similarity, however, important differences exist in the way students of mass death have analyzed the memory of that phenomenon. Although all pay lip service to the need to understand genocide as a means to prevent future occurrences, only Lifton provides the necessary empathetic view that encourages the construction of a framework leading to a more comprehensive understanding of the process by which individuals are persuaded to commit destructive acts. Lifton is primarily concerned with transmitting memory in such a fashion as to preserve the humanity of the witnesses so that future generations will, in turn, be able to preserve their humanity by avoiding the seemingly endless repetition of violence and mass death. Lifton's overall plea for human action and remembrance is in the very best tradition of interpretative social science. With this as a base, the next part will look at the means by which memory is transmitted and the motivation to kill is developed.

---

ment Agency" (1990, p. 47). In fact, he was deputy undersecretary of defense for research and engineering, strategic and theater nuclear forces. Lifton and Markusen probably confuse him with Louis O. Giuffrida, who was head of the Federal Emergency Management Agency under the Reagan administration and who made one of the classic statements about nuclear war: "It would be a mess, but it wouldn't be unmanageable" (Scheer 1983, p. 3).

In addition, Lifton and Markusen often categorize writers according to their presumed heritages, a practice that serves no useful purpose. For example, they identify Raul Hilberg and Hannah Arendt as "prominent Jewish writers on the Holocaust" (p. 232). Hilberg, it so happens, is not Jewish, and even if he were, why is it necessary to include such information? Arendt was also a woman; should she be referred to as a woman writer? Should I indicate Lifton's and Markusen's religion, ethnicity, national identity, or other characteristics? These problems reflect the authors' tendency to overwrite, to create a plethora of categories, and to psychologize all phenomena discussed.

Transmitting Memory

WHY PEOPLE KILL

Memory affects behavior. Accumulated memories and the factors that are involved in the accumulation of memory, which we have discussed in the preceding chapters, construct the environment within which an individual is confronted with choices. But these choices are not presented in a vacuum. Every person does not have an equal opportunity, for example, to become the head of a giant multinational corporation. Such an opportunity is mostly an accident of birth into particular social, economic, political, cultural, national, gender, or class groupings that control the options available to any single person. That person's decisions or choices will be influenced, of course, by this context, which has already largely determined his or her opportunities, as well as by the accumulated and created memories that have been transmitted by the acculturation or socialization process.

As argued earlier, memory is passed from generation to generation, and in each passing, it is changed and in turn passed on again. This process of socialization results in individual and national identity formation, and it serves as the background from which one might move forward to understand how to build a more just, peaceful, humane future without the scourge of mass death. The alternative is to remain imprisoned in the constrictive, reconstructed memory manipulated by states and individuals to serve political ends. The patterns can be broken only if we add this psychological and individual dimension to the understanding of memory. To accomplish this, I examine first how accumulated memories are carried by language, demonstrating how language is a potent political weapon; and second, how the process of political socialization works, using education in Nazi Germany as an example. I then explore the relationship between individual identity, memory, and mass murder.

We are, after all, talking about people, about humans killing other humans. For genocide to occur, there must be a supply of individuals willing to pull the triggers, drop the bombs, turn on the gas, and remove the bodies. How people come to participate in what are generally thought to be immoral acts of torture and murder is surely one of the most enduring and puzzling questions. Memory plays a crucial role in that process, and language, socialization, and identity formation are all integral parts of the process of memory transmission.

The Language of Extermination

THE IMPORTANCE OF LANGUAGE

Steiner (1971) writes: "The apostle tells us that in the beginning was the Word. He gives us no assurance as to the end" (p. 12). If the twentieth century is any indication, the end may result from words used to motivate, justify, and rationalize murder on a scale unprecedented in human history. Words can kill—or at least motivate a person to kill. It is through language that the primal impulses, the likes and dislikes, the hatreds and enmities, the stereotypes and degrading and dehumanizing characterizations of those who are not desirable or are rivals for political or economic power or status, are transmitted. The socialization process, which will be examined in chapter 10, is the psychological process of transmission, but words are the carriers of the deeds. Language, like memory, is a powerful political tool.

The seemingly mysterious connection between words and actions, between language and behavior, has been a puzzle of enduring interest and fascination for scholars of many disciplines. In the contemporary era, this fascination continues as scholars explore what Thomas Mann referred to as the connection between language and human responsibility (Steiner 1977, p. 102). Unfortunately, most of the philosophical investigations of language are written at a level of abstraction that renders their utility as interpretative tools questionable. Those of us interested in how language works in the "real world," in particular in the world of politics and power, have relatively few sources to which to turn.

C. Wright Mills (1984) pointed the way when he noted that "we must approach linguistic behavior, not by referring it to private states in individuals, but by observing its social function of coordinating diverse actions" (p. 13). For at least two reasons, however, the matter is not quite as simple as it sounds. First, language "does not have the fixity or stability of meaning implied by the dictionary definitions of the words that comprise it. The crucial feature of language is that meaning is not fixed—it is emergent—tied to specific situations and constantly changing. The meaning of language is really no more stable than the particular situations it may be used to describe" (Weinstein 1980, p. 17). Second, language is a dialectical phenomenon that both shapes and reflects experience (Bollinger 1980, p. ix). It not only describes events but is itself "a part of events, shaping their meaning and helping to shape the political roles officials and the general public play. In this sense, language, events, and self-conceptions are a part of the same transaction, mutually determining one another's meanings" (Edelman 1977, p. 4). Events, then, are defined by the language used to describe them, and this language, in turn, functions to "create shared meanings, perceptions, and reassurances among mass publics" (p. 65). Perceptions of reality are linguistically created, and meaning derives from the cultural, social, and political context.

In this sense, language may be a potent cultural and political weapon, for it carries the cultural imperatives and transmits the dominant themes of a culture into the minds and hearts of the people. Language is the carrier and formative agent of the ideologies and mythologies prevalent in a culture or nation-state (Poliakov 1971; Mosse 1978; Becker 1975).

LANGUAGE AND MYTH

In chapter 4, I explored the connection between myth and history. At this point, that connection becomes clearer since the myths, transmitted via the socialization process, are expressed in the language of the culture. All states, all cultures, and all societies construct political myths that are usually based upon claims explaining the origin of the people or of the nation-state. Generally, these claims are phrased metaphorically and "suppress the recognition of reality" (Edelman 1971, p. 74). The metaphors eventually become self-perpetuating and serve as mechanisms used by people to organize their views of the world. Usually, the metaphors become myths (Edelman 1977, p. 17). The creation myths very often maintain that the members of the group or the state descend from divine origins or are protected by divine intervention. In the case of groups of people, the group may be said to descend from God or gods or from some mythic hero or animal. When the nation-state is involved, the founding myth is often based on presumptions of divine intervention resulting in divine protection.

In addition, of course, the founders, generally male, are usually the wisest, most beneficent individuals, representative of the best the culture has to offer. In the United States, for example, the Founding Fathers are revered as the "best and the brightest," who created a heavenly mansion on the hill that would be protected by God and would always be on the side of right and justice. They are thought of as superior to average human beings and therefore not motivated by normal human passions. In fact, when I discuss the more mundane motivations of some of the founders in my introductory government class, students often become defensive and accuse me of "ridiculing" the great men. But examining the motivations of humans is not ridicule, whether they built governments or destroyed a group of people. In both cases, and in the example of any founding myth, we are witnessing a very rudimentary type of historical thinking that operates to differentiate the group or the state from other groups or states and to invest the actions of the state or group with a legitimacy beyond that normally accorded the actions of mere human beings. After all, if you are descended from or inspired by gods, your actions cannot be questioned since they are not merely human acts. Such myths of divine origin are sometimes extended to define other peoples as outside the "universe of obligation" (Fein 1979, pp. 4–5). Once it identifies an "out-group," whose members are no longer protected and not among the privileged members of the society, the creation myth becomes a tool of destruction. These tools then become part of the folklore and the "history" of a people or a nation as they are passed from generation to generation. Transmitted along with the myths are the accompanying stereotypes, hatreds, and desires for revenge or redemption, all of which may ultimately lead to destructive acts. These myths, and the propaganda that accompanies them, may function to dehumanize those outside the mythical boundaries—the potential victims—and eventually to justify their extermination. The recurring memory stimulated by these myths helps shape policy in the present. Earlier, I used the example of Israel to demonstrate a society caught in constricted memory, perpetuated by the myth of victimization and the accompanying dehumanization of the Palestinians. Another, perhaps even more obvious, example is the Nazi appeal to what is referred to as "the Aryan myth" to justify and rationalize the killing of the Jews.

Myths such as the Aryan myth simplify a complex political reality. As Edelman (1971) points out, the basic themes often revolve around a threatening out-group conspiracy against the in-group, from which the benevolent political leaders will save the people. Victory, according to the leaders, may be achieved if the group works hard, sacrifices, and, most importantly, obeys its leaders (p. 77). These types of myths, which often form the basis of the language of extermination, perform at least four functions. First, they define the out-group—in this case, the Jews. Second, they call for certain actions on the part of the in-group that are justified by the myth. Third, they require unquestioning obedience to the leaders, who will function, if they are obeyed, as the saviors of the people. Fourth, they disguise reality and justify the acts of destruction.

DEFINING THE OUT-GROUP

When political leaders seek to target a population for abuse, they will produce negative characterizations that can usually be found linguistically in deprecating nouns such as "kike," "wop," "spick," "bohunk," "Jap," "Chink," or "dago" (Bollinger 1980, p. 79). As the out-group picked for destruction, the Jews were portrayed by Nazi propaganda that followed familiar lines. It was part of a cultural legacy that had developed over a long period of time and had been expressed several hundred years earlier by Martin Luther. Luther "was not above advocating overt violence against the Jews and their institutions" (Rubenstein 1988, p. 36). At one point, he wrote: "We are at fault for not slaying them"; at another, "Set fire to their synagogues or schools and . . . bury or cover with dirt whatever will not burn." Yet again he urges, "I advise that their houses also be razed" (quoted on p. 37). This portrait of the Jew, as illustrated by Luther, was not originated by him.

Of all of the diverse forms of prejudice, anti-Semitism is one of the oldest and most persistent. It has deep historical and cultural roots and has been expressed in forms as diverse as the "polite" exclusion of Jews from clubs and schools to the genocide of the Nazis. In order to understand any form of prejudice, it is necessary to know something about its development. Historically, Jews have been accused of, among other deeds, killing God or the son of God; being allied with the Devil and the powers of evil; being hostile and unfriendly toward other religions; desecrating the host; being homeless wanderers; being unclean; being subversive of established religion or state; being carriers of new, potentially dangerous, ideas; being usurers; being revolutionaries; being Communists; being capitalists; poisoning wells; killing Christian children to use their blood in their rituals; and attempting to take over the world. Societies have sought to punish Jews for these imagined crimes by subjecting them to measures including forced conversion, the wearing of badges of identification, boycotts of Jewish enterprise, anti-Jewish laws, isolation in ghettos, pogroms, expulsion from the state or community, and extermination.

Anti-Semitism has its roots in antiquity, particularly in the countries of the Roman Empire. Jews were accused early on of being unfriendly toward non-Jews. Simply because they believed in their own religion, they were viewed as nonconformists who were hostile toward other religions. In the pagan world, before Christianity, Jews were thought to lack respect for other groups. Jews were nevertheless allowed to work and live with relatively little discrimination in the Roman Empire, where rights were granted or denied primarily according to the class to which a person belonged.

As the era of Christianity approached, anti-Semitic prejudice became more vocal and more deadly. After the Christian era began, three policies were used against the Jews: conversion, expulsion, and annihilation (Hilberg 1985). When Christianity became the dominant religion of the state, the state began to carry out church policy based on anti-Semitic mythology. Jews were now defined as being outside the "Christian universe of obligation" (Fein 1979, pp. 4–5), meaning that they were not protected by the dominant religious group or, after 1648, by the state because they were not considered official citizens and therefore did not have the protection of the law. This status is similar to that of African Americans in the southern United States until 1964. Legal victimization of the Jews, as of African Americans, was justified because it was condoned by the law. Consequently, it was "legal" to kill an African American in the South; even during the civil rights years, killings of blacks occurred for which no one was convicted. For example, on August 28, 1955, Emmett Till, a young African American from Chicago who was visiting his relatives in Mississippi, was killed for talking to a white woman, but "justice" was never meted out in this case, as well as many others.

Clearly connections exist, which are not merely theoretical, between different forms of prejudice and the expressions they take. Ideologies of hate and racism function to dehumanize the people at whom they are directed and to prepare the way for oppression or even extermination. Dehumanizing ideologies are justifications for the perpetrators' actions. From their perspective, it is legitimate to discriminate against or kill those they have dehumanized not only because they are not seen as human but also because they are seen as a threat.

This verbal characterization of the Jew remained somewhat constant in anti-Semitic propaganda and mythology and was incorporated into the Aryan myth as stated by Hitler. "The Jew," he wrote, "completely lacks the most essential prerequisite for a cultural people. . . . He is and remains a parasite, a sponger who, like a pernicious bacillus, spreads over wider and wider areas according as some favorable area attracts him. . . . He poisons the blood of others" (cited in Hilberg 1985, p. 12).

Hitler followed Luther and other proponents of Aryan superiority in the belief in a worldwide Jewish conspiracy and the view that Jews were "vermin." It is important to note that they did not say that Jews were *like* vermin—they *were* vermin. This assertion was repeated in Nazi propaganda throughout the period of the mass murder. Many firsthand accounts have verified that it was a widespread belief. For example, a Jewish smuggler who escaped from the Warsaw ghetto provides the following description: "When I was in Aryan Warsaw, I sometimes tried, in spite of the danger, to tear down the large posters showing a hideous Jew with a louse-ridden beard. 'Jew-louse-typhoid,' it said. We were germ carriers, vermin" (Gray 1971, p. 82).

The language used to portray the Jew as a parasite, as vermin, functioned effectively to dehumanize the potential victims and justify their extermination. After all, killing vermin is legitimate and is viewed as self-defense because you are protecting yourself, your family, your people, your nation, from contamination. This is a very clear example of language used as a weapon to define a group that is to become a potential target. This type of terminology of contempt is all too common, and its use is not restricted to Jews or even to religious, racial, or ethnic groups. Bollinger (1980) has drawn up an instructive, if partial, list of such terms:

Farmers: "hick, hayseed, yokel, clod, bumpkin, countryjake, rube."
Women: "slut, slattern, frump, drab, dowdy, draggletail, trollop, bitch."
Older women: "hag, crone, witch, workhorse, biddy." (p. 90)

The use of unfavorable epithets is referred to by Bollinger as "dysphemism." Such epithets depersonalize and dehumanize the subject and are examples of language that might be used to motivate or justify extermination.

Other examples of language that functions to dehumanize involve the use of racist terminology, in particular, color symbolism that communicates a powerful set of negative stereotypes and images. James Baldwin stated that as a black writer in an English-speaking country he was forced "to realize that the assumptions on which the language operates are his enemy. . . . I was forced to reconsider similes: as black as sin, as black as night, blackhearted" (quoted in Bollinger 1980, p. 89). "Black" is synonymous with negative images, with evil, while "white" is symbolically positive and beautiful. Moffic (1988) notes that one might discover the source of the negative connotation of "black" by examining synonyms in the English language. He writes:

> Even before the 16th century discovery of darker people in Africa, the Oxford English Dictionary indicated negative associations to the term black. The meaning of black back then included "deeply stained with dirt, soiled, foul . . . having dark or deadly purposes . . . iniquitous, atrocious, horrible, wicked." Recent studies support the continuation of these associations. The great majority of Roget's Thesaurus' synonyms for "white" embrace positive qualities, while most (at least 60%) synonyms for "black" have negative connotations. Examples of "white" synonyms include pure, moral, fair, and honorable. For "black," in contrast, we have such synonyms as disastrous, repulsive, sinister, and wicked. In Webster's Dictionary, concepts or words hyphenated with the term black are mainly negative, including blackball, blacklist, black magic, blackmail, and black market. . . . For children learning the English language, negative associations to black are quickly reinforced. (pp. 3–4)

This type of racist stereotyping takes additional forms and is not limited to color. For example, "People executed as witches in the seventeenth century and those persecuted in witch hunts in the twentieth century suffered from the definitions applied to them regardless of the correctness of either form of belief in witches" (Edelman 1977, p. 9). Moreover, during the Vietnam War, negative symbolism characterized Vietnamese people as "gooks," "dinks," or "slant eyes" (Lifton 1973; Caputo 1977; Baker 1981). In an earlier period of American history, Native Americans were negatively labeled in preparing the groundwork for their eventual destruction. They were, for example, called "savages," "infidels," "heathen," and "barbarians" (Berkhofer 1978). As understood at the time, a "barbarian" was the opposite of a person who was "civilized"—a term that, as Berkhofer notes, was interchangeable with "Christian" (p. 16).

A prime example of this type of language may be found in a letter sent to England by Alexander Whitaker, a minister in Henrico, Virginia, who wrote in 1613: "Let the miserable condition of these naked slaves of the divell move you to compassion. . . . Wherefore they serve the divell for fear, after a most base manner, sacrificing sometimes (as I have heard) their own children to him. . . . Their priests . . . are no other but such as our English witches are. They live naked in bodie, as if their shame of their sins deserved no covering: Their names are as naked as their bodie: they esteem it a virtue to lie, deceive and steal as their master the divell teacheth to them" (Berkhofer 1978, p. 12).

This use of language would, of course, be of little consequence if it were not accompanied by calls for action. As noted above, the call to the in-group to act is a second function of myths created by the language of extermination.

CALL TO ACTION

A relationship exists between negative symbols and mass murder. The symbols are a legitimating mechanism and a call for action. Once it has been established that the state or group is threatened by vermin or some other mythic creation, however defined, the protection, cleansing, extermination must be put into motion. Leaders prepare their constituents for participation in mass murder by issuing the calls for action and legitimate violent action by declaring it necessary in defense of the state or of a "way of life." A ready supply of people is always willing to act out the hostile impulses if they are reinforced by those in positions of influence. Political authority perpetuates the image of order and stability against a background of potential chaos. In this context, familiar language may be used to "represent traditional standards" or to "change the language because the familiar has failed or appears to be failing" (Weinstein 1980, p. 18). Political leaders are, therefore, like dramatists in that they "can manipulate the common capacity for a willing suspension of disbelief. But whereas people follow the dramatist in his work because nothing is lost if they do, they must follow political leaders because everything may be lost if they do not."

Examples abound. The commandant of the Treblinka concentration camp, Franz Stangl, for example, was profoundly influenced by Cardinal Theodor Innitzer's call to Catholics to "cooperate" with the Nazis. Little or no Christian opposition was ever mounted against the Nazis as Innitzer welcomed them and urged "Austrian Catholics to support them" (Engelmann 1986, p. 121). Stangl also noted that he was affected by the fact that many political leaders capitulated "at once" to the Nazis (Sereny 1974, p. 30). Observing no leadership in opposition to the Nazis, Stangl and other Germans heeded the call to action. No alternative was offered, no other sentiments were legitimated, as the Nazis called for the implementation of the Final Solution. This call was transmitted by the German language, which became a valuable tool. It became, Steiner (1977) argues, "a language used to run hell" (p. 100). The process of transforming the language into one of extermination is described by

Steiner: "Gradually words lost their meaning and acquired nightmarish definitions. *Jude, Pole, Russe*, came to mean two-legged lice, putrid vermin which the good Aryans must squash, as a party manual said, 'like roaches on a dirty wall.'" Certain words were used to call the faithful to action and to cover up the action instead of utilizing specific descriptive terms. The words "killing" or "execution" were never used to indicate the actions carried out against the Jews. Instead, Hitler and his associates used euphemisms such as "removal," "elimination," "clearing up," "special treatment," "treated appropriately," "evacuation," "thinning out," and even "cleansing" to motivate followers to carry out the policy of extermination (Roth 1984/85, p. 89). Thus, the words of the leader were used to induce action and to insure obedience to the commands of authority.

LANGUAGE AND OBEDIENCE

Primo Levi (1986c) has asserted that the "entire history of the brief 'millennial Reich' can be reread as a war against memory, an Orwellian falsification of memory, falsification of reality, negation of reality" (p. 31). In this new reality, as pointed out above, Jews were not killed, they were "cleaned up" or "disinfected." Lifton (1986) states, "For what was being done to the Jews there were different words, words that perpetuated the numbing . . . by rendering murder non murderous" (p. 445). This was particularly true for the language used by the "Nazi doctors" to justify their participation and to suggest that what they were engaged in was "responsible military-medical behavior." Killing, hence, was no longer killing, and since they "lived increasingly within that language [of extermination]—and they used it with each other—Nazi doctors became imaginatively bound to a psychic realm of derealization, disavowal, and nonfeeling."

Language used by the Nazis functioned, then, to obscure the reality of mass murder and to numb the participants (Fleming 1982). The fact that this is a commonplace use of language is depressing and all too often denied. Leaders prepare a population for genocide by positing, as we have seen in the case of Nazi Germany, a connection between the well-being of the country or group and obedience to the leaders. As a result, citizens perceive leaders as "correct" simply because they are leaders. Authority is to be obeyed, the exterminations are to be carried out as ordered. For additional examples of language that functions to insure obedience, we may look to the Vietnam War and to the language of nuclear weapons.

Lt. William Calley, accused of murdering over 100 civilians during the Vietnam War in what became known as the My Lai massacre, illustrates this blind obedience to authority. He explained his actions by claiming that he simply believed what he was told: "I was a run-of-the mill average guy: I still am, I always said, *The people in Washington are smarter than me.* If intelligent people told me, 'Communism's bad. It's going to engulf us. To take us in,' I believe them. I had to. I was sure it could happen: the Russians could come in a parachute drop. Or a HALO drop or some submarines or space capsules even" (Calley 1972, p. 225). Obedience is rewarded, encouraged by "the glory words like duty, honor and valor" (Baker 1981, p. 168). It is also reinforced by indoctrination and the destruction of identity and self-worth. Rituals of induction often function to transmit into the psyches of individuals the words of the leaders. Military training is a prime example. Philip Caputo (1977) describes his military indoctrination into the Marine Corps during the Vietnam War as mental and physical abuse, the objective of which was to eliminate the weak, who were collectively known as "unsats" for "unsatisfactory" (pp. 9–10). The reasoning was that anyone who could not take being shouted at and pushed around could never withstand the rigors of combat. But such abuse was also designed to destroy trainees' sense of self-worth, to make them feel inadequate until they proved themselves equal to the corp's exacting standards.

Once a person's self-worth is destroyed, what message replaces it? Again a perceptive observer, Caputo notes that then "the psychology of the mob, of the *Bund* rally, takes command of his will. . . . In time, he begins to believe that he really does love the Marine Corps, that it is invincible, and that there is nothing improper in praying for war" (1977, p. 12). The result, of course, is obedience. One is not supposed to consider the consequences of acts one is ordered to undertake. Once the orders are executed, the behavior, especially if destructive, must be justified. One mechanism of justification is to manipulate and disguise reality.

LANGUAGE AND JUSTIFICATION

In some cases, acts of human destructiveness are disguised by euphemisms. Jargon is a type of euphemism, functioning "to mask what one does not wish to face. . . . If Pentagon pronouncements speak of structures in Vietnamese villages, people feel better than they would if they read that huts or houses were being destroyed" (Edelman 1971, p. 74). In fact, categorizations were developed to label the Vietnamese so that when U.S. troops entered a village they assigned the villagers to categories according to their supposed involvement with the National Liberation Front (Schell 1987, p. 241). The categories were "confirmed VC," "VC suspect," "VC supporter," "detainee," "refugee," and "defector." Schell goes on to describe what happened when the troops actually entered a village and rounded up the villagers. Those who were to be evacuated were labeled as "VC supporters" or "VC suspects," but when the same villagers were removed to a camp, the army categorized them as "refugees." By the same token, a Vietnamese who had been shot by U.S. troops was almost invariably categorized as a "confirmed VC." (The soldiers had a joke that ran, "Anything that's dead and isn't white is a VC.")

A similar use of language to obscure a distasteful and potentially horrible reality may be found in the language used to discuss nuclear weapons in particular and war in general. One observer has pointed out that the use of obfuscating terminology was given impetus after World War II when the "War Department was officially changed to the Department of Defense; it is easy to oppose war but difficult to object to defense" (Barash 1988, p. 328). It is also easier to support a "defense budget" than a "war budget" and more palatable to promote "national security" than war in any form. Jargon and euphemisms are used to provide safe pigeonholes for what is, in reality, massive destruction of people by blast, fire, wind, and radioactivity. Several observers refer to this tendency as "nukespeak," the function of which is to "obscure and sanitize" nuclear war by draining away the actual horror of the events (Barash 1988, pp. 327–28; Chilton 1986, p. 135). In some cases, nuclear weapons are humanized—they are given names, even families: "They have fathers (Edward Teller, father of the H-bomb), though no mothers; they grow from infants ('baby nukes') to old age (NATO's allegedly 'aging force') and make way for the young ('new generation MX ICBMs')" (Chilton 1986, p. 135). The language of nuclear war includes terms such as "nuclear exchange," "nuclear yield," "counterforce," "nuclear escalation," "megaton," "MIRV," "Polaris," "Poseidon missile" (Lifton 1979, p. 363), and "peacekeeper." Barash (1988) has compiled a chart that compares equivalent terms in "nuclear language" and in "blunt language" (p. 328):

Nuclear language	Blunt language
Nuclear exchange	Nuclear war
Countervalue	City destroying
Collateral damage	Killing innocent civilians
Delivery vehicle	Bomber or missile
Reentry vehicle	Nuclear warhead
Hardware	Weapons
Taking out a target	Destroying a target

The purpose of this language is to disguise reality, to create the illusion that nuclear war is acceptable, to convince people to obey if they are ordered to push the buttons, and to justify massive destruction. The outlook that nuclear war is acceptable is perhaps best capsulized by the statement of an official in the Reagan administration who noted that "it is possible for any society to survive a nuclear war. . . . Nuclear war is a destructive thing, but still in large part a physics problem"; it is possible to "win, in a classical sense," a nuclear war (Scheer 1983, pp. 6, 131). If you can survive, even win in a "classical sense," what is wrong with a nuclear exchange? The destruction of millions, possibly billions, of human beings is disguised in the same fashion that the Nazi rhetoric disguised the murder of the Jews.

CONCLUSION

The language of extermination is not a historical aberration; it is all too common. Used to create myths that function to simplify a complex world, call people to action against specified targets, motivate obedience, and justify destruction, the language of extermination is designed to touch what Steiner (1971) refers to as the "dark places" that are "at the center" of all human beings (p. 31). These dark places are probably not part of the consciousness of most people; after all, few people intend to commit evil. "No eighteen-year-old kid went to Vietnam thinking, 'Oh boy, now I'm going to be evil.' But most of them met their darker sides face to face in that war" (Baker 1981, p. 168). Until we confront and begin to understand how language functions to touch that "darker side," until we understand that the evil of mass extermination is a frequent historical occurrence, we will remain potential victims and executioners. Evil is encouraged and rewarded with symbols that may come in many forms—sometimes medals or honors of assorted types, but most often words. These words are transmitted from generation to generation through the process of socialization, and they perpetuate the myths and negative stereotypes and hatreds that fuel the cycle of violence.

The manner in which the language of extermination operates has been eloquently noted by Steiner (1977), who argued that the German language gave "hell a native tongue" (p. 99). Indeed, he continues, "that is what happened under the Reich. Not silence or evasion, but an immense outpouring of precise, serviceable words. It was one of the peculiar horrors of the Nazi era that all that happened was recorded, catalogued, chronicled, set down; that words were committed to saying things no human mouth should ever have said and no paper made by man should ever have been inscribed with." Not only were these words spoken and written, but they were purposefully transmitted to young people via a conscious attempt at indoctrination through the process of political socialization, which emphasizes obedience to authority as a fundamental value.

All education must have the sole object of stamping the
conviction into the child that his own people and his own
race are superior to all others.

Adolf Hitler, *Mein Kampf* (1925)

We love our Fuehrer,

We honor our Fuehrer,

We follow our Fuehrer,

Until men we are;

We believe in our Fuehrer,

We live for our Fuehrer,

We die for our Fuehrer,

Until heroes we are.

Song sung in Nazi preschool nursery

The Socialization of Memory

Teaching Obedience in Nazi Germany

MEMORY AND POLITICAL SOCIALIZATION

People are not born with memory or with political ideas. As
far as is known, everything we remember is taught to us either formally,
through the process of education, or informally, through the process of cultural transmission. Born into a particular political culture, young people learn
the norms of that culture through the agents of socialization. Generally speaking, these agents include family, educational systems, media, peers, and other
influences such as religion. These norms are taught to every person in order to
try to convince individuals to accept them as "natural" and to exhibit "approved of" or "desirable" forms of behavior. By extension, if this process is
successful, it operates to control what is regarded as "deviant."

The most efficient means of insuring conformity and obedience is to transmit, through political socialization, norms of behavior that are congruent with the dominant ideology in a society. If people can be convinced that these norms are "legitimate," that they define proper behavior, then it will not be necessary for those in power to resort to force to put down dissidents—that is, those who do not conform to the norms. To accomplish this, all states and organizations socialize new members in an attempt to instill their desired vision of reality (Hirsch 1971b; Matthews 1960; Wheeler 1966). One of the most important aspects of this process is the creation of an agreed to or collective memory so that all or most individuals in a nation or society will value positively the same set of symbols and will share a view of what is and is not legitimate. Thus cultures and societies define deviance. Behavior in the political realm that is defined as not legitimate invokes sanctions, and consequently, the populations are controlled.

If most people, for example, regard military service as a virtue and as necessary for anyone running for high office, such as the presidency of the United States, then not serving or avoiding service in a war with which the candidate disagreed may not help the candidate's approval rating. If, in addition, people believe that all or most of the wars in which a nation has fought were "just," or that the nation never started the wars but was provoked and was acting to defend values that are agreed to be positive, such as defending democracy or the free world, then it becomes very difficult to question that memory. People who do challenge such a perception might be subjected to derision or, even worse, to retribution ranging from blacklisting to prevent them from securing certain jobs to, in cases such as the antiwar protesters of the 1960s, violence by the state. One of the most obvious and pervasive examples of this process can be seen in the operations of educational institutions and other organizations for young people in Nazi Germany.

MANIPULATING MEMORY AND TEACHING OBEDIENCE

All societies, all cultures, all states attempt to perpetuate themselves by inculcating into new members the fundamentals of the ongoing set of living arrangements. For the modern state, the most pervasive mechanism for accomplishing this task has been setting up state-sanctioned systems of public education.

Schools in all societies function to train people for the roles they are to play in those societies. Generally, education serves the dominant political and economic forces in a state. The idea that education serves political ends goes back a long way in history—some attribute it to Plato, some to Rousseau.

However far back one goes, it is clear that at one time education was designed to serve the ends of the dominant religious forces—to inculcate "the faith" and insure its continuation.

As the nation-state replaced religion as the major power in the world, this function was inevitably secularized and transferred to the state. Education became the inseparable adjunct of the state. Its function was to serve the state in the same way it had served religion—to perpetuate it by teaching citizens to revere certain memories, which would serve as the basis for policy, and to obey state authority.

Although all systems of public education are geared toward inculcating political views supportive of the existing arrangements, this process is much clearer in totalitarian states. It is important to examine such examples for at least two reasons. First, totalitarian states that consciously manipulate education as a mechanism of teaching obedience remain an important part of the contemporary scene. Second, the extreme cases teach valuable negative lessons by providing examples of more overt practices that operate at a subtler level in less authoritarian settings. With these considerations in mind, the Nazi experience assumes great importance since it is the prototype of controlling and manipulating memory.

In order to understand the workings of a comprehensive system designed to create a quiescent and obedient population through manipulating memory, it is necessary, first, to examine the overall philosophy of education as expressed by the leadership and, second, to attempt to ascertain the specific mechanisms of implementation.

The culture and philosophy of Nazi Germany are well known. Assuming power in 1933, Adolf Hitler proceeded to build a regime based on the twin principles of unquestioning obedience to authority and racial hatred. These principles guided the creation of an education system that one observer referred to as a system of "education for death" (Ziemer 1972). Hitler, as his confidant Albert Speer (1970) notes, was "particularly concerned with the question of how he could assure his Reich a new generation of followers committed to his ideas" (p. 122). His solution, as that of other political leaders in totalitarian settings, was to organize the formal and informal socialization mechanisms so that the youth of Germany would learn to be obedient soldiers and personal vassals of the Fuehrer. The principles upon which Nazi education rested were

Faith in the Fuehrer
Love for the Fuehrer
Hate of enemies (Mann 1938, p. 47)

The Nazi state was to have total control over all individuals. The German child was to be bound to the Nazi party. As a Nazi saying put it:

> When does the Nazi Party become interested in the german Child?
> Before it is conceived. (Ziemer 1972, p. 25)

The German child would attend a Nazi school, belong to a Nazi youth organization, see Nazi movies, play Nazi games,[1] wear Nazi uniforms, and become willing to sacrifice his or her life for the Nazi state and the Fuehrer. *Mein Kampf* became the official guide for education and behavior, and Hitler proceeded to establish a series of institutions designed to lead German youth in the desired direction. In addition to the schools, the Nazis established a comprehensive set of nonschool institutions designed to help the child become an obedient citizen of the Third Reich. The socialization of children was part of the overall totalitarian concept that included controlling all aspects of life—from conception, through childhood, and into adulthood. Institutions were an essential element in maintaining this control.

INSTITUTIONS FOR THE YOUNG

After birth, the first institution a child encountered was the Nazi day nursery (Kindertagesataedte). The party provided food, entertainment, flags, pictures, supervision, and special uniforms for every child who attended—including babies as young as six months. Children could enter the nursery only if they were healthy and of pure "Aryan" descent, which was to be proven by genealogical record. Parents had to sign a document giving the party exclusive jurisdiction over their children while they were in the nursery (Ziemer 1972, p. 49). The nurseries were organized around essentially the same philosophy that guided all aspects of the Reich—training citizens to revere and obey the Fuehrer. This training drew a very sharp distinction between roles to be played by males and females.

Girls were described as inherently weak, while boys were "naturally" strong; female and male roles, therefore, were accordingly different. As a teacher's manual noted: "Boys and girls have nothing in common. Their aims, their purposes in life, are fundamentally different. Boys will become soldiers; girls will become breeders. Co-educational schools are manifestations of decadent democracies and hence are taboo" (Ziemer 1972, p. 16).

---

1. One example of a Nazi game was a variation on "cowboys and Indians" called "Aryans and Jews." It is not difficult to guess which role was considered the most desirable (Grunberger 1971, p. 285).

Boys six to ten years old were regarded as Pimpf or "little fellows." They were provided a uniform composed of "heavy black shoes, short black stockings, black shorts, a brown shirt with a swastika armband, and a trench cap" (Ziemer 1972, p. 16). During this period, the purpose of training was to set the foundation of obedience for the periods to follow when the young boys would enter Jungvolk and Hitler Youth. The Pimpf attended preschool until one o'clock, then participated in party activities, including running errands and performing guard duty. Weekends were devoted to military maneuvers.

Each Pimpf was given a number and an efficiency record book. In this, he was to record his physical development, military activity, and ideological growth. This efficiency record book divided life into activities called "prerequisites," such as

- Ideological schooling
- Promotion examination
- Athletic achievements
- Military accomplishments, including the ability to set up a tent, march, make maps, do spy work, and fire a gun
- Party accomplishments, including knowledge of Hitler songs, Hitler biography, Hitler oaths, and Hitler holidays
- Foreign affairs, including "the names of territories lost by the Treaty of Versailles, knowledge of lost African colonies, names and locations of . . . strategic positions in foreign countries of military value" (p. 55)

School, home, and party life was supervised, controlled, and recorded as the Pimpf participated in many activities designed to reinforce obedience.

When the Pimpf was ten years old, he had to pass a rigid examination before he could be promoted to Jungvolk. If he failed, he was humiliated, and if he passed, he was told to be ready to die for Hitler. The transition from Pimpf to Jungvolk was marked by well-defined rituals of passage and induction. Symbols of blood and violence, such as a flag dipped in the blood of a Nazi killed by Communists, were part of the process. The final step in entering Jungvolk was the taking of an oath: "In the presence of this blood-flag which represents our Fuehrer, I swear to devote all my energies, all my strength to the savior of our country, Adolf Hitler. I am willing and ready to give up my life for him, so help me God. One people, one Nation, one Fuehrer" (Ziemer 1972, p. 59).

Jungvolk was an elaborately organized group divided into 580 Jungbanne. The members were subjected to a series of difficult tests, such as being forced to endure long marches, periods of hunger, and limited privileges. Life was spartan and restricted. These ten-year-olds were provided a coherent ideology that pervaded their entire experience. For example, after a Jungvolk nature class studied an ant hill, the teacher drew their attention to the appropriate moral: "Everywhere you looked you saw how nature employed the Fuehrer Prinzip, the principle of leadership. One thing you did not see, and that is the principle of democracy" (pp. 65–66). As throughout history, the ants obeyed the leader and the strong dominated the weak. The themes were consistent and were reinforced in and out of school. Around the campfire, Jungvolk sang:

> Adolf Hitler is our savior, our hero.
> He is the noblest being in the whole wide world.
> For Hitler we live,
> For Hitler we die.
>> Our Hitler is our lord
>> Who makes a brand new world. (p. 120)

At the age of fourteen, boys left Jungvolk with a ceremony similar to that marking the transition from Pimpf to Jungvolk. After taking the appropriate oath, the fourteen-year-old became a member of Hitler Youth and learned to become a soldier. Hitler Youth studied German culture, Nazi party history, military geography, natural science, chemistry, mathematics, and a foreign language. All subjects, as we shall see, were taught from the peculiarly Nazi perspective. Indoctrination in Hitler's doctrines was also continued. When Hitler Youth turned nineteen, they entered either a university or, more likely, the military.

Girls, although involved in similar organizations, were exposed to different training. In *Mein Kampf*, Hitler stressed that the "one absolute aim of female education must be with a view to the future mother" ([1925] 1943, p. 169). The Nazis attempted to control the entire process from conception to birth to education by controlling women. Women were sterilized if they were determined to be "unfit" mothers, and they had to obtain permission from the state to marry. Women were encouraged and expected to have children, and those with fewer than four were labeled "slackers" (Ziemer 1972, p. 36). Their entire training, as with males, involved total control used to inculcate obedience to the Fuehrer. For example, the Nazi state provided homes for unwed mothers who bore "state children"—that is, illegitimate children—that functioned as propaganda machines. Meals in these homes were preceded by the following prayer:

> Our Fuehrer, we thank thee for thy munificence;
> we thank thee for this home;
> we thank thee for this food. To thee we
> devote all our powers; to thee we dedicate our
> lives and those of our children. (p. 35)

Again, as with the boys, the girls were provided a series of institutional structures. Until they were fourteen years old, girls were classified as Jungmaedel, or "young girls." During this period, they received the basic education that the party considered essential, just enough to enable them to read and write. Most of their education focused on preparing for childbirth and taking care of the home. This training continued into the next stage, when from ages fourteen to twenty-one girls belonged to the Bund Deutscher Maedel—League of German Girls.

The young women wore uniforms and attended classes that were part of a course called "activities of women." These classes included handiwork, domestic science, cooking, and house and garden work. Considered most important was the course on eugenics and hygiene, which was devoted to the study of male and female reproductive organs, conception, birth, racial purity, infant care, and family welfare. Although the girls also learned nursing skills and were taught how to defend the homeland, such skills were secondary to the propagation of the superrace. Since a woman's primary responsibility was to have children, it did not matter whether she was married or unmarried. In fact, monogamy was considered an impediment to the superrace. In an article entitled "Knowledge and the Spirit of Motherhood," Professor Ernst Bergman stated: "Life-long monogamy is perverse and would prove harmful to our race. Were this institution ever really enforced—and fortunately this is almost never the case in reality—the race must decay. Every reasonably constructed State would have to regard a woman who has not given birth as dishonored. There are plenty of willing qualified youths ready to unite with the girls and women on hand. Fortunately, one boy of good race suffices for twenty girls" (quoted in Mann 1938, pp. 138–39).

The Nazi state obviously intended to socialize males and females to meet rigid role specifications. The institutions provided for this training had distinct functions, and the roles of the respective sexes were clearly spelled out, although for both, the primary responsibility was service to the Fuehrer and the state. In order to insure that this plan was successfully implemented and the goals secured, a tightly controlled formal system of education was set up in which teachers were carefully selected and the curriculum was structured to emphasize obedience.

SCHOOLS IN NAZI GERMANY

Kandel ([1935] 1970) points out that during the previous two centuries of German history two political concepts had been in conflict (pp. 3–4). Since the time of Frederick the Great, the idea had existed that the state was absolute and authoritarian and that the will of the state was superior to that of the individual or the people collectively. The power of the state was to be supported by aggressive militarism. An opposing concept, manifested during shorter periods, held that the "state should grow vitally and organically out of the people themselves and that the culture and spirit of a people can flourish better if left to express themselves spontaneously rather than if they are regimented from above." Throughout German history, the former concept had been dominant, and it constituted the core value on which the Third Reich based a system of education.

Education as conceived by Hitler was not to be confined to "stuffy classrooms but to be furthered by a Spartan, political and martial training in the successive youth groups and to reach its climax not so much in the universities and engineering colleges, which absorbed but a small minority, but first, at the age of eighteen, in compulsory labor service and then in service, as conscripts, in the armed forces" (Shirer 1960, p. 248). To implement and work out the details for the total control of education, Hitler appointed Bernard Rust to the position of Reich minister of science, education, and culture in 1934. Rust had been a member of the Nazi party since 1922, and since 1930 had been an unemployed teacher (Mann 1938, p. 48; Shirer 1960, p. 248).[2] Reputed to have been a fanatical Nazi, Rust had boasted in 1933 when he was named Prussian minister of science, art, and education that he would succeed overnight in "liquidating the school as an institution of intellectual acrobatics" (Shirer 1960, p. 248).

The goal, as stated by Rust, was for the German school to become an "integral part of the National Socialist order of living. It has the mission, in collaboration with other phases of the Party, to fashion and mold the National Socialist being according to Party orders" (quoted in Ziemer 1972, p. 17). In order to achieve these ends, Rust proceeded to reorganize the schools and to draw up instructions for teachers. These instructions may be found in the "Official Teacher's Manual" as cited in Ziemer (1972). Since teachers are one of the main agents through which the desired views of the state are communicated, it is important to examine the role of the teacher in the Third Reich.

TEACHERS IN NAZI GERMANY

According to the "Official Teacher's Manual," teachers were disciplinarians who did not instruct but commanded, and their "orders are backed up with

2. Shirer (1960) reports that Rust was dismissed by "local Republicans [in the Weimar Republic] at Hanover for certain manifestations of instability of mind," possibly alluding to his fanatical nazism (p. 248).

force if necessary" (Ziemer 1972, p. 15). According to Minister Rust, successful education had little to do with knowledge. Rather, education was a success if students learned to submit to authority. Within this view, knowledge had only one legitimate end—enhancing the power of the state. The job of the teacher was to indoctrinate all students into Nazi ideology and to teach them to obey the "Fuehrer Prinzip" (leadership principle).

Teachers were supposed to be miniature Hitlers—Fuehrers in their own classrooms, where obedience was the rule. Class discussion was prohibited since, as the minister noted, it often led to faultfinding and criticism. The lecture system was the only form of instruction allowed, and no freedom was permitted because youth often, according to the minister, abused freedom. To be a teacher in Nazi Germany, then, was to be a participant in a system endorsing obvious antiintellectualism. To become such a participant, a prospective teacher had to meet certain requirements.

In the winter of 1933, teachers of "non-Aryan" or Jewish descent were relieved of their positions. On July 11, 1933, an edict was issued ordering teachers to subordinate their wishes, interests, and demands to the common cause and to devote themselves to the study of National Socialist ideology. It also "suggested" that they familiarize themselves with *Mein Kampf*, which became the model for education (Mann 1938, p. 52). After November 1933, all German schoolteachers were required to "belong to a Nazi fighting organization; they were to come to school in uniform, whenever possible, and live in camps; and, during the final examinations, they were to be tested in Gelande-sport—military sport."

By 1937, 97 percent of all teachers belonged to the National Socialist Teachers' Union, and in the spring of 1937, a decree was issued stating that every member of this union must "submit a table of his ancestors in three copies, with official documents of proof, or certified copies of the same." Teachers could not escape indoctrination and control, and by 1938, two-thirds of the teaching force had been sent to training camps (Grunberger 1971, p. 287).

A Nazi teacher served the state and taught the philosophy of that state to the children. As one might expect, the materials teachers used reflected Nazi tenets.

TEACHING MATERIALS FOR NAZI EDUCATION

The courses and textbooks in Nazi schools reflected the goals of the Fuehrer, and teachers were expected to cover the following categories of topics, in order of importance:

- Hereditary tendencies (general racial picture)
- The character (degree of adherence to national socialism)
- The physical makeup of the body (degree of usefulness in the event of war)
- Knowledge (not in the traditional sense, but National Socialist knowledge)

Knowledge, in the traditional sense, was not included on the list, and the stories, textbooks, and formal course work used in the Nazi classroom all reflected its absence.

In a revealing interview, a teacher at a girl's school was asked if students were ever given time to play. The response illustrates the nature of the educational priorities in Nazi Germany: "Play? You mean silly games that have no real purpose behind them? Well, no. They are not infants any more, you know. Life is too serious for play" (Ziemer 1972, p. 95). Not only did play have no place in the curriculum, but knowledge was reduced to education for war and obedience. A high school principal writing in 1935 stated: "Education in relation to weapons, then, is no special branch of general education; rather, it is in point of fact, the very core of our entire education" (Mann 1938, pp. 54–55).

Textbooks and courses naturally reflected these goals. Under the Nazis, the preparation of textbooks was in their total control by 1939. After this time, "books could be published only if they had the approval of a special commission headed by Phillipp Bouhler" (Blackburn 1985, p. 6). By 1941, only one firm was allowed to produce textbooks—the German School Press (Samuel and Thomas 1949, p. 163). In many respects, Nazi textbooks continued and built upon the traditions manifest in German culture prior to the rise of Hitler—hero worship, glorification of war, obedience, and Germany's encirclement by a hostile world. Additional dimensions included the vilification of the Weimar Republic and the increased emphasis on Jews, socialists, and internationalism as antipatriotic (pp. 87–88). Textbooks were also increasingly replaced by propaganda pamphlets and books written to inculcate the Fuehrer Prinzip and the military spirit.

For example, a young child was usually exposed to a primer that clearly showed the priorities "in word and picture, with camp life, marching, martial drums, boys growing up to be soldiers, and girls to take care of soldiers" (Mann 1938, pp. 56–57). A supplement to the primer was entitled *Trust No Fox on Green Heath! And No Jew on His Oath!*: "On the bright red cover are two pictures with the title. One is of the fox, peering around a corner maliciously eager for his prey; and the other, a typical Nazi caricature of the Jew, beneath a Star of David—huge nose, thick lips and bleary eyes, swearing his false oath with fat fingers raised." The words the authors wished their readers to remember were printed in red: "Devil," "Jews," "thick-lips," "gangster." This anti-Semitic book was a basic educational tool and was typical of the material provided for young children.

Course content was likewise oriented toward the same goals. Art had to involve military themes. Drawing, for example, included lessons such as aerial defense. Chemistry focused on how to use and defend against chemical warfare. Chapter titles in one textbook of chemistry experiments, *School Experiments in the Chemistry of Fighting Materials: A Book of Experiments in Protection against Poison Gas and Air Raids*, were "Gas Weapons," "Eye Irritants," "Lung Poisons or Choking Weapons," "Skin Poisons," and "Nose and Throat Irritants" (Mann 1938, p. 27). Physics was also Nazi physics or the "physics of weapons." One Nazi physicist summed up the reasoning by noting that, "Science is and remains, like everything else, created by the human mind, racially bound and a result of blood" (p. 95). A typical physics problem read: "A coast artillery gun is firing at a ship steaming at a speed of thirty knots diagonally toward the point where the cannon is. How great is the approach? The average speed of the projectile is to be as 600 meters per second" (p. 96). Mathematics too served the Nazi state. In *The National Socialist Essence of Education*, a German educator wrote that mathematics was "Aryan spiritual property; it is an expression of the Nordic fighting spirit, of Nordic struggle for the supremacy of the world beyond its boundaries" (quoted in Mann 1938, p. 66). Most math problems involved airplanes, bombs, cannons, and guns or used historical and racial propaganda. Two examples follow:

1. Germany had, according to the Versailles Treaty, to surrender all her colonies (An enumeration of colonies and mandates, with estimates of population and area, is given)
   A. What was Germany's total loss in population and territory?
   B. How much did each mandatory power receive in territory and population?
   C. How many times greater is the surrendered territory than the area of Germany?
   D. Compare the population of Germany with the population of the lost territories.
2. The Jews are aliens in Germany—in 1933 there were 66,060,000 inhabitants in the German Reich of whom 499,682 were Jews. What is the percentage of aliens? (pp. 67–68)[3]

3. The first problem is taken from *National Political Practice in Arithmetic Lessons* and the second from *Germany's Fall and Rise: Illustrations Taken from Arithmetic Instruction in Higher Grades of Elementary School.*

Not only science courses but also courses in history, geography, and religion were given over to inculcating obedience and racial hatred. In a religion course, students would be told that the Nazi state was willed by God. The premise was that "Hitler had come to his people directly from God. . . . His planes are God's planes, his methods God's methods, and his will God's will." Jesus became a war hero who "waged war on the Jews until he was killed by them" (Mann 1938, pp. 86–87). Children were provided with slogans to learn and recite. One example is, "Judas the Jew, betrayed Jesus the German, to the Jews" (p. 90).

Geography emphasized German superiority and race purity. The general viewpoint was that race purity made Germany superior to other nations. According to this outlook, since the United States was a melting pot, composed of "undesirables" from Europe whose children had mingled with Jews and blacks, its citizens were sinking ever lower on the scale measuring the superiority of beings. In one class observed by an American teacher in Germany, the German teacher elaborated on this theme:

There are many other weaknesses as a result of this lack of racial purity. Their government is corrupt. They have a low type of government, a democracy. What is a democracy?

Democracy is a government by rich Jews.

A democracy is a government in which there is not real leadership.

A democracy is a government that will be defeated by the Fuehrer. (Ziemer 1972, pp. 68, 69)

History was a cult of personality based on a romanticized past. It was great men and military battles and had the twin goals of fixing race consciousness and insuring blind obedience. As one essay entitled "History as the Essence of Political Education" noted: "The crown of all teaching of history consists of nothing but following the Fuehrer" (Mann 1938, p. 58). Nazi history was, in short, history reconstructed to fit the Nazi model and preconceived ideology. It was memory rewritten, and it is one of the most obvious examples of the state attempting to manipulate memory to serve its own ends. Nazi education was devoted to support of the Nazi state. Teachers, textbooks, and the conduct of classes were all mobilized to promote the values of militarism and obedience. Yet, in the end, it did not survive.

CONCLUSION

In the finale of World War II, the Allied bombing offensive of 1943 tumbled German education into chaos. By autumn 1944, when the Allies entered

Germany, "Education was virtually at a standstill" (Samuel and Thomas 1949, p. 163). Even though the entire political edifice of the Third Reich disintegrated, the fact remains that the Nazis had attempted a rather remarkable experiment in manipulating memory through totalitarian education. The question of the impact of this education, consequently, must be addressed.

Even though Nazi policies could not have been implemented 100 percent in every school in Germany, millions of German youths were exposed to Nazi thought and to Nazi schools. Children who began their education in 1933, at age six, would be in their sixties in 1993. Millions of present-day Germans, therefore, experienced at least some of their early socialization within the context of the Nazi school system. Questions concerning the long-term effect of this exposure have generated two interpretations.

The first view asserts that, since the entire edifice of Nazi education was overturned—the Reich Ministry of Education was abolished and sixteen new states were created, each with its own Ministry of Education—the "Nazi educational materials made no permanent impact upon the mind of most Germans" (Blackburn 1985, p. 184). The second interpretation maintains that nazism did have a significant educational impact. Blackburn (1985) sums up this view: "It is not possible to separate classroom instruction from education in the more inclusive sense. Measured by that broader gauge, the Nazis' educational program aimed at nothing less than changing the nation's view of the world and of reality itself. The short term successes of the Nazi regime were certainly impressive. . . . It took the greater part of the world's armed might to bruise the head of that serpentine force, whose legions had been schooled for the contest in one of the most unique and far-reaching experiments in educational history" (p. 184). In addition, as discussed in chapter 4, Germany has failed to deal forthrightly with the period of the Holocaust. Renn (1983) has shown in his analysis of contemporary German textbooks that most textbooks repress discussion of the Nazi period (pp. 157–77).

Given the overall trends of denial and manipulation of memory, it is likely that the Nazi experiment in totalitarian education had some lasting effect. Of course, the long-term effect of exposure to the Nazi education system cannot be addressed without major in-depth retrospective interviews with those who participated in the system. It is possible that German citizens simply adapted to the changing historical/political circumstances within their nation-state and coped to the best of their ability. This is not implausible since it is probably the predominant response of individuals forced to accept history reconstructed by a powerful and supposedly beneficent state. Most citizens, as Primo Levi aptly noted, are "one-eyed men in the kingdom of the blind" and do not confront the lies and the pollution of memory. The socialization of reconstructed memory is an ongoing, modern problem. All states attempt to insure their continuity by manipulating memory and by controlling the mechanisms that transmit memory to succeeding generations. Whether the reconstruction of memory is a success, as defined by the state, depends on the result of the process of political socialization. A "successful" product, from the perspective of the state, would produce quiescent subjects—citizens who will not question authority and who will obey the orders given to them. As we shall see in the next chapter, the socialization of obedience and the resulting psychology of obedience are prime factors in motivating individuals to participate in genocidal incidents.

> The choice to say no ... ultimately rests on our saying yes
> to some of the distinct qualities that make us human: a
> sense of personal agency, an awareness of the consequences
> of our actions, and a caring attitude toward our fellow
> human beings.
>
> Herbert C. Kelman and V. Lee Hamilton, *Crimes of Obedience:*
> *Toward a Social Psychology of Authority and Responsibility* (1989)

Learning to Obey

Creating the Conditions for Genocide

If all nation-states attempt to socialize citizens to obey authority without question, and if, as I will demonstrate, obedience to authority is a prime motivator for participation in genocide, one might have thought that the social science disciplines would express great interest in this crucial set of issues. On the contrary, they have, for the most part, demonstrated little concern. Even modern psychology, which might have approached this topic through its focus on memory and learning, has shown little interest in autobiographical memory and even less in history. Of course, a few conspicuous exceptions have been concerned with exploring why people commit mass murder. Although as a whole contemporary psychology is more focused on experimentation and clinical practice, some insightful analysis has emerged that is clearly suitable as a foundation upon which to endeavor to construct a more comprehensive explanation of individual participation in mass murder.

Three works are of particular importance: Milgram's pioneering work, *Obedience to Authority* (1974), which will be discussed later, Staub's *The Roots of Evil* (1989), and Kelman and Hamilton's *Crimes of Obedience* (1989). The two latter works reveal Milgram's contribution, although not always acknowledging it, and they start with the assertion that many of the greatest crimes against humanity are committed in the name of obedience. As a result, much of the focus has been on explaining the roots and results of unquestioning obedience to authority.

Kelman and Hamilton attempt to account for the apparent repetition throughout history of what they call "crimes of obedience" by focusing on "the consequences that often ensue when authority gives orders exceeding the bounds of morality or law" (1989, p. xi). According to their definition, an act of obedience becomes a crime of obedience "if the actor knows that the order is illegal, or if any reasonable person—particularly someone in the actor's position—'should know' that the order is illegal" (p. 47). An act of obedience is a crime if the orders issued by superiors cause or justify the act of violence. The issues involved thrust us into the uncharted and precarious terrain of individual and collective responsibility.

As one of their prime examples, Kelman and Hamilton begin with the crime of obedience committed at the village of My Lai on March 16, 1968, by a company of U.S. soldiers commanded by Lt. William C. Calley. After examining the massacre, the military code of justice, and the trial of Calley, Kelman and Hamilton attempt to explain this particular crime of obedience, which they refer to as "sanctioned massacre." In discussing their analysis, I will place it more directly within the context of the already-existing literature, which the authors refer to from time to time but often leave out when it seems most relevant. In so doing, I do not intend to make light of their contribution but to connect their book and this one with the larger narrative and explanatory tradition of work in this area.

According to Kelman and Hamilton, "sanctioned massacres" are "violent acts . . . of indiscriminate, ruthless, and often systematic mass violence, carried out by military or paramilitary personnel which engaged in officially sanctioned campaigns, the victims of which are defenseless and unresisting civilians, including old men, women, and children" (1989, p. 12). Sanctioned massacres, they argue, have occurred throughout history and examples include the actions of U.S. troops in the Philippine war, the massacres of the Native Americans, the Nazi extermination of the European Jews, the extermination of the Armenians by the Turks in the period from 1915 to 1917, the liquidation of the Russian kulaks, and the massacres that have taken place in Indonesia, Bangladesh, Biafra, Burundi, South Africa, and Cambodia—clearly there is no paucity of examples. Genocide, as this type of crime of obedience has been labeled since the term was first coined by the international lawyer Raphael Lemkin in 1944, has, according to Kelman and Hamilton, certain common features. They focus on two particular features: context and target.

All sanctioned massacres, they argue, occur "in the context of an overall policy that is explicitly or implicitly genocidal: designed to destroy all or part of a category of people defined in ethnic, national, racial, religious, or other terms" (1989, p. 13). The massacres themselves may not be explicitly planned, but the overall policy sanctions the violent acts as a strategic necessity. Second, the authors point out that the targets or victims are "often defenseless civilians," and the primary question they ask is why "so many people are willing to formulate, participate in, and condone policies that call for the mass killings of defenseless civilians" (p. 15). To answer this difficult and most important question, Kelman and Hamilton identify three social processes that tend to create conditions under which sanctioned massacre occurs: authorization, routinization, and dehumanization.

Sanctioned massacres are authorized by an authority situation within which "a different kind of morality, linked to duty to obey orders, tends to take over" (1989, p. 16). This condition was apparently first identified by Stanley Milgram (1974) when he noted that people acting under orders do not lose their moral sense but that the moral sense "acquires a radically different focus" (p. 8). Moral concern shifts to a consideration of how well a person is living up to the expectations that the authority has of her or him. "In wartime," Milgram notes, "a soldier does not ask whether it is good or bad to bomb a hamlet; he does not experience shame or guilt in the destruction of a village: rather he feels pride or shame depending on how well he has performed the mission assigned to him." In short, as Kelman and Hamilton, and Milgram, argue, individuals see themselves as agents, as having no choice but to accept the legitimacy of orders they are given. This, in turn, allows them to be relatively free of guilt when their actions cause harm to others because they are required and permitted to do so by the authorities from whom the orders came. Acts of violence are thus legitimated, and the perpetrators are rendered free of guilt because they are acting out the orders of higher authority.

The second condition, routinization, "transforms the action into routine, mechanical, highly programmed operations" (1989, p. 18). Routinization operates at both the individual and organizational level as the performance of a job is broken down into steps and divided among different offices. Responsibility is consequently diffused. This is very close to Weber's (1946) classic arguments about the nature of bureaucracy. Weber notes that bureaucracy is characterized by hierarchy and levels of graded authority, in which the responsibility for a job is divided and there is a firmly ordered system of super- and subordination (p. 54). Routinization normalizes atrocity and masks it with language (as argued in chapter 10), rendering it seemingly harmless.

The third condition is dehumanization. Dehumanization is necessary, according to Kelman and Hamilton, because the usual moral inhibitions against killing can be overcome once the victims are "deprived in the perpetrator's eyes of the two qualities essential to being perceived as fully human and included in the moral compact that governs human relationships: *identity*— standing as independent, distinctive individuals . . . and *community*—fellow membership in an interconnected network of individuals who care for each other and respect each other's individuality and rights" (1989, p. 19). When people are denied these qualities, the moral restraints against killing them are weakened.[1] Once again, however, these notions were developed earlier, and Kelman and Hamilton's work should be tied to this previous study.

The idea of the "universe of moral obligation" was first developed by Helen Fein (1979) in the very important work, *Accounting for Genocide*. Fein was the first to point out that excluding fellow humans from the universe of moral obligation loosened the restraints on violence and defined them as likely victims of sanctioned massacre.

Next, I broaden Kelman and Hamilton's analysis to ascertain if there are more inclusive conditions under which genocide might occur.

CREATING THE CONDITION FOR GENOCIDE

"So you didn't feel they were human beings?"
"Cargo . . . they were cargo."
"There were so many children, did they ever make you think of your children, of how you would feel in the position of those parents?"
"No . . . I can't say I ever thought this way. . . . You see . . . I rarely saw them as individuals. It was always as a huge mass."
—Franz Stangl, commandant of Sobibor and Treblinka extermination camps, interviewed by Gitta Sereny, *Into That Darkness* (1974)

As memory is transmitted from generation to generation in the ongoing process of renewing the species, the myths, legends, and other assorted likes and dislikes that persist in a culture are also transmitted. As we have seen in

1. At this point in the book, Kelman and Hamilton (1989) abandon their more comprehensive focus to examine in detail the process of authorization. Going well beyond

previous chapters, these elements are transmitted through language by the process of political socialization. If memory is to serve as a warning and to act as the foundation on which to build a more humane world, it is important to understand how people become killers. The bluntest possible confrontation with the most depressing possibilities is called for so as not to disguise the realities. We must, therefore, begin with the realization that mass murder does not occur in a vacuum and is not committed by "other" people. For people to die, other people have to pull the triggers, release the gas, and drop the bombs. How they are convinced to undertake such actions knowing full well what the end result will be is a question of enduring significance. The search for answers might very well begin with a consideration of Raul Hilberg's classic work, *The Destruction of the European Jews* (1985).

Hilberg notes that in order for mass murder to occur, mechanisms must be developed to short-circuit traditional concepts of individual morality. Psychologically, people must not be allowed to feel guilt or pain, or empathy, when they destroy others. Lifton (1987), as noted in chapter 8, refers to this as "numbing," while Duster (1971) discusses the "conditions for guilt free massacre" (pp. 25–36). These terms mean essentially the same thing—namely, that mechanisms are developed to justify and rationalize the destruction of the targeted group. In short, the planners of the proposed massacres must motivate participation in order to bring about the desired result—extermination. To accomplish this, certain conditions must be created. These conditions, as we shall see, allow the perpetrators to successfully carry out their planned actions while at the same time providing a means to dissipate guilt and explain why such horrible acts were necessary.

Although Duster identifies six conditions,[2] I have narrowed them to three

My Lai, they extend their focus to numerous other examples, including Watergate, and ultimately decide that crimes of obedience occur most often within structured contexts of authority. They examine the forces that both *bind* individuals to authority and cause them to *oppose* authority. They also analyze responses to a series of questionnaires that asked the general public to react to the My Lai massacre and the Calley trial. It is during these discussions that the previously coherent narrative begins to break down. The data analysis is presented in mind-numbing detail, complete with repetitive discussions and abbreviated classification schemes that can only serve to confuse general, non–social scientist readers. This, as I argued earlier, draws attention away from their early formulation of how people are motivated to participate in sanctioned massacres.

2. The six conditions Duster (1971) identifies are the denial of the victims' humanity, the subordination of the individual to organizations, the connection between individual responsibility and rules of organization, secrecy and isolation, the existence of a target population, and developing the "motivation to commit a massacre" (pp. 25–36).

broader, more inclusive categories—three conditions under which the state will be able to motivate participation in mass murder. Lacking more descriptive terminology, I call them cultural, psychological, and political conditions.

CULTURAL CONDITIONS

Cultural conditions are usually tied to the myths and ideologies stressed in a culture or a nation-state, which are used to rationalize or justify the destructive activity of the state.[3] As we saw in the previous discussion of language, every society claims a genealogy, an explanation grounded in mythology of the origin of its people or of the state. Generally, these myths hold that the members of the group or the state descend from divine sources or are protected by divine intervention. This type of thinking differentiates the group or the state from all other groups or states and thus serves as a reason for dehumanizing those perceived as "the enemy," against whom the state wishes to pursue aggressive action. The fact that "enemies" are not protected by or descended from the same bloodlines and do not have the same pedigree may serve as a justification for genocide.

In other words, the myths and ideologies stressed in a culture or state are expressed in the language of the major authority figures and are transmitted, through the process of acculturation or socialization, to the people living within the bounds of the state. As they absorb and begin to believe these myths, they are conditioned so that when ordered to engage in acts they might not have considered moral in other circumstances, they are willing to obey the orders because of the elaborate system of justification that has been constructed. These cultural conditions for mass murder are related to psychological conditions, which focus on the explicit mechanisms through which citizens are taught to obey authority.

PSYCHOLOGICAL CONDITIONS

The psychological conditions for participation in acts of atrocity focus directly on the possibility that, given certain circumstances, individuals might find themselves in a position in which their sense of individual morality, of right and wrong, is compromised. The basic psychological conditions necessary for mass murder involve obedience to authority; following orders takes

3. The relationship between racial myths, culture, and oppression is explored in Poliakov (1971) and Mosse (1978). The connection between culture and genocide or oppression is examined in Harris (1973), Henry (1965), and Becker (1975).

precedence over all other considerations. Under these conditions, individuals no longer view themselves as responsible for their actions, and they define themselves as instruments for carrying out the wishes and commands of those in positions of authority (Milgram 1974; Moore 1978). The classic example, of course, is Adolf Eichmann.

After his arrest for war crimes, Eichmann never expressed guilt or remorse for the acts he committed. His position, according to the transcripts of his interrogation (Lang 1984), was that he had never killed any Jews: "I had nothing to do with killing the Jews. I never killed a Jew, but I never killed a non-Jew either—I've never killed anybody. And I never ordered anybody to kill a Jew, or ordered anybody to kill a non-Jew. No, never" (p. 101). Eichmann, however, left little doubt that if he had received such an order he would have done so. In fact, he recalled that he would have felt remorse only if he had not done what he had been ordered to do—that is, organize the transportation of millions of men, women, and children to their death "with great zeal and meticulous care" (Arendt 1965, p. 25). Eichmann has become the prototype of the person whose sense of individual morality has been reoriented so that he or she feels shame or pride according to how efficiently he or she carries out orders. Efficiency in carrying out orders remains a highly desired value in contemporary society. In fact, Milgram has argued that morality takes on a different shape in the highly bureaucratized, hierarchical states that characterize our times. Morality is now defined, as it was for Eichmann, in terms of how well a person carries out the tasks assigned to him or her—no matter what they may entail.

The implications of this view are that acts of human destructiveness are not necessarily committed only by deranged psychopaths. Rather, a viewpoint that has come to be referred to as the "banality of evil" stresses that evil is most likely committed by very ordinary people. One biographer of Heinrich Himmler, head of the SS, has noted that, although it is difficult to accept, we must begin to understand that many of the great monsters of history, such as Eichmann and Himmler, were not unusual examples of their culture. They were, as he characterized Himmler, "pedestrian, unimaginative—in a word, ordinary" (Graber 1978, p. 211).

Similar examples of banality or ordinariness pervade the decision-making bureaucracy in the contemporary United States. For example, Thomas K. Jones, a deputy undersecretary of defense in the Reagan administration, is quoted in Scheer (1983) as saying that "the United States could fully recover from an all-out nuclear war with the Soviet Union in just two to four years" (p. 18). He declared that nuclear war was not nearly as devastating as we had been led to believe and went on to say, "If there are enough shovels to go around, everybody's going to make it." Scheer points out that the shovels were "for digging holes in the ground, which would be covered somehow or other with a couple of doors and three feet of dirt thrown on top, thereby providing adequate fallout shelters for the millions who had been evacuated from America's countryside." Jones claimed, "It's the dirt that does it."

How did Jones appear as he talked about nuclear destruction? Scheer describes him in a manner reminiscent of Arendt's depiction of Eichmann:

> Do not misunderstand. There was nothing deranged or hysterical about Jones' performance that night, nothing even intemperate. Jones' manner is circumspect. His house reflects a Spartan life-style. . . . His looks are clean-cut, if plain, and he's trim for his forty-nine years. He seldom raises his voice and tends to speak in a drone, sometimes inaudibly. This studied, matter-of-fact style persisted even when he discussed the deaths of hundreds of millions of people, as if he were attempting by the measured tone of his voice to deny the ultimate horror of it all. I have listened many times to the tapes of this interview, and what startles me most is how easily Jones seemed to make the subject of mass death almost boring. (Scheer 1983, p. 22)

These observations recall the discussion by Lifton and Markusen (1990) of the role of professionals in committing acts of destruction and the mechanisms used to blot such acts out of their memory and consciousness, to numb them to the consequences of their actions. The banality of evil, then, is clearly not confined to the Holocaust. In the nuclear era, contemporary bureaucrats were engaged in planning the destruction of the planet in a calm, almost disinterested, "almost boring," fashion. The individuals who program and play war games seem to be able to consider the possibility of mass death, involving millions of people, without realizing or caring that they are dealing with human flesh and blood. They reduce destruction to abstraction, unleashed in the name of duty, patriotism, "national security" (Landau 1988), and "doing one's job." Obviously, if one is following orders aimed at preserving the national security, then the responsibility for the ultimate horror of mass destruction is not one's own but belongs to the state or the leaders.

The real impact of banality is to render trivial and acceptable the most horrendous acts. When responsible individuals talk about mass death as though they were discussing the weather, they are communicating acceptance and lack of concern.

But government decision makers are not the only people engaged in these processes of justification and rationalization. Citizens on a large scale appeared unwilling to confront the reality of death by nuclear incineration. As

German citizens supported and did not question Hitler's orders, U.S. citizens did not question the president's orders or even his intentions. Whatever the president does is to be supported simply because he *is* the president.

These are, of course, controversial notions because they force us to focus on our own vulnerability and to question the circumstances of our own obedience. Where, for example, does one draw the line in obeying authority? Are there different types of authority? Moore (1978), for example, divides authority into positive and negative categories. Does a person follow orders even if the ultimate result is evil? Such questions are tied closely to the third set of conditions—political conditions.

POLITICAL CONDITIONS

Politics is tied to culture and psychology. The way people view politics and a political system and the way they learn to relate to authority are connected to what they learn as they are growing up. As children, we are all exposed to the cultural and political myths and legends common to our environment. These myths, which we learn through the process of political socialization, act as foundations upon which our adult views of the world and our adult behaviors are based.

Children learn and internalize the existing norms of their culture. If people are convinced that these norms are legitimate, that they are the accepted views of the majority, and particularly of political and social leaders, then they will obey those leaders who communicate the ideas that appear congruent with those norms. The cues that reinforce obedience are sent by people occupying important social, cultural, and political positions. If a strain of the national mythology emphasizes obedience, it is quite possible for leaders to attempt to manipulate that strain in order to convince potential participants that mass destruction is justified. Hence, if people in high positions spread dehumanizing symbolizations of another state or group of people, they send a message that it is justified to act aggressively against that state or group. Many people will always be willing to act out hostile impulses if they are reinforced by those in high positions.

During the Holocaust, the continued description of Jews as vermin and bacilli was a prime example of dehumanizing symbolization. Anti-Semitism was also reinforced by the lack of opposition to the extermination of the Jews. The fact that political and religious leaders did not object seemed to confirm the legitimacy of the destruction. As mentioned in chapter 9, the commandant of Treblinka, Franz Stangl, provided a striking example when he noted that he was profoundly affected by Cardinal Theodor Innitzer's call to Catholics to "cooperate" with the Nazis as well as by the fact that many political leaders capitulated "at once" to the Nazis (Sereny 1974, p. 28). Leaders, consequently, may prepare a population for genocide in this fashion.

This process is no less true today as political figures and their advisers (reinforced by social and religious leaders) discuss war as "policy" and use terminology such as "ethnic cleansing," as in the case of the Serb massacre of the Bosnian Muslims. This form of discussion contributes to the acceptance of genocide as a desirable policy to achieve the goals of the leadership. Political leaders and their advisers thus act to legitimize genocide as an instrument of policy that is not only acceptable but also likely to be used. The state, as was the Nazi state, is turned into an executioner state as the leaders engage in the process of justification and condition the people to participate in and accept the large-scale destruction of their companions on the planet.

CONCLUSION

Obedience may thus be enhanced under three broad types of conditions (Hirsch 1988). The first involves the development of cultural and racial myths and stereotypes that function to dehumanize the target population, in essence identifying the victims. Psychological conditions, the second set, require obedience to authority by individuals—that is, the people who pull the triggers and carry out the orders. The third type of conditions, political conditions, combine the giving of orders with justification of the acts of destruction. Ultimately, if we view mass murder as being carried out, at least in part, in response to these conditions, we are left with the profoundly disturbing conclusion that acts of large-scale destruction of human life may be committed by any individual or nation under the "right" cultural, psychological, or political circumstances.

Understanding the conditions that promote participation in genocide does not necessarily guarantee that these acts will not occur again. Yet we must understand the past and incorporate as an integral part of our learning experience information about genocide and mass murder so that our memory is not reconstructed by the state or those in power who may wish to convince us to kill others. How individuals respond to the language of extermination, how they react to the attempts to socialize obedience, is not predetermined. Humans respond to authority in a great variety of ways. As we shall see in chapter 12, this variety is related to the self, to a person's identity, which is often formed within the crucible of politics and is heavily influenced by the politics of memory.

The ease with which the self adapts its identity to a

surrounding situation threatens the notion that spiritual

value is the primary incentive for human conduct.

Lawrence Langer, *Holocaust Testimonies:*

The Ruins of Memory (1991)

12

Memory and Identity

Developing Self in the Context of Politics

As an individual reconstructs his or her biography through memory, that biography becomes the basis for identity; the same is true of nation-states. Thus it is that the identity of the individual and that of the state form the background upon which the motivation to do good or evil may be imprinted. The type of self that emerges is affected by socialization patterns and by how a person has learned to relate to authority. The connection between memory and identity is dialectical because memory both shapes the content of what is communicated by the socialization process and is formed by that process. Ultimately, the self does not develop in a vacuum.

Although this simple notion seems obvious, scholars interested in the development of identity often neglect important contextual environments within which the self develops and which have important effects on that development throughout the life cycle. Attempts to measure and analyze self or identity have, as one observer notes, "often run aground in a conceptual fog" (Adam 1978, p. 68) because they ignore the context of politics. Any discussion of identity or comparison of levels of self-esteem among different ethnic, racial, or class groups has no significance without examining the conditions surrounding the subject. All social phenomenon are, after all, embedded in social and political structures, and any research that hopes to be remotely isomorphic with reality must consider these structures an integral part of the conceptual framework. In fact, identity is manifestly political since it reflects and is influenced by the social, economic, and political circumstances within which a particular individual or group of individuals finds himself or herself.

Identity becomes a sociopolitical creation when it is tied to power and to the dominant or subordinate position in which an individual or group is placed (Adam 1978, p. 10). For example, access to or denial of opportunities in a society is generally related to the characteristics that have been declared by that society to be valued as either positive or negative. Value might be placed on the color of a person's skin, religion, or gender. These "subjective" judgments are transformed into "objective" categories as they are used by those occupying positions in society that allow them to bestow or withhold the rewards of the system. In short, seemingly objective criteria are actually the result of highly subjective political evaluations that have developed within a society over time. Once these criteria are established, groups will engage in political warfare to maintain or change them and to pass them on to succeeding generations. The criteria for status and success become embedded in the memory and become part of the conventional wisdom and dominant ideology of a culture or state. Hence, they also become political means and ends and are tied to the maintenance of the status quo or to change. The battles over these definitions may become heated and occasionally violent and, in turn, have an impact on an identity developing within that context. In other words, self-esteem cannot be divorced from politics, and research on self-esteem is more complete if it is analyzed within the context of politics. This chapter will examine the process of identity formation as it operates within boundaries formed by the political environment. To accomplish this, it is first necessary to define that environment.

THE POLITICAL ENVIRONMENT OF IDENTITY FORMATION

Terrence Des Pres writes, "To pass from civilization to extremity means to be shorn of the elaborate system of relationships—to job, class, tradition and family, to groups and institutions of every kind—which for us provides perhaps ninety percent of what we think we are" (1976b, p. 214). Even though he was referring to the experience of concentration camp survivors, in a very real sense his comments are applicable to the development of self in the modern world. He identifies the foundations of identity as well as the agents that transmit, through the process of socialization, the cues that will be vital to the formation of individual identity. This process has been elaborated in detail in previous chapters, but what was omitted was any attempt to outline the "political" in political socialization. Even though historically it has been foolhardy to attempt to define precisely what the term "political" means, it is necessary to venture into that territory if one is to have any notion of the context within which identity is formed.

Political thinkers have grappled with the problem of defining "politics" for thousands of years. From Aristotle to Marx, they have offered a multiplicity of definitions. Most contemporary definitions involve the concept of "power"—which itself is very difficult to define. Other definitions use terms such as "influence" and attempt to distinguish between influence and power. These efforts at definitional clarity ultimately, in modern political science, give way to attempts to frame the concepts in mathematical symbols and thus to make them "scientific." Although "scientific" definitions are useful for empirically based studies, especially if they are grounded in theory and based on historical understanding, very often the method becomes an end in itself and results in trivialization in the name of science. As we saw in chapter 7, method replaces content and human emotions and feelings are reduced to techniques of measurement. Since I believe that the human being must be the primary focus of inquiry (Hirsch 1989), the definition I wish to use is that of a humanist.

Terrence Des Pres, whose perspective was delineated in chapter 6, approached politics by writing about poetry. He once defined politics as "acts and decisions that are not our own but which nonetheless determine how we live; events and situations brought about by brute force or manipulations of power. . . . Politics, then, as the condition we find ourselves in when, without consent, we become the means to others' ends—politics as endured by the victims, as seen by the witnesses, as beheld by the poet" (1981b, p. 73). For Des Pres, politics is manipulation of people by agents of power, generally of the modern nation-state. His view of the "political" means that identity formation takes place in an environment in which people are unable to escape the penetration of politics into their everyday lives because politics is, as Des Pres notes, "insistent," "penetrating," and "widespread" (p. 74). Even if the individual does not personally experience incidents such as terrorism, violence, political chaos, and uncertainty, he or she cannot escape "knowing" about such facts, and the mere "knowing" "changes the way you feel about being in the world." Politics now intrudes on all aspects of life, and there are no more bystanders. The personal has been transformed into the political, and the disintegration of the boundary between them has left the individual face-to-face with the power of the modern state.

This further means that memory is influenced by the political environment, for, as we saw in chapter 4, the state is the ultimate manipulator of memory as it reconstructs history to justify policies it wishes to pursue and to rationalize actions it has taken in the past. The reality created by this erosion of boundaries means that a person is no longer isolated and that his or her identity is formed within a crucible of political turmoil and unpredictability. The realities of contemporary political life intrude upon the formation of identity and may be destructive or constructive—they may destroy or preserve life. If we adopt Des Pres's definition and focus on the acts of power directed toward generally powerless people, the realities are often unpleasant.

Reflect for a moment on some of the more somber realities. Within the United States, individuals face poverty, homelessness, environmental destruction and disintegration, growing gaps between rich and poor, unemployment, recession, drugs, violence, disintegrating cities and infrastructures, and increases in the incidents of racism, sexism, and other forms of ethnocentrism. Internationally, individuals are confronted with war, nationalism, ethnic hostility, a widening gap between rich and poor nations, increasing interethnic conflict, starvation and famine, the destruction of the rain forest, and genocide against indigenous populations. The list is almost beyond comprehension and immediately depressing. These are, of course, balanced by countertrends that are also part of the political context, which, quite naturally, varies over time. For example, in the late 1960s and early 1970s, the context of identity development included political movements seeking to broaden the base and exercise of political power. These movements were devoted to empowering previously powerless people and undoubtedly had an effect upon the development of identity. At present, in the international context, certain hopeful and positive signs exist, such as the restructuring of the former Soviet Union, the apparent decline of totalitarian regimes, peace talks in Southeast Asia and the Middle East, and the quest for self-rule and democracy.

These political episodes are part of our daily dose of overwhelming information and become embedded in our memory. But our memories, as our experiences, differ widely and radically. As noted earlier, each person's experience has confusing and complicated aspects that vary according to such factors as gender, religion, nation of origin, or accident of birth. Although some might maintain a sense of psychological balance between the apparent tranquillity of their everyday life and the chaos and violence of the political context, others experience no tranquillity since their everyday life is composed of violence, chaos, and a struggle to survive. Even those who do not experience the direct effects of violence can become aware of it secondhand. Television news and daily newspapers inundate the mind with information—most of it concerning death, tragedy, and war. Knowing such facts not only changes the way a person feels about being in the world but also must influence the type of person he or she becomes. Politics, thus, intrudes into the process of identity formation and has important repercussions for the developing identity. It is therefore important to explain how identity is formed in the political cauldron of contemporary civilization. As noted in chapters 10 and 11, the process of socialization is the process by which identity is formed.

POLITICAL SOCIALIZATION

Our earlier discussion of political socialization demonstrated that people learn to perceive political reality and assimilate their political ideas and opinions through a process called political socialization. Although the process is the same as the psychological processes of learning, the content of what is transmitted and learned differs markedly from culture to culture, from state to state. Extensive research documents the impact of culture on political socialization.

Perhaps the clearest demonstration of cultural differences may be found in the study by Lambert and Klineberg (1967) in which children from several nations were asked, "What are you?" The cultural differences in the responses are interesting and demonstrate how one's sense of self is influenced by culture. Many, but not all, of the students interviewed by Lambert and Klineberg described themselves by referring to gender. This was true for American, English, and Canadian students, who also mentioned their role as students (p. 91). Describing oneself in terms of gender was also characteristic of the Brazilian, French, and German six- and ten-year-olds and for the fourteen-year-old Bantu children, who also identified themselves by racial background. Israeli fourteen-year-olds, however, referred to themselves primarily as "children" and generally emphasized the fact that they were persons and students. As Israeli children got older, they referred more often to their national and religious backgrounds (p. 94). Turkish children rarely described themselves as boys or girls, identifying themselves instead as children, persons, or students. Lebanese children did mention gender but also used religion as a reference point. Finally, Japanese six-year-olds described themselves as persons, and ten- and fourteen-year-olds typically referred to themselves as "Japanese boys or girls."

These data clearly indicate that culture influences conceptions of self and that the use of national, racial, gender, or religious categories places these descriptions within a political context. Cultural differences in the content of what is socialized are not limited to intercountry comparisons. In the United States, for example, a child born and raised in an Appalachian (Hirsch 1971b), African American (Abramson 1977), or Hispanic (Hirsch and Gutierrez 1977) community does not view the police, or political authority in general, in the same way as a child born into a white, middle-class context. These variations mean that the process is more complex than usually thought and emphasize the importance of the context in determining the boundaries of the process of socialization.

In addition, one complicating factor is that, along with an individual self-concept, people have a collective self. This means that self-esteem must be analyzed as it operates at both the societal and individual levels (Staub 1989). In short, a person may manifest low individual self-esteem, which might result in high societal self-esteem, or some other variation of the possible combinations. This means that both high and low self-esteem may lead to visions of superiority or inferiority and could conceivably provide a justification for hostility toward other groups. Or as Staub puts it, "Both an inflated and a weak self-esteem can enhance threat" (p. 55).

For example, low self-esteem may intensify the need to compensate for your own perceived inferiority by seeing your own group as superior to others. Individuals who vary in self-esteem "may share a belief in the superiority of their culture, nation, society, or way of life" (Staub 1989, p. 54). The relationships between types of self-esteem are much more complex than generally thought, and high self-esteem does not necessarily lead to a concern for others. In fact, in some cases high self-esteem may mask self-doubt and may also "be associated with limited concern for others" (p. 55). The collective or societal self-image of a people "includes shared evaluations of their group, myths that transmit the self-concept and ideal self, goals that a people set for themselves, and shared beliefs (e.g., about other groups). It may also include or mask uncertainties, insecurities, and anxieties" (pp. 104–5). This analysis is very close to our earlier discussion of the elements of memory, and it suggests that states or groups attempt to socialize and transmit memory that will attempt to bind individuals to the collectivity. In other words, when a member of a group is dependent on the group for bolstering his or her self-esteem and confidence, he or she will be more likely to follow the group's decisions (Janis 1982, pp. 257–58).

When identity is wrapped up tightly with the actions of the group or community, any perceived threats to the group or community become more real and potentially more devastating and, thus, more likely to motivate a behavioral response (Sigel 1989, p. 381). On the other hand, the more atomized and disconnected people are, the less linked they may feel to the community, and therefore it is more likely they will be unconcerned about the individual members of the community. The great puzzle is how one maintains a feeling of belonging and connection without becoming a person willing to obey the leaders and commit atrocity or participate in genocide. This struggle is especially difficult when group identification and self-esteem are related to the nation-state and are coupled with militarism or a streak of authoritarianism that emphasizes unquestioning obedience to authority (as argued in chapters 10 and 11). Belonging to groups, and in the modern era, to nations, "is of profound significance for human beings. It fulfills deep needs and provides satisfactions inherent in connections. It provides a feeling of security. It is essential in defining the self: as a member of a family, a profession, a religious group, voluntary associations, a nation. Individual identity is defined and the self gains value and significance through identification with groups and the connection to others that membership provides" (Staub 1989, p. 252).

In short, individual identity and collective identity are influenced by the cultural and political context within which those identities take shape. This context often involves questions of power, which are tied closely to the dominant or subordinate positions to which groups within a society are assigned and to which groups or nations are assigned within the international political community. As I noted earlier, this assigning of position might very well be related to any number of factors, including skin color, religion, and gender.

How individuals, groups, even nations are described and perceived influences the way they are treated, which, in turn, influences their perceptions of their own identity. Very often attributes such as skin color, religion, and gender are used as the basis of myths that may function to dehumanize those stigmatized as possessing less desirable characteristics. Examples of such myths were discussed in chapter 9, where we saw that they could be found in every historical epoch. The example of the Aryan myth was shown to give rise to a terminology of contempt that depersonalized and dehumanized the subject of the negative stereotypes. In this chapter, I demonstrate that this same variety of language cannot help but have profound effects on the formation of a person's identity.

The assigning of negative attributes not only shapes the identity of the individuals or groups to whom the negative characteristics are assigned but also significantly influences the manner in which these groups are viewed by members of the dominant group—as well as the way the dominant group perceives themselves. Obviously, as pointed out in the earlier discussion of language, if the subordinate group are "savages" or "vermin," it becomes viable and justifiable to deal harshly with them or even kill them. Vermin, after all, carry disease, and savages may be a threat to the dominant group's existence. In addition, the dominant group is clearly superior and stronger. Hence, the self-image of the dominant group may be elevated, or at least defended, by repressing or killing the subordinate group. In this fashion, self is related to the political context transmitted to succeeding generations via the process of political socialization, which forms the memory to be transmitted over and over again. The content of what is transmitted is, as I argued in chapter 9, carried by language. This language, in turn, seriously influences memory, which is the ultimate basis for individual and state behavior. In fact, identity is connected to both mass and elite political behavior in circumstances involving dominance and subordination, and it may be a crucial factor in determining how a person will react to authority. The factors that influence whether a person becomes either a Hitler or Himmler or one of their followers are undoubtedly related to the identity that is the product of a process of socialization within a particular cultural and political context. Killers, victims, and people who risk their lives to save victims all have identities. If we can understand how these widely divergent forms of behavior are related to identity, we might begin to understand more about the relationship between memory and identity and the commission of violence.

IDENTITY AND MASS MURDER

Several persistent questions concern whether identity is involved in the production of positive or negative, constructive or destructive, behavior and how it is influenced by, or influences, behavior in dramatic or extreme circumstances. Generalizations concerning these questions are, once again, often based on psychoanalytic concepts that have given rise to an entire industry devoted to explaining, in individual terms, why, for example, people such as Hitler became mass murderers (see, for instance, Fest 1970 and Bullock 1992). A major problem with psychoanalytically derived explanations of violent leaders is that they focus on destructive behavior as a manifestation of individual pathology or as caused by some significant event from the leader's childhood. This is too easy and ignores the possibility that given the "right" set of conditions, any person might be motivated to become either a victim or a killer (Hirsch 1985). Conceptions of self figure prominently in attempts to isolate the causal factors.

Staub (1989), for example, argues that low self-esteem is related to violent crime and that "a poor or shaky self-image, easily threatened, and a tendency to see the world, other people, or institutions as hostile may cause a constant need for self-defense and elevation of the self. People with such characteristics may be especially sensitive to life problems. A low level of well-being and much frustration and pain—a negative hedonic balance—heighten the desire to enhance the self. Diminishing others raises at least one's relative well-being" (p. 70). But in the modern era, the self is diminished by the constant assault of politics as the intimate connections within which the self is formed are exposed to the chaos and disorder of the contemporary political world. Within this context, attachments to smaller units such as the family may be in the process of being replaced by connections to the nation. As the smaller units have lost their importance or been transformed, the individual's sense of allegiance and belonging has been shifted to the nation-state, which, as I demonstrated earlier, controls memory and rewrites history to try to insure a ready supply of obedient citizens. This identification with the state has, as Staub notes, "destructive potential if the members stop questioning" its "beliefs, values, ideals, policies, and actions" (p. 253). Self-concept is related to views of "the other," of outsiders. "If groups do not have valid ways of defining themselves on the basis of their past history, tradition, values and customs, they will have to define their identity by contrast to outside groups." Groups and nations set themselves up as "good" by setting others up as "bad." This process is related to identity, according to Staub, in the sense that "the more a group has succeeded in encoding most aspects of its experience into its self-concept, and the more this self-concept is realistic and moderately positive, the less likely that it will give rise to nationalism as an important goal. There will be less need to protect and enhance the nation by 'purifying' it or by enlarging its territory or power" (pp. 253–54). According to Staub and others, these needs for protection and purification were some of the elements that combined in the Third Reich. It was, as Staub notes, "the elevated German self-concept" that became dangerous when combined with these other factors (p. 108).

In a similar fashion, the Khmer Rouge demonstrated a sense of superiority along with "underlying feelings of inferiority and vulnerability" (Staub 1989, p. 199). The notion of having a mission to create and implement the "true" people's communism based on a model of the glory of the rural worker, along with the conviction that the entire world was against them, lead the Khmer Rouge, from 1975 to 1978, to kill over 1 million of their own people (Becker 1986). But concepts of identity are only one of a rather complicated set of contributing conditions.

Clearly, the Germans may have had an elevated sense of self, but without the historical conditions of postwar instability and the historical development of anti-Semitism along with cultural hierarchy, this sense of superiority would not have been translated into the deadly mix that lead to the extermination of the European Jews. Similarly, the past history of the Khmer people provided a glorification of militarism and a romanticization of a warrior tradition that combined with the feelings of inferiority and vulnerability on the one hand and superiority on the other to lead to violence. This combination is not unknown in contemporary history. Elevated or low self-esteem in and of itself is not sufficient to cause mass murder. Self-image becomes of particular importance in the formula when one realizes that it not only influences the behavior of leaders who are involved in programming and manipulating the murderous mix of conditions but is also an important element motivating the followers, who are, in many cases, only too willing to carry out the destructive acts.

In addition, identity is influenced by the context created by the destructive situation. We must, therefore, now ask what happens to the individual self when it experiences the trauma of war or repressive incarceration in a concentration camp. This issue is of extreme importance because the exposure to such extremity provides a very definite environment within which to examine the development of identity and also to ascertain how identity affects or is affected by its context.

IDENTITY IN WAR AND CONCENTRATION CAMPS

Identity is not always formed under conditions of apparent autonomy. Very often, identity emerges out of conditions involving violence. This is especially true for minorities—either racial, sexual, or ideological. What is most important here is the "limitation of life possibilities" (Adam 1978), which are not equally experienced by all people. Participation in violent acts, either as a willing or coerced perpetrator, or as a victim, appears to function as a kind of primitive socializing event in a person's life. Studies have shown that trauma has a quite profound impact on people's sense of who they are—especially on their identification with various types of authority and their predilection for participating in political violence. Laufer (1989) writes:

The literature on the survivors of war indicates that exposure to the trauma of war leaves lasting scars on individuals and potentially serves as a turning point in life trajectories. What we know about the experience of war indicates that the resources, beliefs, and experiences individuals bring to it are wholly inadequate to cope with the actual experience. Warfare in the imagination cannot compare with warfare in situ; and the latter, especially modern warfare, is without romance, glamour, or melodrama, it is terrifying beyond imagination, horrifying beyond what is known in civil society and, for those trapped in its grip, inescapable. The experience of warfare is so overwhelming that individuals rapidly find it necessary to develop a new repertoire of adaptive coping mechanisms for functioning in the warfare environment, i.e., the situation imposes a new subjective reality on the neophyte. (p. 418)

The effect of modern warfare is so overwhelming that even the military estimates that most individuals cannot endure sustained exposure for "more than thirty to fifty days" (p. 419, citing Marlowe 1983; see also Fussell 1989). The parallels to incarceration in any total institution are obvious.

Inmates in a Nazi concentration camp faced a similarly overwhelming experience for which nothing in their backgrounds could have prepared them. As Des Pres (1976b) summarizes, "In the camps prisoners lost their possessions, their social identity, the whole cultural matrix which had previously sustained them. They lost, in other words, the delicate web of symbolic identifications available to men and women in normal times. In Nazi camps they lost even their names and their hair. They were reduced to immediate physical existence through a process of de-sublimation so abrupt and thorough that—in the plainest, starkest sense—nothing remained of what the self had been" (p. 214). Those exposed to war and the concentration camps are reduced to "primal acts and to an awareness circumscribed by primitive needs. They are naked to the roots, radically compressed to their essence as creatures of flesh" (p. 223). Even time is destroyed as the usual habits and "rhythms of change and motion," of seasons, work, cultural rituals, are lost. The person in war or in the camps has no idea how long the ordeal will last, and the situation often appears to be endless. As Des Pres notes, "The death of time destroys the sense of growth and purpose, and thereby undermines faith in the possibility that any good can come from merely staying alive" (p. 12).

In extremity, then, two basic problems of existence have a major impact on identity: first, "how not to despair," and second, "how to keep moral sense and dignity intact" (Des Pres 1976b, p. 16). These are crucial to the maintenance of a semblance of what one might call a civilized self as opposed to the development of a war or concentration camp self. Undoubtedly, people experiencing either of these extreme situations will have to adapt, and that is, in fact, what happens. What is important, however, is whether they are able to reassert their civilized self at the conclusion of the extreme events.

Laufer (1989) identifies nine factors that might influence the results of exposure to the extremity of war. All involve the experience of one or another form of stress, including direct experience of combat; loss of buddies; proportion of unit suffering casualties; witnessing abusive violence or atrocities;

direct participation in abusive violence or atrocities; age of person exposed; performing dangerous assignments such as graves registration or demolition; knowledge of personally killing enemy soldiers; and length of time in war situation (pp. 419–20). In order to survive horrible experiences, a person must develop mechanisms to adapt. Lifton (1986) and Lifton and Markusen (1990) assert that both perpetrators and victims develop a new version of the self through a process they call "doubling." In chapter 8, I pointed out that doubling was, in reality, the process of learning to adapt or cope with adverse circumstances, as in discriminatory learning or learning to play a role that helps a person to survive.

In a concentration camp, Lifton points out, the perpetrators developed an "Auschwitz self" that allowed them to go about their jobs of destruction; likewise, the prisoners of the camps developed a self that aided their survival. Through what Lifton calls doubling or numbing, the perpetrators were able to adapt to an environment that was highly unusual while at the same time being able to invoke the prior self when they made periodic visits to their wives and children (Lifton and Markusen 1990, p. 13).

Doubling involves the "division of the self into two functioning wholes, so that a part-self acts as an entire self" (Lifton and Markusen 1990, p. 106). These selves acquire a logic and purpose that seems appropriate to the environment even though the environment is extreme. The self is, therefore, able to adapt to almost unbelievable conditions and to, consequently, engage in and justify acts of great cruelty or great courage. The "Nazi doctors" at Auschwitz were able to justify their actions by investing their work with such great significance that any feelings of guilt were diffused. This, as Lifton (1986) notes, is "part of a universal proclivity toward constructing good motives while participating in evil behavior" (p. 458). Lifton identifies several elements involved in the doctors' construction of their Auschwitz selves. These include force of routine, the justification that they were the ultimate biological soldiers doing important medical work, blaming the victim, and the overall emphasis on performance that seems, according to Lifton, to be characteristic of the male ego. By extension, one suspects that similar justifications are created by persons asked to engage in warfare and, in particular, by those ordered to undertake actions that in normal civilian circumstances would be morally suspect.

Therefore, when a civilian is exposed to the military and to "basic training," his or her civilian self is erased as the doubling or adaptive process occurs. Obviously, it is not desirable to completely erase the civilian self since it is necessary at some stage to reintegrate the citizen-soldier back into society. This problem is delayed for a longer period in the case of the professional soldier. In general, Lifton argues, professionals are particularly susceptible to doubling. He includes physicians, psychologists, physicists, biologists, clergy, generals, statesmen, writers, and artists and points out that they have a "special capacity for doubling. In them, a prior, humane self can be joined by a 'professional self' willing to ally itself with a destructive project, with harming or even killing others" (Lifton 1986, p. 464).

Lifton assumes that two selves exist, that, in essence, the person is basically moral or good, and that the "bad" or evil self is created through the process of doubling. Assuming that he is correct—an assumption necessary to maintain one's hope for the species—to some degree we are doubling every day. Our work self and our home self may be quite different from each other. Doubling is role-playing, and we learn to discriminate or play different roles according to the conditions or the circumstances within which we find ourselves. To a very large extent, how we play these different roles—how, in short, we double and what type of acts we are willing to pursue when ordered or given the opportunity to do so—depends upon the type of internalized self that exists at the moment of choice. Doubling, in fact, is similar to Staub's notion of the individual and collective self. The collective self, the societal self, may be that doubled self, the self developed to allow the person to adapt to extreme circumstances. In this case, the doubled or the societal or institutional self a person develops may very well be dependent upon the prior individual self or upon the memories and myths to which that person has been exposed. In other words, our self-image or identity affects how we react in extreme situations.

In a similar fashion, extreme experiences become a filter through which subsequent events may be given meaning (Laufer 1989, p. 445). Experiencing the trauma of war, for example, is related to delayed stress reactions.[1] Any exposure to extreme events such as war or incarceration in a concentration camp would likely have an impact on the self. The problem is how to reinte-

1. Although precise connections are difficult to substantiate, there is evidence of "psychopathology associated with the trauma of war," including problems with careers and marriages and delayed stress reactions. Laufer (1989) does note that "although the vast majority of Vietnam Veterans continue to function without institutionalization, the evidence indicates that war stress irreparably alters the intrapsychic life trajectories by creating series of identity crises whose resolution requires the integrations of serial crystallized selves that often can only be partially integrated. The early adult development crisis around the integration of the serial self creates confusion in social relations, career development, and parenting which, because they often come close together, negatively affect interlocking life trajectories" (p. 435).

grate into the less violent civil society. Just such a conflict faced the Nazi doctors who conducted experiments at Auschwitz.

At the conclusion of World War II, the Nazi doctors had to find some way to establish a postwar self. They had to discover how to cast off their "Auschwitz or Nazi self and to see themselves (and of course represent themselves to the world) as essentially decent and moderate postwar German burgher-physicians of a conservative stamp" (Lifton 1986, p. 457). In doing so, they had difficulty confronting the Nazi or Auschwitz self and found themselves without moral clarity concerning their contemporary self. Because of these difficulties, as with soldiers who have experienced combat, they were not all successful at reintegrating themselves into civilian society. Some committed suicide after the German defeat, some were tried and executed, some served prison sentences, a few escaped, and "a considerable number returned to medical practice and continued until retirement or natural death" (pp. 456–57).

In short, the relationship between extremity and self is complicated. Clearly, common sense dictates that we recognize that exposure to horrible events must significantly affect identity. What those effects are is not clear, however. Nevertheless, we can say with some assurance that, while the individual experiences the events, the self adjusts. Whether we call it doubling, numbing, the development of an institutional or societal self, or some other term, it raises important questions about the relationship between identity and memory.

If an individual is able to adapt to virtually any situation, is it possible to create a self-image, an identity, that blocks participation in atrocity? Do human beings develop "good" and "bad" selves depending upon the conditions of their socialization? Moreover, if memory is shaped by and shapes the socialization process, the experience of war or confinement in a concentration camp must surely be one of the most significant type of events, which are permanently imprinted on a person's memory. As such, the events become central in shaping both the individual and the world as we look back and reconstruct, through the testimony of survivor and witness, what took place. If we remember the horror and through an empathic reaction resolve to try to never allow such events to be repeated, then a certain lesson is learned. If we numb ourselves and engage in abstract definitional recall of the events, we might derive the lesson that genocide works and that the survivors got what they deserved—if we acknowledge that the genocide happened at all. Perhaps we do both at the same time—that is, perhaps we remember what is most desired or rewarded by the society in which we live. Perhaps Milgram (1974) is correct in pointing out that morality in contemporary times has been redefined so that it is determined by how well we execute orders given to us by authority. How we behave must be related to what type of identity we have developed. The remainder of this chapter will first discuss the relationship between identity and altruism and then present an alternative view of the development of self in a political context.

IDENTITY AND ALTRUISM

Not everyone helps to kill. Although most of research on violence has focused on war and the perpetrators of violence, some scholars have examined why, in the midst of violence and evil, some people are willing to help others even though they may be risking their lives. Generally, this type of act is referred to as "altruistic behavior." Examining altruism in the face of malevolence provides a needed counterbalance to the focus on violence and evil. After all, if identity is related to the commission of "evil," it must also be related to the commission of "good."

Philip Hallie (1979) quotes the American poet John Peale Bishop as saying that the tragic thing about war is that it destroys the "tragedy of death" (p. 274). The prevalence of war and violence causes people to lose their "awareness of the pricelessness of life" because they become accustomed to killing. This, he argues, "destroyed the foundations of a life-and-death ethic. War substituted military heroism for dignity." It is quite probable, given the fact that violence has become commonplace, that this demise of a life-and-death ethic has spilled over into modern life in general—that the prevalence of state-sanctioned mass murder and the technology of death have created a commonness of violence that continues to erode our awareness of the pricelessness of life along with our capacity for outrage at injustice and cruelty, which appear, in the modern period, to be the "normal" state of human existence. People are numbed and no longer react with horror and disgust at the massive destruction of life. Once again, the events in Bosnia serve as a telling example of unconcern. If this is the case, the people who resist death, those who actively refuse to participate in the killing and take action to oppose it, deserve the status of modern heroes, and we need to not only celebrate their acts but also attempt to understand the development of their motivations to the same extent that we examine those of the killers. Resisters could very well provide an alternative focus for memory. We might consider replacing the heroes who kill with those who refuse to kill. This would, of course, necessitate a massive change in national and cultural values as the entire reward structure of a society would have to be radically transformed.

Scholars have conducted rather extensive research on different aspects of what is often referred to as altruistic or helping behavior. For the most part, as is common in contemporary social science, many have anchored the idea of helping others with heavy weights of academic jargon. Instead of looking for good or evil in events that take place in people's lives, they begin with definitions and proceed to examine trivial and mundane forms of behavior, usually in artificially created situations. For example, Tec (1986) notes that most studies of altruism define it as the exhibiting of a certain kind of behavior, such as "picking up unmailed letters and mailing them (Forbes 1971), dimming one's headlights for an approaching car (Ehlert et al. 1973), writing letters on behalf of others (Harris 1972), picking up someone's dropped groceries (Schneider and Mokus 1974), giving money when approached by a stranger in a supermarket (Bickman and Kamzan 1973)" (pp. 150–53), and intervening in someone else's crisis (Latane and Darley 1970).

Most of the studies of bystander intervention have been conducted by psychologists who have offered a number of hypotheses to explain why people refuse to intervene. These include the belief that the victims are to blame for their suffering and hence "deserve" their fate (Lerner 1970) and that others will or can help so they do not have to—the diffusion of responsibility (Latane and Darley 1970). Also, the longer an emergency continues without help being offered, the less likely it will be forthcoming (Piliavin, Rodin, and Piliavin 1969). Other hypothetical determinants of altruistic behavior include an optimistic as opposed to a fatalistic vision of the future (Sorokin 1950) and an internal locus of control (Midlarsky 1986).

Clearly these types of acts bear no resemblance to actions taken in the real world. In particular, actions taken in the laboratory or in a supermarket could not be further from actions taken in a situation such as the Nazi destruction of the Jews because, as Tec (1986) notes, "the price to be paid is insignificant when compared with the risks of one's own life" (p. 151). Consequently, a more relevant examination of altruism would focus on helping in a real-life situation such as the Holocaust and raise what is perhaps the most important question: "Why did some people during that era resist Nazism by rescuing and in other ways helping Jews often at great risk to themselves and their families while the majority of the population remained passive bystanders or, worse, active participants in genocide?" (Baron 1986, p. 307).

As Baron (1986) notes, most of the attempts to explain why people helped the Jews "operate at a macroscopic level and, hence, reveal little about either the type of individuals who engaged in Jewish relief or the reasons which motivated them to do so" (p. 239). Generally, there have been two broad approaches to studying why people helped Jews. The first deals with "the historical conditions that fostered collective rescue operations at the national and local levels. The second analyzed the psychological traits and sociological profiles of individuals who rescued Jews as revealed in intensive interviews with them" (p. 238). Neither considers the role of identity or self directly, but the discussions will allow us to draw some tentative conclusions about the role of self in rescue.

The general, historical approach considers examples such as the Danish rescue of the Jews, concluding that the Danes helped the Jews because of "Denmark's long heritage of democracy and religious toleration, the high degree of social integration and acceptance achieved by native Jews, the lenient nature of the German occupation until 1943, the timing of the Nazi attempt to deport the Jews which coincided with the imposition of martial law on the increasingly unruly Danes who resented growing German economic exploitation, and finally the proximity of neutral Sweden which publicly offered to receive the escaping Jews" (Baron 1986, p. 238). In short, the Danes viewed the Jews as humans who were entitled to all the rights of citizens, and they set about to rescue the Jews. Omitted from these general historical observations are any ideas concerning why individuals were willing to help—what factors motivated them to offer aid.

Additional studies of those who helped Jews during the Holocaust have been able to identify a number of different factors and suggest several explanations. Baron (1986) cites a German study in which letters and other evidence were gathered from seventy Germans who helped Jews (p. 240). A group portrait based on age, gender, marital status, geographical distribution, religious affiliation, vocation, political outlook, and involvement in other forms of resistance against nazism revealed that many of the rescuers were born before 1910 and had achieved adulthood prior to the Nazis' assuming power. They were, thus, not as susceptible to the influences of Nazi propaganda manifested in the socialization process, but they were still a distinct minority. As the major finding of this study, this conclusion clearly reveals the inability of this type of study to uncover more in-depth reasons people were willing to risk their lives to help Jews.

Another study (Gordon 1984) examined data from 452 Gestapo files on individual opponents of racial persecution in the district of Düsseldorf (p. 211). These files included 203 files on "individuals who aided Jews," 42 on "critics of racial persecution," 30 on "individuals suspected of aiding Jews," 137 on "Germans who had sexual relations with Jews," 40 on "persons who were suspected of having sexual relations with Jews," and 255 on "Jews arrested for these reasons." Gordon found that German males over fifty years old were the most active in helping Jews and hypothesized that this happened because the political socialization of older men occurred when anti-Semitic movements were not as strong and because older men had access to the financial resources and contacts that helped them to hide Jews. Once again Gordon's analysis does not offer any insight into individual reasons for helping Jews and certainly says nothing about the role of self. In order to approximate some understanding of individual motivation, it is necessary to turn to in-depth interview studies of individuals who rescued Jews.

Nechama Tec (1986) interviewed Polish rescuers and attempted to ascertain what influenced them to help Jews. She looked at social class, political beliefs, degree of anti-Semitism, extent of religious commitment, the prospects of monetary reward, and friendship with Jews. She found that, although each of these may have offered a partial explanation, none was a "wholly reliable predictor of precisely who would attempt the protection of Jews" (p. 150). As a result, she proceeded to look for "core characteristics," eventually identifying the following six characteristics:

1. Individuality or separateness (p. 188). By this Tec means "the inability of the rescuer to blend with the environment." This closely resembles an earlier finding of London (1970) that rescuers are socially marginal to their societies, but Tec points out that marginality has a negative connotation, and she prefers to describe the characteristic as "individuality" or "separateness" (p. 154).

2. Independence or self-reliance. This "causes these individuals to pursue personal goals regardless of how these goals are viewed by others" (p. 154).

3. "Broad or long lasting commitment to stand up for the helpless and needy" (p. 188). This commitment began before the war and "included a wide range of activities" (p. 154).

4. "A matter-of-fact attitude toward rescue that sees it as a mere duty, which explains the repeated denials of rescuers that their protection of Jews was extraordinary or heroic" (p. 154).

5. "An unexplained beginning to rescue efforts" (p. 154), which "could either have happened gradually or suddenly, even impulsively" (p. 188). In other words, rescue was not premeditated and was spontaneously undertaken.

6. "A universalistic perception of the needy; the ability to disregard and set aside all attributes of the needy except their . . . extreme suffering and need" (pp. 154, 188).

Tec then derives three hypotheses to explain what she calls selfless rescue of the Jews. First, individuals who are freed from the constraints and control of their community are more likely to resist the pressures for conformity and act independently (1986, p. 190). Second, these independently acting individuals may be motivated by moral imperatives expressed as a strong desire to help the needy. This is often, as we shall see shortly in the case studies of two rescuers, learned through early socialization from parents. Third, helping behavior becomes a habit. "The longer people act in accordance with such strong moral imperatives, the more likely are these actions and values to become traditional patterns. The more firmly established such actions become, the easier they are to follow and the greater the likelihood that they will be taken for granted as natural reactions and as a duty" (p. 191).

Rescuers appear, therefore, to be independent thinkers, freed from obedience and conformity, willing to follow their moral conscience to "do the right thing" even in the face of threats to their own lives. Although identity is never mentioned as a factor, it is logical to believe that individuals possessing the above characteristics would have a very strong sense of self. This likelihood becomes very clear when we turn our attention to two individuals who devoted their lives to rescuing Jews during the Holocaust. Pastor André Trocme and the people of the French village of Le Chambon-sur-Lignon sheltered and saved hundreds of Jewish children (Hallie 1979). Herman "Fritz" Graebe, a German engineer, also used his courage and ingenuity to save Jews during the period of Nazi domination (Huneke 1985). Their stories are not only inspiring but bring us closer to an understanding of the relationship between self-image and altruism.

In all the literature on altruism and rescue, self or identity was specifically discussed as possibly contributing to altruistic behavior in only one case, even though some allusion to identity was clearly present in others. Discussing the events that occurred at Le Chambon, Sauvage (1986) conjectured that to help Jews despite the horrible penalties meted out by the Nazis required a "very secure, very anchored sense of self—a spontaneous access to the core of their being—that resulted in a natural and irresistible proclivity to see the truth and act upon it" (p. 256). Rescuers of Jews came from many different backgrounds but appear to have had in common a "caring human concern for the suffering of others and the ability to endure personal risk in order to alleviate the suffering" (Henry 1986, p. 318). How this concern was developed is the important question.

As Sauvage notes, it is critical to recognize that "to care about other people is also to care about yourself" (1986, p. 259). Caring about oneself may be indicative of a strong sense of identity. Surely one cannot undertake dangerous acts such as the rescue of Jews from the Nazis without a strong inner core of identity. If this is the case, if a strong sense of self is a characteristic of those who helped Jews, then how did it develop?

Huneke (1985) and Grossman (1984) suggest that parental and role models were responsible for inculcating an ethic of tolerance, justice, and equality. One observer argues that "the type of parenting [rescuers] received endowed them with an acute sense of personal responsibility, a great deal of empathy toward others, and the independence and confidence to act upon their feelings and values despite the legal or social consequences" (Baron 1986, p. 242). The recollections of the rescuers were that they learned these traits from communicative and nonauthoritarian fathers and affectionate mothers who established warm and trusting relationships with their children. As might be expected, children who had "experienced security, acceptance, and love could readily empathize with another human being in trouble" (p. 243). It is, consequently, not so much "what a child is taught, but how it is treated which determines the kind of human being he or she will be, and the way he or she will relate to others." In-depth interviews with specific rescuers reinforced this idea.

The study of German engineer Fritz Graebe led to the identification of a number of factors related to rescuing. Among these, the most important was thought to be the influence of a moral parental role model (Huneke 1986, p. 323). Graebe is said to have learned his moral values of compassion from his mother, who "taught him to be an independent thinker and to care for the less fortunate and for those who were the victims of society. She showed him how to be hospitable and instilled in him a profound sense of justice that enabled him to resist ill-willed, inhumane authorities" (Huneke 1985, p. xviii). As Graebe noted, he grew up "in a world of distinct right and wrong, but that sense of righteousness was always tempered by an equally strong sense of charity, a willingness to understand and appreciate the position of the other person" (p. 6).

A second characteristic identified in the study was social marginality or independence. This finding is similar to the ideas of London and Tec. Marginality is defined in terms of social class, political affiliation and viewpoint, economic status, religious beliefs and practices, educational status, geographic location, family style, and personal characteristics. Graebe was taught to be an independent thinker, and he had the confidence to not conform, to be marginal. At one point, he noted: "I marched to my own tune. I was not taught to be political. Therefore, I did not oppose or support National Socialism on ideological grounds. I became opposed to it when I personally witnessed its injustice and inhumanity" (Huneke 1986, p. 324). Graebe did what he thought was right and did not seek the approval of authority figures.

A third value "strongly emphasized in the Graebe household was the virtue of hard work and diligence" (Huneke 1985, p. 7). Graebe overcame a problem with stuttering and worked hard to become a licensed engineer, a position he then used to help rescue Jews.

From this examination of Graebe and other rescuers of Jews during the Holocaust, Huneke (1986) identifies "seven traits of the caring person—the rescuer" (p. 325).

1. "Empathic imagination," or the "ability to place oneself in the actual situation or role of another person and to imagine the long-term consequences of the situation or the role on that person."
2. A "person's ability to present himself or herself and control a critical situation." Graebe had trained as an actor and was able to seize control of situations and play different roles as needed to further his efforts at rescue.
3. "Previewing for a purposeful life" (p. 326). "In order to be altruistic, a person must be both proactive and prosocial. Proactive (its opposite is reactive) and prosocial (its opposite is anti-social) behavior is characterized by (1) careful planning to act in a cooperative and responsible way; (2) anticipating opportunities for having a positive and beneficial impact in the lives and circumstances of others; and (3) actively promoting the well-being of self and others."
4. "Significant personal experiences with suffering and death prior to the war" (p. 327). Graebe, for example, remembers watching the returning veterans of World War I, in particular, "one bandaged young man . . . , much of whose face had been blown away by a bullet, . . . [and] recalls thinking that this man and others like him were going through such unnecessary and wasteful suffering." These experiences sensitized him to death and tragedy and heightened his empathic identification.
5. "Ability to confront and manage their prejudices."
6. "Development of a community of compassion and support."
7. "Ability to offer hospitality."

Emerging from all of these studies is the very clear impression that those courageous individuals who risked their lives to attempt to save or help Jews during the Holocaust must have had, as was noted of Fritz Graebe, a deep "faith in [their] own abilities" along with a "capacity for difficult, sustained work" (Huneke 1985, p. 8). This deep faith in one's own abilities is another way of referring to a strong and positive sense of identity or a positive self-image. Whatever term is used, the act of rescue must have come from a deep inner core of self, and sustaining it in the face of the German atrocities must have necessitated calling up all of the strength of character a person possessed.

The example of Graebe clearly indicates the important role of memory in bolstering this strength of character. Graebe remembers his mother's example. He remembers seeing the wounded veterans of World War I marching home.

He remembers his first view of the injustice and inhumanity of the Nazi cadres. Memory appears to be a very important ingredient in the mix that is stirred to create helping behavior. Yet the motivations of both killers and helpers are complex and remote. Although we can identify characteristics of both, we can come to no definitive outline of the character and motivations of each group.

There are essentially two basic arguments concerning the difference between rescuers and killers. One is that there is an "unbridgeable difference" that exists "between those who can torture and destroy children and those who can only save them. Under such an ethic, no verbal bridges may be erected connecting these two kinds of people. Between them there is only profound conflict" (Hallie 1979, p. 275). Others argue that it is important to find the underlying causes for both forms of behavior and to ascertain what accounts for the differences because it is possible, given the right set of conditions, that any person might become either a killer or a rescuer. This perspective, which is closest to my own, examines the heart of the person to try to find why some express the dark side while others reveal the light. Perhaps the best we can do is to attempt to outline some thoughts on the adaptive self.

ADAPTIVE IDENTITY

Whatever lies at the heart of a human being remains an enigma. All the academic debates over nature and nurture, whether human nature is "good" or "bad," have not helped illuminate the self and how it relates to politics. In-depth case studies of individuals have, however, provided some directions to follow in trying to untangle the complex knot of motivations. At least there is now information on some of the background characteristics of victims, killers, bystanders, and rescuers. In addition, the realization that most previous theoretical models were inadequate has led scholars to develop alternative perspectives.

The most generally accepted perspective is that people are socialized or learn an image of themselves that is reinforced and transmitted by the culture and political context in which they live and to which they must adapt. If it is true that the self is adaptive or malleable, then individuals can adapt themselves to war, to concentration camps, and to politics of all forms, and within every person there exists the capacity for both great good and great evil. Where, in that case, does one find one's "true self" if one can survive as either an inmate or a doctor at Auschwitz? Conceivably, in our pursuit of identity we have asked the wrong questions.

An individual is not, as Lifton (1986) points out, "inherently evil, murderous, [or] genocidal" (p. 497). Yet under certain conditions, virtually any person is capable of becoming all of these. Just as there are many different types of people, there may be different selves—even within the same person. A self is not a single fixed entity but a representation or symbolization of the way people perceive themselves, the way they think others see them, their identifications with groups, nations, and other institutions, and the survival and adaptive mechanisms they have developed. Since these factors are all related to the context of development, it is also important to ascertain how identity interacts with, influences, or is influenced by the political context through the explication of the lived-out roles. Particularly important is the notion of choice. In fact, the focus on choice reinstates the individual as a responsible actor and puts the person and the self back into the calculations of political behavior. As Des Pres (1976b) puts it: "People still free must decide how much their 'freedom' is worth: how many lies they will live by, how far they will acquiesce while their neighbors are destroyed. The choice is always there" (p. 18). Although one cannot argue that the person victimized by a strong oppressor necessarily has much choice, it is true that just as the murderers make choices, the victims also have choices, though they may be more limited. They do not choose to become victims, but once they are placed in that role, they then must choose how to behave. The essential "distinction is between those who live at any price, and those who suffer whatever they must in order to live humanly" (p. 19).

Killers do not have to become killers, and even victims can, until choice is taken from them by the killers, decide how to structure their survival. In short, a direct and reciprocal relationship exists between the self and the environment. The previous self, which is recalled through memory, determines the types of choices one makes, while the context influences the self that will be formed. It is in the choices that one makes that the individual identity surfaces. Thus, educating people to be aware of and critically evaluate the contextual importance of the many choices they will face throughout their lives becomes a determining factor in the developing self. Although most of the choices one must make appear on the surface to be insignificant, they are, in reality, part of a larger pattern.

By ignoring inhumanity, however small—for example, racist or sexist jokes—a person may become accustomed to ignoring oppression and injustice and eventually may lose the ability to recognize inhumanity when it confronts him or her, consequently losing his or her sense of outrage at acts of oppression and injustice. We can learn or relearn a sense of justice and compassion in the institutions that most intimately affect our everyday lives. It is in the seemingly small areas of everyday life that we find protection and relief from the reach of the intrusive state and from the sad realities of political life. Our day-to-day existence is a buffer separating us from confrontation with the negative realities, and it allows us to develop attachments and a sense of identity. Yet these attachments to the objects of love and affection do not exist in a void. They are part of the larger context within which we must learn to forthrightly confront injustice and inhumanity so that we can develop the capacity to make the choices between destruction and preservation of life. People who do so also develop a positive self-image as they realize that they have a form of empowerment—they are not powerless, they do have choices, and if they are joined by others who choose preservation of life, they can influence local, national, and perhaps international politics. As Albert Camus has noted, if we all choose to be neither victims nor executioners, those who wish to make us either will have a difficult time sating their appetites for destruction.

In short, certain ethical rules exist that revolve around matters of life and death—around killing. Hallie (1979) sees them as falling into two categories: "negative commandments and positive ones. In an ethic of life and death, there is an ethic of refusal and there is an ethic of positive action" (p. 281). This means that an ethical person not only refuses to obey or participate in the killing but takes action to prevent it and to help those in danger. How we might move from a world in which genocide and mass killing appear to be common examples of state policy to one with an ethic of life is the topic of the final section of this book.

What is frightening is to realize how content we feel because we suppose there are deeds that cannot be repeated. . . . The holocaust will be understood not so much for the number of victims as for the magnitude of the silence.

Jacobo Timerman, *Prisoner without a Name, Cell without a Number* (1981)

Today the state assumes its own rationale. Holding its will as preeminent, it has become a sacred phenomenon, intent upon sacrificing private interests and personal life at the altar of global competition. A stand-in for God, the state is now a providence of which everything is accepted and nothing expected.

L. R. Beres, "Genocide" (1985)

THREE

Preserving Life

After devoting twelve chapters to the still enigmatic connection between memory and genocide, we must return to the question posed at the outset: If we have so many memories of so many genocides, why have so few lessons been learned? This, of course, assumes that knowing about past destruction of life will necessarily contribute to insuring that it will not happen again. Conceivably, this assumption may be incorrect. It is possible that the lesson learned is how to kill more efficiently next time. Smith (1992a), for example, points out that "would-be perpetrators of genocide have seen what has happened with the Armenians: they know they can commit genocide and get away with it, and through denial eventually erase any recollection of their crime. And by ignoring the Armenian Genocide, knowledge important to the prevention of genocide was, for too long, lost" (p. 13). Smith's lament appears to be only too true. One need merely look at the situation in Bosnia at the time of this writing to confirm that the lesson appears to be that the world does not really care and that genocide is, in fact, a viable policy for gaining political objectives.

In a newspaper report on November 27, 1992, a Serbian nationalist soldier related his memory of a recent incident: "We told them not to be afraid, we wouldn't do anything to them, they should just stand in front of the wall. But it was taken for granted among us that they should be killed. So, when somebody said, 'Shoot,' I swung around and pulled the trigger, three times on automatic fire. I remember the little girl with the red dress hiding behind her granny" (Burns 1992, p. A1). He was confessing to the fact that he, along with two companions, executed ten members of a Muslim family from a distance of about ten paces. Even though he expressed some remorse and claimed that he remembered Muslims who had been kind to him, his memory was shaped by Serbian leaders who filled his mind with propaganda. He was, for example, reminded that Serbians had viewed Muslims as a threat as far back as the Middle Ages when Serbs were defeated by the Ottoman Turks (p. A13). He claimed that Serbian political leaders told him that the Bosnian Muslims were "planning to declare an 'Islamic republic' in Bosnia" and that Muslims "would also require Serbian children to wear Muslim clothing." The leaders declared that "we would have to cleanse our whole population of Muslims. That's what we have been told, that's why it has been necessary to do all this."

This soldier expresses the same type of sentiments about and motivations for killing, invoking the same sort of memories, as those we have discussed in this work and which humankind has witnessed throughout its relatively brief period of consciousness. Seeing genocide repeated again, as in the example just cited, inevitably leads to the pessimistic conclusion that the political, social, cultural, educational, and religious institutions of the twentieth century have failed to solve or even to confront the most grievous problems facing individual human beings; starvation, sickness, war, and genocide, the four horsemen, still gallop over the globe. The "magnitude of the silence" about the Holocaust referred to by Timerman (1981) insures repetition; silence is the destruction of memory.

The only way to begin to break this silence is to confront forthrightly the magnitude of the destruction of human life historically and in the twentieth century, for genocide is certainly not a new phenomenon. Mass murder did not commence with the Nazi extermination of the Jews, and it did not stop when these horrible events were made public. Genocide has been an ever-present and persistent phenomenon that has occurred in every historical epoch.

Biblical and other accounts of ancient times clearly reveal the precedents—as enumerated in Smith (1987) and in Chalk and Jonassohn (1990). For example, after Melos refused to surrender to its Athenian conquerors, the Athenians put to death all men who were of military age and sold the women and children into slavery. Similar examples abound, since in ancient times genocide was used to make an example of rebellious peoples. Conquerors admitted proudly to the act, as did the sixteenth-century Mogul emperor Akbar who constructed a wall of human bodies out of the corpses of those he conquered to deter anyone who might contemplate rebellion. Just as examples of mass murder exist, examples of attempts to stop the slaughter—to preserve life rather than destroy it—also exist, although they are far fewer. The ubiquity of genocide throughout history must, however, give pause to anyone considering possible mechanisms to preserve life rather than destroy it. It would appear that humans are more readily motivated to follow orders and kill than to disobey and rescue. How then does the concerned person and the world get from the "slaughterhouse of history" to the preservation of life?

The first step is to explore mechanisms for changing the way we view our fellow inhabitants of the planet. My basic argument is that if life is to be preserved, humanity must develop, inculcate, and internalize a life-preserving ethic based on the universal acceptance of human rights. The second step is to create both the long- and short-term conditions for implementing this ethic by instituting a life-preserving politics. This is necessary because, in the short run, there must be some means to stop, or at least moderate, the prevalence and intensity of the violence. Life must be preserved as the broader, more comprehensive ethic is developed.

13

Where Do We Go from Here?

Memory and Resocialization to Preserve Life

Throughout history, and with increasing ferocity and deadliness in the twentieth century, genocide has been condoned by the modern nation-state, which has made few if any moves to prevent or punish that crime. This chapter examines the relationship between how individuals learn to view the state and techniques that might help to temper nationalism and contribute to internationalizing worldviews so that individuals begin to see themselves as experiencing the same problems, frustrations, and desires as their fellow beings. If this basic sense of likeness, of empathic identification, can be communicated and internalized, then basic changes might begin to occur.

Since nationalism is the psychological foundation upon which international perceptions are currently constructed, it must be modified by instituting a process of political resocialization that changes the focus from nationalism to internationalism. The mechanism suggested to accomplish this goal is the socialization of "covenanted internationalism" through an emphasis on international human rights.

LEARNING TO LIVE TOGETHER

The relationship between memory and the nation-state was first explicated in chapter 4, where state manipulation of memory via a series of different techniques was discussed. In chapter 14, I will explore the complex relationship between memory and the political obstacles to preserving life. My basic argument is that historical reconstruction is a mechanism used by the state to socialize its citizens and to create an obedient population. As I noted earlier, one of the primary tools for socialization is the establishment of a system of education that transmits the basic values of the group in power. The state inculcates nationalist ideas that serve as the psychological foundation upon which perceptions of the world are structured. Whether future generations will live together peacefully or continue the outrage of mass murder depends to a very large extent upon how the generations learn to perceive the state and whether educators and political decision makers work to increase people's awareness of human interdependence.

This view of the source of international perceptions is not new. In 1926 George Bradford Neumann wrote: "International relations are of far greater importance now than ever before in peace times and there does not appear any indication that this importance will decrease, but it rather appears that it will continue to increase" (p. 5). Neumann enumerated selected indicators of the growing importance of international relations and noted that social scientists and educators were focusing ever greater attention on international concerns. In a surprisingly contemporary comment, he pointed out that "modern technology is causing the world's physical distances to shrink . . . [but this] does not necessarily mean that world brotherhood will result" (p. 7). In fact, he argued, only "the development of more friendly attitudes in the nations and people concerned" can lessen hostility.

Neumann noted that new perceptions of the international state system were lacking: "New attitudes toward humanity in general and other nations in particular must take the place of those which have obtained—a new loyalty, an internationalistic loyalty, not simply a nationalistic loyalty" (1926, p. 6). If this sounds vaguely familiar, it is not surprising. Contemporary scholars have once again discovered the importance of international perceptions and knowledge

(Delli Carpini and Keeter 1989; Grosvenor 1989; Ravitch and Finn 1987) and are asking questions first posed over fifty years ago by Neumann: "Are the people of the nations being prepared for these new conditions . . . ? Or are the youth of today being attitudinally prepared to live in a social order which is rapidly ceasing to exist?" (1926, pp. 6–7).

In chapters 9, 10, and 11, I noted that political attitudes and views of the world are learned through the process of political socialization, which occurs within a definite cultural context. This context includes the national culture, which bends international perceptions in certain nationalistic directions. Children are taught the politically constructed boundaries of the international nation-state system. Indeed, it would not be an exaggeration to say that national identity is learned early in life along with some of the more basic socialization experiences.[1] Our identity becomes intertwined with the nation-state, and we use leaders and patriotic figures and rituals as guidelines to place ourselves within the international political community. When children internalize nationalistic identifications and international orientations, they formulate a worldview based upon the reconstructed memory of their nation's history and its affiliation with or hostility to other nations. Unlike the indoctrination to the nation-state, which fosters total loyalty and identification, attachment to the international domain is more selective and, therefore, more disconnected.

It is, consequently, disingenuous for scholars to decry the lack of international knowledge or identification when there are few or no agents from which to acquire these perceptions. It is unlikely that any nation-state will include, as part of the process of memory construction or socialization, information that presents a positive view of international attempts to override the power of the individual state. This is supported by the findings of research studies that continuously indicate the strength of nationalist sentiments.

In 1926 Neumann surveyed 110 high school students and found "a strong tendency toward nationalism" (1926, p. 89). When Lambert and Klineberg

---

1. Many of the studies of political socialization tend to confirm that children's early experiences provide them with their basic view of the world. The first six years of a person's life influence the way in which they will define "reality." They learn their socially defined roles, but they also begin to acquire a political identification. In particular, among the first political perceptions learned are views of authority—that is, perceptions of political leaders—and orientations toward relating to authority. Although it has not been adequately tested, it is possible that national identity—identification with the nation-state—is also learned early and reinforced by later agents such as the school and the media (Hirsch 1971b).

asked American children what nationality they would "most like to be if they were not American," most said they would like to be British, Italian, or Canadian (1967, pp. 32–33). The people they most often considered similar to them were also British, Canadian, French, Italian, or German. Those they most often thought of as different were African, Chinese, Japanese, or Russian. In addition, a study conducted by the Educational Testing Service (Pike and Barrows 1976) found what the authors called a "we-they" view among American fourth-grade children, with the United States set far apart from all other countries. The United States was seen as the most desirable, richest, strongest, and largest country by the respondents (p. 108). Clearly, these different studies yield remarkably similar results. Among the common threads, also found by Lambert and Klineberg (1967, p. 102), are the very definite stereotypes, based on nationalism, that are attached to these perceptions. As far back as 1926, Neumann noted that nationalism was a pervasive and important ideology. Acknowledging its complexity, he nevertheless defined it as a "reverence bordering in sacredness for the political institutions. Often symbols such as the flag or Constitution are regarded as sacred and any criticism is seen as unpatriotic" (pp. 17, 18). Similar perceptions remain today.

One study (Hirsch and Hirsch 1990) disclosed that the American students interviewed categorized the United States as a "free country," as opposed to Communist countries, which were seen as "not free" and "bad." Communism was also viewed as a form of social organization that does not reward or encourage individuality or competition; it makes everyone "the same as everyone else." Conversely, the United States was thought of as a free nation where people can choose to be different, and it was considered less warlike than other nations. Thus, Americans were described as "good, wealthy and free," as were the Canadians, French, and Germans. These perceptions are, quite clearly, not based on information or knowledge but on vague, and sometimes incorrect, perceptions of reality.

Perceptions of reality are, as argued in chapter 9, linguistically created, and individuals derive meaning from their cultural, social, and political context. In the social construction of reality, language transmits the cultural imperatives into the minds, feelings, and habits of the people. Language is the carrier and formative agent of the ideologies and myths that form the basis of perceptions.

All cultures and nation-states construct political myths that involve glorification and romanticization of the nation-state. Whether in war or in peace, the state is correct, and the enemies of the state—any other state—are wrong. Moreover, as Mosse (1990) and Fussell (1989) note, "God" and righteousness are always on the side of one's own state. Nationalism and Christianity created myths to justify violent action by one state against another, and the myth was further extended to justify the death of an individual in service to the state as a worthy, sometimes Christ-like, sacrifice (Mosse 1990, p. 35). Nationalism became the new religion as love of the father- or motherland replaced love of God as the new mythology with which people could identify. These myths, as we pointed out in chapter 9, are phrased metaphorically and "suppress the recognition of reality" (Edelman 1971, p. 74). They eventually become self-perpetuating and serve as mechanisms used by individuals to organize their views of the world, which are based on nationalism.

Overall, it seems quite remarkable that, given this evidence of deep-seated nationalism, research continues to uncover hope for a peaceful future—even in the face of absolute tragedy. In his remarkable book, *Children of War* (1984), Roger Rosenblatt found a similarly hopeful phenomenon. Many of the children he interviewed who had been exposed to the most unspeakable inhumanity and cruelty expressed kindness and hope instead of a desire for revenge. This suggests that, even though the world is now locked into a system of international politics that operates on the imperatives of nationalism and the nation-state system, some young people would like the future to be different. In turn, this might imply that the power of memory to chain people to stereotypic responses and to perpetuate hate and hostility might be mitigated by some, albeit slim, hope for the future. Is it possible that, if people realize they must share their fate on this small planet, the seemingly continuous cycle of violence might somehow be broken? My argument is that transforming national loyalties into international and human loyalties is one hesitant step toward creating a more peaceful planet. Ascertaining how to transform these international perceptions based on nationalism into truly international perceptions is the task at hand.

POLITICAL SOCIALIZATION AND
INTERNATIONAL PERCEPTIONS

Having just noted the historical importance of the nation-state and the overwhelming presence of nationalistic themes, it is now necessary to examine how these themes can be transformed into perceptions more compatible with international harmony. How, in other words, can the process of political socialization be recast from one in which international perceptions are actually based on nationalism to one in which they are truly international?

Chapters 10 and 11 explored the extensive literature on how people learn about politics—the process of political socialization. For the most part, studies have focused on national identity and have ignored or paid little attention to international concerns. Although the international political system has under-gone a remarkable and swift transformation since the end of World War II, our perceptions of it appear to remain mired in the morass of nationalism. If international perceptions remain tied closely to national identity, and if the process of political socialization does not begin to focus on the formation of international identity instead of national identity, it is unlikely that narrow nationalism will be decreased. Fortunately, it is not difficult to see how this process of change might occur.

Political socialization studies generally find that knowledge and attitudes are transmitted to young people via a series of socialization agents. These include the family, the peer group and other significant groups, the media—in particular, television—and education. In molding international perceptions, all of these agents could have an impact, but education would appear to be the most logical agent of transformation.

Formidable obstacles, however, exist. Political decision makers view educa-tional institutions as extensions of the state (see chapter 10). For them, schools should function to train people for the role they will play in society. Histor-ically, education fulfilled this function as it served the dominant political and economic forces in a nation-state and taught citizens to identify with the nation. Consequently, nations, in the persona of the political decision makers, think of education as a means to achieve national aspirations. As a result, the focus remains centered on national sovereignty and is not conducive to the creation of a truly international identity. In fact, "As long as the framework for international education is based on the notion that education, like military power, is but a means to achieve national ambitions, progress in building better cross-cultural and global relations among people and nations is likely to be incidental and haphazard. Education viewed solely as a matter of getting ahead is divisive at local, national and international levels. The need is to devise a system that educates all comers, rich and poor, foreign and domestic, to full humanity" (Becker 1973, p. 106).

One way to attempt to achieve this "full humanity" is to try to change the content of socialization from competitive nationalism to cooperative interna-tionalism. The single best way to inculcate cooperative internationalism is by focusing on the "world's first universal ideology"—international human rights (Weissbrodt 1988, p. 1).

HUMAN RIGHTS AND POLITICAL SOCIALIZATION

All observers, as Forsythe (1991) points out, do not agree that human rights is a universal ideology (pp. 1–26). Some argue that the very idea of individual human rights is culture-bound and tied to Western ideology. Proponents of cultural relativism and those who hesitate to apply human rights principles to their own situations because of their use of power to abuse individual rights, do not accept human rights standards as universal. In fact, some argue that "indigenous-aboriginal peoples have achieved both dignity and, equally important, a harmony with nature without the conception of rights" (Forsythe 1991, p. 3). Certain nation-states, such as Saudi Arabia, go even further and argue that rights such as freedom of religion and freedom from sexual discrimination violate their cultural traditions and are not appropriate for a multicultural world. In short, they claim it is their right to cut off a person's hand for stealing or to stone a woman to death for committing adultery, for example, without outside interference in their affairs. Ideas of human justice and equality are, these critics argue, tied to imperialistic notions of the West. What is left out is the important consideration that individuals must have some protection from the all-powerful state. The rise of the nation-state placed the individual face-to-face with the state, and, as we have seen, the state has repeatedly killed and dominated ever larger numbers of people. Without the protection offered by safeguarding human rights, the individual is at the mercy of the modern state.

Whereas most political, religious, philosophical, or economic ideologies have been tied to a particular tribe, group, nation, or group of nations, human rights represents a more universal idea that offers one method to protect the individual from the all-pervasive power of the state. Despite the growing need for this protection, political education, which is one aspect of political socialization, seldom portrays identity or rights as international. The nationalistic orientation of almost all history and civics courses means that human identity and human rights are not seen as international, and rarely are international documents studied to the same extent as national documents. For example, it is far more common to learn the Declaration of Independence or the Preamble to the Constitution than the Universal Declaration of Human Rights. In other words, schools prepare students to fit into the particular national context and to venerate the nation-state. Studies find over and over again that this type of "nationalistic education incorporates instruction designed to portray the most positive views of the nation-state and the most negative views of ideas, symbols, and people considered to be contranational" (Nelson 1980, p. 270). These national identifications, as I have repeatedly argued, are not completely compatible with true international identity. What is needed is a new way of looking at the relationship between the individual and the international community.

Young people, Schaar (1981b) argues, "need a clear and intelligent comprehension of life to guide their earnestness, their seeking, . . . and their indignation. . . . If the larger community does not provide out of its own resources of ideas and experiences the material for the fabrication of such identity-forming ideologies, young people will find their material elsewhere" (pp. 278–79). Some may "escape into a private utopia," some may submerge their nascent identity into the consumer fads of America, and still others— "especially those on the economic, ethnic and cultural margins—will develop negative and hostile ideologies" (p. 279). Young people need points of positive identification, and since little positive attention is focused on international identity, young people may find their identity in virulent forms of patriotism and nationalism. Perhaps a new definition of patriotism or nationalism is needed.

A model of patriotism that is in fact compatible with humanism and internationalism does exist. Schaar (1981a) argues that "covenanted patriotism" is the only "conception of patriotic devotion that fits a nation as large and heterogeneous as our own" (p. 293). Covenanted patriotism, he argues,

> sets a mission and provides a standard of judgement. It tells us when we are acting justly and it does not confuse martial fervor with a dedication to country. . . . The covenant is not a static legacy, a gift outright, but a burden and a promise. The nation exists only in repeated acts of remembrance and renewal of the covenant through changing circumstances. Patriotism here is more than a frame of mind. It is also activity guided by and directed toward the mission established in the founding covenant. This conception of political membership also decisively transcends the parochial and primitive fraternities of blood and race, for it calls kin all who accept the authority of the covenant. . . . This patriotism is compatible with the most generous humanism.

Covenanted patriotism is an alternative to the blind adherence to patriotic ritual devoid of critical and moral reasoning that has traditionally characterized nationalism.[2] Since it is based on knowledge of, for example, the Bill

---

2. Nationalism became ascendant in the modern era. Schaar (1981a) identifies four factors involved in the rise of nationalism:

1. "The decline of religious faith as the basic bond among people and as the primary source of cultural life."
2. "The breakdown of cultural isolation consequent upon the development of improved means of transportation and communication."

of Rights, covenanted patriotism could be socialized in a manner similar to that in which patriotism is inculcated today. In addition, the notion could be extended to include what I call "covenanted internationalism," whereby international identity, like covenanted patriotism, would be guided by and directed toward the mission established in international human rights covenants, specifically, the numerous eloquent documents adopted by the United Nations (Davies 1988).[3] Covenanted internationalism would also be based on teaching the common history of human rights. Thus, the historical basis of human rights as espoused in documents such as the Declaration of Independence, the U.S. Constitution, and the Declaration of the Rights of Man (France, 1791) would be included as the foundation on which all people, and children in particular, would begin to construct their international identity.

Memory would be built upon an invocation of these documents as the common framework of human identity and as the common hope for a better life for all people. For, as Smith (1992a) eloquently argues,

---

3. "Consolidation and growth of centralized state power."
4. "The dissolution of the monarchical and dynastic principle of political legitimacy." (p. 299)

3. These documents include United Nations Charter (1945); Universal Declaration of Human Rights (1948); Convention on the Punishment and Prevention of the Crime of Genocide (1948); Convention Relating to Status of Refugees (1951); Convention Relating to the Status of Stateless Persons (1954); Declaration of the Rights of the Child (1959); Convention against Discrimination in Education (1960); Protocol Instituting a Conciliation and Good Offices Commission to Be Responsible for Seeking a Settlement of Any Disputes Which May Arise between States Parties to the Convention against Discrimination in Education (1962); Declaration on the Elimination of All Forms of Racial Discrimination (1963); International Convention on the Elimination of All Forms of Racial Discrimination (1965); Declaration on the Promotion among Youth of the Ideals of Peace, Mutual Respect, and Understanding between Peoples (1965); International Covenant on Economic, Social, and Cultural Rights (1966); International Covenant on Civil and Political Rights (1966); Declaration on the Elimination of Discrimination against Women (1967); Protocol Relating to the Status of Refugees (1967); Declaration on the Rights of Mentally Retarded Persons (1971); International Convention on the Suspension and Punishment of the Crime of Apartheid (1973); Declaration on the Rights of Disabled Persons (1975); Declaration of the World Conference to Combat Racism and Racial Discrimination (1978); Declaration on the Elimination of All Forms of Intolerance and of Discrimination Based on Religion or Belief (1981); and Convention on the Elimination of All Forms of Discrimination against Women (1981).

recognition and remembrance involve more than regard for truth: they express compassion for those who have suffered, respect for their dignity as persons, and revolt against the injustice done to them. In the deepest sense, recognition and remembrance are related not only to what happened, but to questions of who *we* are, what *society* is, and how life and community can be protected against visions that would destroy both. To remember those who have come before us is an expression of ourselves—our care, our capacity to join in a community, our respect for other human beings. And through our capacities for memory and foresight, a community comes to include those who are living, those who have died, and those yet to be born. (p. 14)

This vision of memory and community can only come about through a profound change in the way we socialize our young people. A process based on covenanted internationalism and stressing human rights may be a viable alternative. Covenanted internationalism alone is not sufficient, however; it must be part of a larger ethic, an ethic aimed at the preservation rather than the destruction of human life. Two recent attempts have been made to determine how the development of such an ethic might occur. Lifton and Markusen (1990) devote their efforts to examining the development of what they call a "species mentality" (pp. 255–79), while Kelman and Hamilton (1989) are more concerned with ways to break the habit of obedience (pp. 307–38).

"SPECIES MENTALITY" AND BREAKING THE HABIT OF OBEDIENCE

Lifton and Markusen (1990) argue that the species mentality is the " 'moral equivalent' to the genocidal mentality: an alternative that serves similar psychological needs in ways that are life enhancing" (p. 255). They define species mentality as "full consciousness of ourselves as members of the human species. . . . Species consciousness contributes to a sense of self that identifies with the entire human species. But the self cannot live, so to speak, on the human species alone. Its traditional forms of immediate identification—other people, family, work, play, religion, ethnic groups and nation—give substance to the species identification and are necessary to it" (p. 258). To achieve this mentality, the human being has to realign elements of the self so that concern and caring are now extended from the immediate self and family to the species as a whole. Although the authors do not specifically discuss the political changes needed to transform the present mentality into the species mentality, they do identify several traditions of species consciousness. They point out that "species consciousness has been advocated over the centuries by spiritual traditions of moral and intellectual power" (p. 263). Their list of examples includes Mohandas Gandhi, Karl Marx, Sigmund Freud, Martin Luther King, Jr., religious traditions such as the Hindu, Muslim, and Jewish faiths, and the reaction of the world to Nazi atrocities after World War II. In the long run, their concern, like that of most students of genocide, is to stop the murder. To accomplish this, they call for all people to "join in a vast project—political, ethical, psychological—on behalf of perpetuating and nurturing our humanity. . . . We become healers, not killers, of our species" (p. 279).

It is difficult to find fault with such resolve to stop the epidemic of mass death. Indeed, my quarrel is not with that resolve, but with what is lacking in Lifton and Markusen's analysis. Without acknowledging the power and the politics of memory, and without indicating how to transform the accumulated generations of hatred and distrust supported by created myths and reality, it is unlikely that the genocidal mentality will undergo the miraculous change so desired by Lifton and Markusen. As with most attempts to suggest alternative worldviews, they neglect to discuss, in convincing fashion, how to get from the "genocidal mentality" to the "species mentality." I suggested above that an alternative socialization pattern built upon covenanted internationalism might serve as one mechanism of transition, but it remains necessary to spell out in more detail additional aspects of the life-preserving ethic. How, for example, do we break the habit of obedience?

Kelman and Hamilton (1989) are more interested in identifying psychological mechanisms to deter obedience than in proposing a general-purpose ethic (pp. 307–38). Their view, as I understand it, is that if the habit of obedience is broken, the next step will be the creation of the species mentality. Kelman and Hamilton offer a detailed analysis of obedience. Specifically, they explore how the habit of obedience might be broken by changing social structures, increasing political participation, changing the socialization process, and creating "collective support systems that are needed to develop a more responsible citizenry—a citizenry prepared to apply human values and moral principles in evaluating the political authorities' policies and demands" (p. 308).

According to Kelman and Hamilton, individuals are bound to authority systems, in a manner originally identified by Milgram (1974), by role definitions, the chain of command, and the general bureaucratic hierarchy. Potential victims are dehumanized or neutralized, and individuals respond differently to authority situations according to their conceptions of responsibility and their political orientation. In severing this bond, it is important to promote personal responsibility, and Kelman and Hamilton recommend two means to reduce what they call rule- and role-oriented behavior and to induce or encourage value-oriented behavior.

The first method is to decrease the impact of forces that bind the individual to an authority system by reducing the "individual citizen's distance from authority, so that they will be more familiar with it and feel more capable of judging its demands" (Kelman and Hamilton 1989, p. 322). It is also necessary, the authors argue, to modify the social structure, the education experiences, and the group support structure so that individual citizens will be empowered and begin to feel a renewed sense of personal efficacy. According to their formulation: "Empowerment means having the opportunity and the right to make decisions about one's own life and to participate in decision making on public issues. Efficacy means possessing the skills, the knowledge, the material resources, and the social supports that enhance people's ability to determine their own fate and to influence public policy" (p. 323). Empowerment and efficacy are related, and the way to enhance them is to disperse authority by increasing decentralization of political and economic institutions.

The decentralization of authority is a key concept in Kelman and Hamilton's theory, and they claim decentralization would have a "liberating effect" because those who experience having some authority would be less likely to abuse that authority and less likely to obey other authority figures. But this assumption fails to recognize the sad reality that the structure and hierarchy of the system repeatedly combine to induce and encourage obedience. Lt. William Calley, one of their primary examples, was clearly in a position of authority, as were Himmler and Eichmann, but nevertheless proceeded to abuse that authority. Simply dispersing authority will make little difference in a system in which the emphasis to obey remains strong.

Kelman and Hamilton (1989) then argue that education promotes empowerment and enhances efficacy (p. 325). Although this may be true, empowerment and efficacy do not necessarily enhance morality. Einsatzgruppen, or mobile units that followed the Nazi army into communities in Eastern Europe with the sole purpose of killing Jews, were composed of highly educated individuals who were willing to obey and kill. Education, even at the highest levels, does not necessarily mean that people will not obey. Heidegger supported, and at first celebrated, the Nazi rise to power (Farias 1989), as did numerous professors, lawyers, physicians, and other highly educated citizens of the Third Reich. To offset this potential criticism, Kelman and Hamilton reason that it is also necessary to expose people to different perspectives and to change the structure of decision-making groups by breaking down the boundaries and emphasizing dissent as an obligation of citizenship. The ideal of citizenship, they argue, should promote dissent, and the citizen should have allegiance to multiple authorities (p. 330). This concept is similar to my idea of covenanted internationalism and to Lifton and Markusen's "species mentality." Kelman and Hamilton refer to it as developing a "global perspective" (p. 331).

Generally, Kelman and Hamilton (1989) sum up their analysis of obedience by noting that "mindlessness in response to authority needs to be replaced by mindfulness—by heightened, active information processing, and attention to multiple perspectives" (p. 333). Individuals must reacquire a sense of personal responsibility, perceiving themselves as personally causing harmful outcomes. They propose as a corrective education directed toward individualizing potential victims so that they are no longer seen as "anonymous members of stereotyped categories" (p. 337). This reflects Lifton and Markusen's idea of a species mentality and the sentiments expressed by rescuers in chapter 12. While Kelman and Hamilton are most interested in finding ways to reduce obedience to authority, Lifton and Markusen operate at a more general and abstract level, detailing a more encompassing ethic. Neither, however, examines the political and psychological reality of memory. Although a life-preserving ethic must surely incorporate the elements discussed in these two fine works, it must also include much more. It must start by recognizing the world as it is and proceed from there. Recognizing the impact of memory and its role in stimulating death leads one to consider its use in preserving life. A life-preserving ethic begins with a solid recognition of the role of memory in stimulating death.

MEMORY AND A LIFE-PRESERVING ETHIC

Possibly the first step in creating a life-preserving ethic is to free individuals from their bondage to systems of authority. Hence, Kelman and Hamilton's discussion serves as a foundation upon which to begin construction. Although their ideas about how to increase empowerment and efficacy are important and necessary, they neglect the great irony, pointed out by Storr (1991) and Milgram (1974), that "the virtues of loyalty, discipline and self-sacrifice that we value so highly in the individual are the very properties that create destructive organizational engines and bind men to malevolent systems of authority" (Milgram 1974, p. 188). Loyalty is equated with obedience, with doing one's duty, with being a good soldier or a good citizen. Disobedience becomes synonymous with disloyalty and is made to appear "morally reprehensible" (Storr 1991, p. 106) as well as a threat to the very essence of society.

In other words, society encourages conscientious behavior, or following orders, without conscience. Baum (1988) notes that "conscientiousness can take the place of conscience very easily" (p. 56). A person may be very conscientious about his or her behavior and act with complete moral indifference.

Moral indifference is the opposite of moral responsibility, which involves concern about the consequences of one's actions. Missing in modern society is what McCollough (1991) refers to as the "moral imagination" (p. 16), which "may be understood as the capacity to empathize with others and to discern creative possibilities for ethical action." If the communal value system of a society or culture does not esteem such empathic identification with one's fellow human beings, very grave questions may be raised about the morality of that society.

Political culture, McCollough (1991) argues, "forms our understanding of who we are as citizens" (p. 91) and, therefore, influences what type of decisions we are most likely to make. If we are not motivated by empathy for our companions but by objectives like national honor, national security, or company security, it is possible that a "propensity for moral indifference may be woven into the social fabric of modern life" (Baum 1988, p. 57).

Many students of modern society have noted the ways in which the specialization of work roles organized in bureaucratic hierarchies disperses responsibility and reinforces norms of obedience. There is no place in the organization for nonconformists, and whatever one is ordered to do must be done; one must obey or risk one's job. Authority is impersonal and uncaring, and as Hannah Arendt has noted, modern society is ruled by nobody since there is no place to affix responsibility. We are all agents for carrying out orders and conveying paperwork from one point in the hierarchy to the next, and we tend not to be aware of, or not to care about, the concrete consequences of our actions. In Lifton's sense, we become numb to the tragedies around us, and it becomes easier not to care.

To reverse this dismal state of affairs, it is first necessary to acknowledge them and then to move forward to develop new ideas. As Baum (1988) notes, "Ideas have consequences, they have given us nuclear arms and heart transplants, the possibility of final death and the reality of the gift of more life. But as every sociologist knows, mere ideas have never altered the psychosocial nature of man" (p. 83). Therefore, we must use what we know to remember accurately—to base memory on the human stories of overcoming "troubles" so that we may begin to learn that, just as memory may lead to genocide, it may also lead us away from genocide. We must begin to *understand* what it means to confront the reality of memory.

Rosenberg (1988) draws a useful distinction between "knowing" and "understanding." "*Knowing*," he argues, "refers to factual information or the process by which it is gathered. *Understanding*, on the other hand, refers to systematically grasping the significance of an event in such a way that it becomes integrated into one's moral and intellectual life" (p. 382). This type of morality is not derived from logic but is, as Kren (1988) notes, "socially created" (p. 254). Just as moral indifference is socially constructed, so too is moral imagination.

The idea of the state as the source of justice, law, and sovereignty is based on a consensus among states, among those who wield power. Modern societies do not allow individuals to make decisions regarding whether or not they want to obey orders. It is easy to carry out immoral orders because they are justified by a higher good and because one does not see the consequences of one's actions. The great irony is that in the name of good, evil is committed. As Kren (1988) argues, "The primary source of violence is found in the willingness of individuals to be self sacrificing for an ideal, ideology, or cause. When individuals speak of a willingness to die for a cause, they also mean a willingness to kill. 'Give me liberty of give me death' is soon followed by 'give me liberty or I will give you death' " (p. 255).

The desire of an individual to bring about his or her own particular vision of a "better" society, to change the world from what it is to what he or she thinks it should be, may also be a source of destructive behavior. Just as Christianity led to the Crusades and the Inquisition, visions of an ideal democracy, the "city on the hill," and manifest destiny led Anglo-Americans to exterminate and steal the land of Native Americans. But, although Kren and others argue that it is the vision and the willingness to die for a cause that result in the violence, one must ask whether it is instead the means of implementation.

The conditions developed within a group or society as a means to move toward the vision create the environment within which certain kinds of behavior are rewarded and others discouraged. Force and violence win out and become the consensual tools to achieve success. In international politics, genocide becomes a tool of success as Bosnians are killed by Serbs and their land is confiscated while the world watches and does nothing. Power triumphs. What is most important are the sets of behaviors receiving the institutionalized rewards of a society, national or global, and the kinds of models that are created. As you look into your memory, if you see that rewards are offered only for violence, for war and aggression, that is the form of behavior you will most likely display. If, on the other hand, you see violence and aggression punished and peaceful negotiation rewarded, you will conclude that peaceful actions are the desired behavior. One does not need to be a very perceptive observer to note which type of behavior is now rewarded and celebrated.

Of course the dilemma is that in a world that rewards an ethic of violence, counterviolence is necessary to protect against the aggression. As Storr (1991) points out, although we would all like to "rid ourselves of our proclivities for violence," if we did, we "might find that we could no longer stand up for ourselves or assert our separate identities. Aggression seems closely linked with self-preservation, self-assertion, and self-affirmation. An aggressive attack upon another individual involving the use of physical force is a crude, extreme example of self-assertion at the expense of the other" (p. 7). The paradox is similar to Moore's (1978) notion of positive and negative authority and extends to the concept of being willing to die for a cause. If one is not willing to die for a cause and use violence to overthrow an unjust state, then the injustice will continue. On the other hand, if one uses violence, then the question remains as to whether a nonviolent society is possible. The problem becomes even more complicated when we remember that the violence is justified by higher moral principles. If a transcendent vision of a good society leads to the ultimate evil of mass death, how are repressive or totalitarian societies to be changed? Are we left with speechless silence and inaction? I think not. Evil, such as that of the Nazi regime, must be opposed, and violence is often necessary. Unfortunately, the world is not a perfect place, but that does not mean that one cannot work toward improving it while trying to stop the greater evils from occurring. Creating and implementing a life-preserving ethic is obviously not an easy task.

ETHICS, LAW, AND LIFE

Ethics are not laws. Even though ethical judgments often use words similar to those used in courts of law, they are different from laws. Law, as Hallie (1979) notes, "moves and lives in public institutions; life-and-death ethics (which is the area of ethics closest to criminal law) moves and lives in individuals" (p. 270). Laws are made and enforced by public institutions, whereas ethical judgments are personal and there are no mechanisms of enforcement. Law and ethics may occasionally be in harmony, but usually the needs of the state are placed before those of the ethical conscience of the individual. Ethics are not, however, entirely private; they are based on some concept of community (p. 271). Ethics, on occasion, may bring people together as in Le Chambon (as discussed in chapter 12), during the Vietnam War, or in groups such as Amnesty International, which opposes torture. Ethics and law, when applied in a nation with ethical principles, if such a nation exists, have the same common goal—to restrain the destructive power of humans (p. 272).

Law and ethics both rest on fundamental principles—beliefs that are accepted by a society or group. A principle such as "innocent until proven guilty" is a presumption of U.S. criminal law, while the "presumption at the foundation of life-and-death ethics is that all human life is precious" (Hallie

1979, p. 273). The Nazis operated on the basis of presumptions that were exactly the opposite. Hallie cites the official handbook of the Hitler Youth Organization, which says: "The foundation of the National Socialist outlook on life is the perception of the unlikeness of men." Hallie concludes, "The distance between this belief and the tenet that all human beings are precious is the ethical distance between the Nazis and the nonviolent" rescuers of Jews at Le Chambon.

Law and ethics also have codes that make demands upon individuals to learn to control certain "passions." Law threatens punishment from without, by the state, for violations, while ethics are supposed to be based on internalized controls. When the moral law within you rules your passions, you are good. When your inward government is in chaos, in anarchy, you are bad" (Hallie 1979, p. 278). In short, ethics involve human character and are based in a community. They cannot be divorced from history or from action since they must concern themselves with how human beings behave.

Starting with the individual and with systems of authority, it will be necessary to build a community based on an ideology encompassing the ideas of international human rights and covenanted internationalism in order to implement a life-preserving ethic. Members of a community in which a life-preserving ethic has been socialized and internalized—that is, accepted as the basis for behavior—will, as Oliner (1986) notes,

> share voluntary and personal linkages with each other. Moreover, individuals in a community are bound to each other through emotional ties which may include in varying degrees of intensity a sense of common interests, responsibilities, fellowship, affection and even love. Unlike the state, in which the central relationship of individuals is to their government, the central relationship of individuals in a community is to each other. It is out of a sense of community that people are more likely to engage in those acts of kindness, civility and helpfulness which enhance the quality of life. It is in the context of community consciousness that individuals begin to feel expansive responsibilities towards each other. (pp. 396–97)

The character of this new community would be very different from the character encouraged in communities based on the state or religion. In this community, citizens would seek mutually supporting consensus to help each other and the primary relationship would be among individuals, whereas in communities based on the state or religion, the primary relationship is either between the individual and the government or the individual and God, however defined. Religion and the state have, consequently, alienated individuals from each other and pushed them into a relationship based on authority instead of one based on a ethic of life—an ethic that encourages mutual cooperation instead of zero-sum competition. But the key question remains: If a life-preserving ethic, based on covenanted internationalism and a new sense of community, is to be implemented, how does that process occur in a real world dominated by nation-states and ruled by the incentives of power and violence—how, in short, do we learn to live together?

CONCLUSION

Of course, several obvious obstacles to peace exist. First, nationalism still predominates, and human rights are still abused by many nations. As I note in the next chapter, the United Nations, though eloquent in its defense of human rights, has not abolished violations of those rights. This contemporary reality will remain until a life-preserving ethic based on covenanted internationalism replaces the virulent form of old-fashioned patriotism. Without international identity, there can be no international authority to supersede the nation-state and enforce the claims to human rights.

A second problem is that the topic of international human rights occupies a very minor place in the overall socialization patterns of most nation-states. Even formal courses such as history, civics, or political science at the collegiate level remain nation-centered with a focus on country and national identity. Moreover, Hahn (1987) notes that "most curriculum guides, syllabuses, text-books, and examinations still emphasize descriptions of national governmental and political institutions and elite political actors (mostly male)," and teachers are generally unfamiliar with international human rights documents. If education is to become truly international or global, "political education about, for, and in the spirit of human rights can and should begin early and continue throughout the school years" (p. 184).

Political socialization research could provide insight into how the process might work. One way to conceptualize the process of political socialization is to see it as involving two steps: first, political awareness and personalization, and, second, institutionalization (Niemi 1973, p. 121). In the first step, political awareness and personalization, the young person learns that there are authorities above and beyond the family and school and that those authority figures help them personally. At this stage, children have little awareness of the actual operation of politics or political institutions. The second step, which occurs as the child grows older, is institutionalization. In this stage, the young person becomes aware of political institutions and how the political process works.

Socializing a life-preserving ethic could very well follow a similar sequence, beginning with teaching about people as individuals and moving away from the emphasis on leaders and wars. Examining the similar problems experienced by all human beings and personifying these problems by giving specific examples representing experiences in everyday life would provide a point of identification for young children. In addition, examples could be presented demonstrating the differences between history as it was lived and history as constructed by selected leaders. Following this, international political institutions and, in particular, human rights documents would be examined, emphasizing the fact that we are all entitled to the protections offered by these documents and must work together to establish these protections throughout the world community. The identification of common problems and common protections may then provide the basis for building a sense of community founded on covenanted internationalism. Such a community sense would then become the base for the spreading of the life-preserving ethic.

As Shafer (1987) points out, education aimed at fostering international identity must incorporate other forms of education, such as multicultural education, peace education, and education that focuses on transnational concerns such as the environment and energy resources. However, the fact that these areas are viewed as separate, as indicated by their discrete labels, demonstrates that there is presently no integrated approach to changing the perspective of socialization. Implementation of these changes is not a simple matter; few enough people believe that humanity must move in this direction in order to forestall the repeated cycles of destruction, and even fewer people are qualified to teach and communicate the knowledge base. For example, in 1988 when California mandated a very fine curriculum on the teaching of human rights and genocide, one of the primary authors of that curriculum reported that few, if any, teachers were qualified to implement the necessary courses (Kuper 1989).

Despite such problems, attempts to move toward a peaceful existence must continue and be more widely diffused throughout the world. In pursuing the desired results, Hahn (1987) states, three central questions must be answered:

> Does the existing political education produce obedient and compliant or alienated citizens who let an elite rule and do not themselves exercise their rights to participate in public policy decision making? Does the existing approach produce citizens who repeat the rhetoric of "rights for all" but who are not supportive of these rights in concrete situations? Or will young people grow up respecting international human rights both at home and abroad and possessing knowledge, skills, and attitudes that will lead them into active citizen participation? (p. 185)

When we can honestly declare that obedience is not the overwhelming product of the socialization process and that memory is focused on recalling the saving of life instead of destroying it, perhaps then young people will grow up respecting human rights at home and abroad instead of displaying outdated nationalism that results in hatred and hostility.

To achieve this admittedly idealistic goal, a system of education must be created to transmit international identity based on covenanted internationalism. The development of an effective world community of legal, political, economic, and educational institutions will then carry the message of common humanity, signifying a transformation of the nation-state system. Such a transformation of the socialization process will signal that a new historical era has dawned. The age of the preeminent state, "intent upon sacrificing private interests and personal life at the alter of global competition" (Beres 1985, p. 397), will be replaced by an age of "understanding, tolerance and friendship among all" (Universal Declaration of Human Rights, 1948).

Although this note of optimism is necessary to reinforce the hope that humanity has the capability to move to a more just, humane, and peaceful future, a dose of realism must be added. The obstacles are many and difficult to overcome, and the reality of the international state system must be confronted. Hundreds of nations are members of the United Nations, and countless ethnic and national groups fervently desire to become nations. These nation-states and groups are well armed—some with nuclear weapons, others with sophisticated weapons that their leaders do not hesitate to use to pursue goals and exterminate people. Ethnic and national violence are increasing rapidly since the collapse of the Communist empires, and the world is ever more unpredictable. These facts make the need for an international identity all the more pressing, but that identity cannot flourish within an environment of political violence and hatred. In the short run, political action must be taken to create the conditions within which a life-preserving ethic may be constructed.

> What there was, from the start, was the great silence,
> which appears in every civilized country that passively
> accepts the inevitability of violence, and then the fear that
> suddenly befalls it. The silence which can transform any
> nation into an accomplice.
>
> Jacobo Timerman, *Prisoner without a Name,*
>
> *Cell without a Number* (1981)

14

Memory and the Politics
of Preserving Life

Preventing Genocide in the Post–Cold War World

The nation-state retains its position as the center of international politics, and one does not have to be particularly perceptive to discern that the nation-state and its accompanying ideologies have not served humanity well. The tide of human destruction that has washed over the world is of such depth and force as to leave little doubt that the nation-state has been the primary threat to human life in the twentieth century. If that tide is to ebb, then change must be both political and psychological.

In chapter 13, I pointed out the ways in which the psychological change might occur. I argued that the first step toward halting the cycle of violence and destruction must be to begin to change the foundation of human perceptions from narrowly defined nationalism to covenanted internationalism. This change is important because memory is constructed upon the myths created by a reconstituted history largely shaped by the nation-state or by those holding power or occupying leadership positions. To revise these myths, it will be necessary to change the socialization process. In itself, however, altering the socialization process is certainly not a sufficient condition for ending the historical horror of genocide. Memory runs deep, and without some mechanism to prevent and punish abuses of power—that is, in the short run, to control the destructive impulses of states and individuals—long-term solutions will continue to be illusive. Without a politics to preserve life, the deep-seated nature of memory will assure that the slaughter of innocents is allowed to continue.

The sometimes stretched analogy between the nation-state and the individual is, in this instance, illuminating. The identity of a nation, like that of an individual, may be defined by the memory or reconstruction of events that caused pain. The example of Germany remembering World War I and the "unjust" peace is a prime illustration, as is the U.S. memory of the Vietnam War, which emphasizes the courage of the troops but neglects to confront the outcome and why it ended as it did.

As I noted in chapter 4, nation-states manipulate memory and derive lessons from history to justify their present policy. For example, during the 1950s, 1960s, and 1970s, any confrontation between the United States and the Soviet Union was viewed in terms of the Cold War, and references were often made to the effort to appease Hitler at Munich, implying that it was useless to try to appease the Communists since appeasement failed to prevent World War II. Following the end of the Cold War, a new meaning has been attached to the Vietnam War, and U.S. foreign policy has been calibrated accordingly. What did we learn from the Vietnam War? We have determined that the lesson of the war is that if the United States is going to commit troops in a conflict, it should go all-out, rally the nation, restrict the press—in fact, do everything just the opposite of the way it was done in Vietnam. Recognizing the painful reality that the United States lost the Vietnam War creates an identity problem for a nation that aspires to be the single greatest power in the "new world order."

Remembering perceived past injustices or crises that create an identity problem for the nation-state in turn may lead to intense nationalism as a reaction to the memory of pain and as a mechanism to overcome the perceived adversity. Staub (1989) argues that this nationalism reflects the "desire to protect and enhance the nation economically and to maintain or increase its power, prestige, and purity" (p. 252). The irony is that the values deemed virtuous in one case may lead to mass death in another. This is true of both nations and individuals in whom loyalty, discipline, and self-sacrifice, as Milgram (1974) notes, "are the very properties that create destructive organizational engines of war and bind men to malevolent systems of authority" (p. 188). These memories of pain and the stimulus to overcome them, to engage in action to rectify the past situation, are likely to come to the fore in times of a crisis, for, as Storr (1991) notes, "when threatened we look for saviors and devils" (p. 122). Selected people or groups, other nations, or one's own nation are endowed with either positive virtues or intensely negative virtues. In such a crisis, a minority is always willing to lead the majority, who assume a passive role. If that authority proposes a solution that involves exterminating another state or people, it will usually appeal to the past and present for justification. The memory of the past is invoked to justify the violent action, while, in the present, the reigning leader is portrayed as the inheritor of the mantle who will restore the power and prestige of the past. These images may be powerful tools to bind the people to authority and motivate them to participate in the proposed, and sometimes final, solution. In such a time of crisis, access to some mechanism designed to control the violence and to provide intervention to save lives is particularly important. Just as laws within nation-states and groups punish certain crimes—in particular, homicide, even though the question of whether punishment prevents murder is still hotly debated—there must be a body of international law and an organization to enforce it that would have the same ability to punish and prevent crimes of mass murder.

In other words, even if individuals come to recognize that they share the same planet, it will be necessary to establish political institutions to deter evil. The most logical step would be to create within the United Nations institutionalized procedures to prevent genocide. The remainder of this chapter will examine how to prevent genocide in the post–Cold War world.

THE POLITICS OF PRESERVING LIFE: THE PRACTICALITY OF MORALITY

Most of the harm in the world is done by those who are dogmatically certain that they are right. For being absolutely right means that those who disagree are absolutely wrong. Those who are absolutely wrong are of course dangerous to society and must be restrained or eliminated. That is the beginning of the road to the torture chamber and the gas oven.
—Anthony Storr, *Human Destructiveness* (1991)

If the incentives to kill are reinforced by memory and politics, if they remain strong and are reinforced by the state and the authority structure of the state, is there any protection against the killing in national or international law—how, in short, do we stop genocide? Once again it is difficult to avoid drawing the conclusion that human beings have learned that genocide is a potentially successful method to achieve certain desired political ends. The failure of the international community to stop the massacres in Bosnia and the inability to regulate violence around the world without the intervention of a superpower must lead one to conclude that the mechanisms to control the violence are very tenuous.

Just before the invasion of Poland in 1939, Adolf Hitler spoke to his military commanders, noting the failure of the world to remember the Armenian genocide: "Who after all, speaks today of the annihilation of the Armenians? . . . The world believes in success alone" (Bardakjian 1985). It will not be long before another Slobodan Milosevic or Radovan Karadzik asks: "Who after all, speaks today of the annihilation of the Bosnian Muslims?" The unwillingness of the world community to take action to end genocide and political massacres is not only immoral but also impractical. Foreign policy, in this age of reawakened ethnonational violence, must be dominated by the "practicality of morality." Action to halt and prevent genocide and political massacres is practical because without some semblance of stability, commerce, travel, and the international and intranational interchange of goods and information are subjected to severe disruption. It is, therefore, in everyone's interest to end that disruption and create an environment of peaceful interchange. In short, moral imperatives are, in this new post–Cold War environment, the most practical way to pursue our national interest and to lay the groundwork for the creation of a life-preserving ethic.

Indeed, if we are to explore the uncharted paths of what director of the CIA James Woolsey referred to in 1992 as a new world situation in which the dragons have been slain but in which numerous poisonous snakes lie in our path (Waller 1993, p. 30), it will be necessary to take three broad steps to develop a coherent strategy to prevent genocide in the post–Cold War world. First, we must devise a multilateral strategy to curtail and prevent genocide and political massacres. This will be facilitated by assembling a coalition of support to halt the violence by developing a policy to bring together the international laws of war and the 1948 U.N. Convention on the Prevention and Punishment of the Crime of Genocide, or the Genocide Convention. Second, we must develop an "early warning system" and instruments of humanitarian intervention to recognize and to prevent future genocides and political massacres. Third, a system of punishment of instigators of genocide and political massacres should be implemented, demonstrating to the world that violence is not an acceptable means to achieve political ends.

INTERNATIONAL LAW AND THE PREVENTION OF GENOCIDE AND POLITICAL MASSACRES

If the prevention of genocide is ever to become a reality, it is essential to create, within the United Nations, a set of institutions that have the power to act to prevent mass killing. These should be based on international law and on a reformulated and strengthened U.N. Convention on the Prevention and Punishment of the Crime of Genocide.

Smith (1992b) is no doubt accurate when he argues that international law sets norms and expectations for state behavior but will accomplish little until "governments redefine 'national interest' to include prevention of genocide" (p. 232). Remedies in international law must be created that will guarantee that perpetrators of genocide will be brought to justice and that international violence will not be seen as a legitimate mechanism to achieve territorial or other aspirations.

International law has been virtually powerless to stop the large-scale destruction of human life primarily because international politics is dominated by the nation-state and the idea of sovereignty. In fact, international law is often defined as "the body of rules that nations recognize as binding upon one another in their mutual relations" (Slomanson 1990, p. 1). The result of consensus among nations, international law is what the nations of the world agree it is. Nations observe international law when they "believe their national interests are best served by observing rules established by international consensus" (p. 8). Any program to stop the violence will have to confront the nation-state's claim to sovereignty within its own borders and its right to use force, to go to war, to defend its interests.

This objective cannot be accomplished unilaterally but will require the kind of coalition building and support inducement manifested in the Persian Gulf War. It will be necessary to assemble a coalition of support for the policy of uniting the Genocide Convention and international laws defining crimes of war in order to punish perpetrators and to demonstrate to the world that international violence is not to be tolerated by the world community. There are precedents for such action.

THE NUREMBERG PRINCIPLES

At the conclusion of World War II, the victors decided that it was necessary to punish the losers and to demonstrate to the world that certain actions would not be tolerated by the international community of nations. In pursuit of this goal, thousands of war crimes trials were held. Trials were conducted by the International Military Tribunal at Nuremberg (IMT), the International Military Tribunal for the Far East at Tokyo, the U.S. Military Tribunal at Nuremberg (NMT), the U.S. Military Commissions sitting at various places in Europe and Asia, the General Military Government Court and Intermediate Government Court of the American zone in Germany, British military courts sitting in various places in Europe and Asia, the French permanent Military Tribunal sitting in various places in France, the French Court of Appeal and the General Military Government Tribunal of the French zone in Germany, the Australian Military Court sitting at Rabaul, the Canadian Military Court sitting in Germany, the Netherlands Temporary Court-Martial and Special Courts, the Norwegian Court of Appeal, the Supreme Court of Norway, the Chinese War Crimes Court, and the Supreme National Tribunal of Poland (Tutorow 1986, p. 5). Before the U.N. War Crimes Commission was phased out, it reported the following number of war crimes trials: 809 American, 524 British, 256 Austrian, 254 French, 30 in the Netherlands, 24 Polish, 9 Norwegian, 1 Canadian, and 1 Chinese.

In addition to the war crimes trials, thousands of denazification proceedings were conducted in Germany. The denazification laws were not designed to "punish Germans who had been Nazis, but to remove them from, or keep them out of, positions of postwar leadership. The accused were classified as either major offenders, offenders, lesser offenders, or followers" (Tutorow 1986, p. 7). The number of cases tried under these laws was huge. Thirteen million people in the American zone alone had to register; approximately 3 million were found subject to classification and over 930,000 defendants were eventually tried by denazification tribunals. West German courts also prosecuted 12,982 defendants as war criminals between 1945 and 1963. Although records are haphazard, a "German government publication reported on January 7, 1964 that in the American Zone alone 1814 people had been sentenced, 450 to death; in the British zone 1085, 240 to death; and in the French zone 2107, 104 to death. More than half of those receiving the death sentence were actually executed" (p. 8). In addition to all of this activity, numerous trials were conducted for which records are difficult to find.

Information on trials in Eastern Europe and the former Soviet Union was previously virtually impossible to obtain but may now become more available. Carefully staged "show trials" of Nazi leaders were held in Czechoslovakia and Poland, and a number of defendants were prosecuted for acts committed in the concentration and death camps. The major cases involved six camps: Dachau, Mauthausen, Flossenburg, Nordhausen, Buchenwald, and Mühldorf. All told, there were close to 88,000 war crimes cases "opened in West Germany between 1945 and 1983" (Tutorow 1986, p. 8). The most important and well known were the trials now often referred to as the "Nuremberg trials."

In 1946 the General Assembly of the United Nations adopted resolution 95 (1), which incorporated the judgment of the Nuremberg court, or the Nuremberg principles,[1] into international law. "Under this principle, a nation that

1. The Nuremberg Principles are found in Falk, Kolko, and Lifton 1971, pp. 106–7.

THE NUREMBERG PRINCIPLES OF 1946

1. Principles of International Law Recognized in the Charter of the Nuremberg Tribunal and in the Judgment of the Tribunal

As formulated by the International Law Commission, June–July 1950.

Principle I

Any person who commits an act which constitutes a crime under international law is responsible therefor and liable to punishment.

Principle II

The fact that internal law does not impose a penalty for an act which constitutes a crime under international law does not relieve a person who committed the act from responsibility under international law.

Principle III

The fact that a person who committed an act which constitutes a crime under international law acted as Head of State or responsible government official does not relieve him from responsibility under international law.

Principle IV

The fact that a person acted pursuant to order of his Government or of a superior does not relieve him from responsibility under international law, provided a moral choice was in fact possible to him.

Principle V

Any person charged with a crime under international law has the right to a fair trial on the facts and law.

Principle VI

The crimes hereinafter set out are punishable as crimes under international law:

A. Crimes against peace:

(i) Planning, preparation, initiation or waging of a war of aggression or a war in violation of international treaties, agreements or assurances.

(ii) Participation in a common plan or conspiracy for the accomplishment of any of the acts mentioned under (i).

B. War crimes:

Violations of the laws or customs of war which include, but are not limited to, murder, ill-treatment or deportation to slave-labour or for any other purpose of civilian populations of or in occupied territory, murder or ill-treatment of prisoners of war or persons on

wages aggressive war commits the supreme international crime, punishable by any nation able to bring that nation's planners to justice. Its leaders incur criminal responsibility—arising directly under *international* law—for their conduct that causes the state to be liable under international law. They may thus be tried and punished for their participation in the unlawful use of force against other states" (Slomanson 1990, p. 413).

Nuremberg clearly established that an individual can be the subject of international law. Although the idea of trying an individual for war crimes was first applied in the Versailles Treaty following World War I when the Allied and Associated powers arraigned William II of Hohenzollern, formerly the German emperor, for a "supreme offense against international morality and the sanctity of treaties," he was never brought to trial. It was the Nuremberg judgment that established the precedent that an individual could be tried for violating international law.

The Nuremberg tribunal specifically rejected the notion that international law covers only the actions of states and cited the case of *Ex Parte Quirin* (317 U.S. 1, 63 S.Ct. 2 [1942]), in which individuals were charged, during World War II, with landing in the United States for purposes of spying and sabotage. As a result, the tribunal concluded that "crimes against international law are committed by men, not by abstract entities, and only by punishing individuals who commit such crimes can the provisions of international law be enforced" (Falk, Kolko, and Lifton 1971, p. 101).

The liability of the Nazis was based on the theory that there "was a direct relationship between the individual and international law. The defendants claimed that they had no obligations under international law: their only duty was to the Nazi state which, in turn, would bear responsibility under international law" (Slomanson 1990, p. 338). The tribunal disagreed: "Individuals have international duties which transcend the national obligations of obedience imposed by the individual state [to which they owe allegiance]. He

---

the seas, killing of hostages, plunder of public or private property, wanton destruction of cities, towns, or villages, or devastation not justified by military necessity.

C. Crimes against humanity:

Murder, extermination, enslavement, deportation and other inhuman acts done against any civilian population, or persecutions on political, racial or religious grounds, when such acts are done or such persecutions are carried on in execution of or in connexion with any crime against peace or any war crime.

Principle VII

Complicity in the commission of a crime against peace, a war crime, or a crime against humanity as set forth in Principle VI is a crime under international law.

who violates the laws of war cannot obtain immunity while acting in pursuance of the authority of the State if the State in authorizing action moves outside its competence under international law."

After the original trials of the high-ranking Nazi officials at Nuremberg, President Harry Truman turned the remaining war crimes trials over to the Office of Military Government in Germany. Twelve trials were held over a period of three years, during which 185 defendants were indicted. Several were given death sentences, which were later commuted, while others received prison terms.

The Nuremberg military tribunals were based on a series of laws passed by the Allied Control Council, which finally turned over the power to try war crimes cases to the German judiciary on November 25, 1949. The NMT generally "followed the guidelines laid down by the IMT, but there were several significant differences" (Tutorow 1986, p. 12). One involved the definition of crimes against peace, which was broadened to "include initiations of invasions which were not resisted, for example, those of Austria and Czechoslovakia." A second difference toughened the definition of a war criminal by stating that anyone who was a member of an organization defined as a criminal organization by the IMT charter was a war criminal. If this provision had not been modified to state that the accused had to have personal knowledge of the criminal purposes and acts of the organization, it would have applied to about 2 million Germans. A third difference was that the NMT was staffed completely by American judges.

These cases reaffirmed the Nuremberg Principles, which were given another classic expression in the Einsatzgruppen case: "Nations can act only through human beings, and when Germany signed, ratified, and promulgated the Hague and Geneva Conventions, she bound each one of her subjects to their observance" (Tutorow 1986, p. 12). These cases also reaffirmed the principle that crimes against peace had a basis in international law and rejected the defense of superior orders.

Surprisingly, these hundreds of cases, involving thousands of defendants, were not the only war crimes trials to take place after World War II. An equal or greater number of cases were heard in the Far East.

WAR CRIMES TRIALS IN THE FAR EAST

The two most important trials in the Far East were the trial of General Tomoyuki Yamashita in the Philippines and the Tokyo war crimes trials that opened on May 3, 1946. These trials, especially the Yamashita trial, were much more controversial than the Nuremberg trials.

When the war in Europe ended, the Allies turned their attention to Japan. The Potsdam Declaration of July 26, 1945, stated: "We do not intend that the Japanese shall be enslaved as a race or destroyed as a nation but stern justice shall be meted out to all war criminals, including those who have visited cruelties upon our prisoners." This "stern justice" had already been meted out in the trial of General Yamashita, who was convicted of permitting his men to commit atrocities.

Yamashita was the commanding general of the Fourteenth Army Group of the Imperial Japanese Army in the Philippine Islands. On September 3, 1945, he surrendered and became a U.S. prisoner of war. Charged with violating the law of war, he pleaded "not guilty" on October 8, 1945, and was tried before a military commission of five army officers appointed by order of Lieutenant General Styer.

As described on his appeal to the U.S. Supreme Court, Yamashita was specifically charged with permitting "members of his command" to "commit brutal atrocities," including "a series of acts, one hundred and twenty-three in number," that were considered to be a "deliberate plan and purpose to massacre and exterminate a large part of the civilian population of Batangas Province, and to devastate and destroy public, private and religious property therein, as a result of which 25,000 men, women, and children, all unarmed noncombatant civilians, were brutally mistreated and killed, without cause or trial, and entire settlements were devastated or destroyed wantonly and without necessity" (quoted in Falk, Kolko, and Lifton 1971, pp. 142–43).

The specific charge against Yamashita was that "while commander of armed forces of Japan at war with the United States of America and its allies, he unlawfully disregarded and failed to discharge his duty as commander to control the operations of the members of his command, permitting them to commit brutal atrocities and other high crimes against people of the United States and of its allies and dependencies, particularly the Philippines; and he . . . thereby violated the laws of war" (quoted in Falk, Kolko, and Lifton 1971, p. 142). The U.S. Supreme Court concluded that "the allegations of the charge, tested by any reasonable standard, adequately allege a violation of the law of war and that the commission had authority to try and decide the issue which it raised" (p. 146).

The Yamashita case has since fallen into obscurity. The reason for its disappearance is clear—any officer whose men commit atrocities would be liable under this precedent. It may, in fact, be the only precedent of its kind.

The Tokyo war crimes trials, which convened on May 3, 1946, were similar to the Nuremberg trials. Eleven nations[2] and eleven justices tried twenty-eight defendants in these trials. Many of the defendants had been generals in the Imperial Army or held other high office, but civilian defendants, including former prime minister Tojo Hideki, were also tried (Minear 1971). The defendants were charged as individuals or as members of organizations with crimes against the peace, conventional war crimes, and crimes against humanity. Since the charges set important precedents, it is necessary to examine them in a bit more detail.

The charge of crimes against peace, which involve murder and "conspiracy to commit murder," accused the defendants of conspiring to "kill civilians and members of the armed forces of certain nations by the initiation of unlawful hostilities in violation of the Hague Convention of 1899" (Tutorow 1986, p. 15). The charge of crimes against humanity accused the defendants of "conspiracy to *permit* the armed forces of Japan to violate the laws and customs of war and of criminal failure to take adequate steps to secure observance of these laws and customs" (emphasis added).

The prosecution began the case by outlining the structure of the Japanese government so that responsibility could be ascertained. The trial would last two and a half years, and when an opinion was finally rendered on November 4, 1948, it was 1,218 pages long and had taken seven months to prepare. Generally, the verdict was "guilty." Seven defendants were sentenced to death by hanging, and the sentences were carried out on December 28, 1949. Sixteen were sentenced to life imprisonment, one to twenty years in prison, and one to seven years in prison. (Two defendants died during the long trial, and one was declared unfit for trial; cases against these three were dismissed.) All prisoners were released on April 7, 1958.

As with the Nuremberg trials, the Tokyo trials were only the most famous. Altogether, there were approximately "5,700 Japanese tried on conventional war crimes charges and 92 percent of these men were executed" (Minear 1971, p. 6). The important fact to keep in mind is that the European and Asian trials constitute a record of applicability and demonstrate that, if the will is there, the precedents exist to hold individuals responsible for violations of the laws of war or other crimes under international law. In fact, literally uncounted numbers of documents and records of the various trials exist.

The official record of Nuremberg alone was published in forty-two volumes in *Trial of the Major War Criminals before the International Military Tribunal* (1947–49). For the IMT Nuremberg trials, about 100,000 docu-

2. These nations are Australia, Canada, China, France, India, the Netherlands, New Zealand, the Philippines, the Soviet Union, the United Kingdom, and the United States.

ments were collected and about 10,000 were published. The word-for-word transcript covers over 17,000 pages. These trials were based upon a common set of precedents and on international law as it existed at the time. Nevertheless, there were critics of the war crimes trials.

The critics made essentially three broad objections. First, they claimed that the neutral and defeated nations should have been included on the various tribunals. Second, some argued that the laws under which defendants were tried were "ex post facto or nonexistent laws, and they argued further that no laws defining war crimes existed until after World War II" (Tutorow 1986, p. 22). Third, some maintained that the standards used in the war crimes trials were not as rigorous standards of justice as those used in the domestic law of most nations. In particular, the specific argument was that in most nations a unanimous jury is required for a death sentence and in the war crimes cases individuals were sentenced to death, in one case at Nuremberg with a vote of 3 to 1 and in Tokyo with a vote of 6 to 5, with dissenting opinions (pp. 22–23).

These objections notwithstanding, the precedents have been set, massively documented, and incorporated into international law. Although it may be debatable whether there were laws defining war crimes before Nuremberg and Tokyo, remedies now exist in international law.

INTERNATIONAL LAW AND WAR CRIMES

Most international laws relating to war are based on treaties, custom, judicial decisions, national manuals of military law, and the writings of legal specialists on the subject. The basic premise behind these laws is that, since it appears unrealistic to believe war will be abolished, the next best thing is to attempt to control the worst effects of warfare by maintaining standards of civilization by which conduct is to be judged. Although participants in war do not always adhere to the laws governing warfare, certain basic ideas have gained widespread acceptance. For example, prisoners of war may not be killed and must be treated humanely; hospitals may not be considered targets; noncombatants, persons not taking an active part in the conflict, such as children, may not be harmed; and torture is not allowed.

States and armed participants comply with the laws for a variety of reasons. These include the desire to avoid negative world public opinion, which might condemn gross violations, the fear that if the laws are violated there will be military or other reprisals—including political consequences such as the loss of friends and allies—and the fear of possible judicial consequences such as war crimes trials, which, although they may not have enforcement sanctions, could very well brand the perpetrators as pariahs in the world of international politics. Even when international law does not appear to be effective, it provides standards of behavior to be considered in the policy-making process.

The basic idea that war is governed by rules appears to have existed in almost all societies, but it was only in the second half of the nineteenth century that laws to regulate war were codified. Since that time, the international agreements regulating war have taken the form of declarations, conventions, and protocols.[3] These precedents established the concept that international law applied to individuals as well as nations. Using them as a foundation, it should be possible to create institutions to prevent future genocides and to punish perpetrators. This, in turn, may contribute to creating an environment within which the life-preserving ethic may flourish and begin to create a new form of memory—memory of the common struggles to implement international law to protect the rights of all individuals.

Laws governing war cannot eliminate the threat of genocide alone, however, because of certain specific weaknesses. First, legal provisions are subject to different interpretations. Second, written law does not adequately deal with all forms of warfare, and there are limitations in application and enforceability. Third, the technology of destructive forces has advanced so rapidly that the written laws cannot cover all of the many possibilities (Roberts and Guelff 1989, p. 15). If the violence is to be stopped, permanent international institutions must be developed, empowered, and operationalized.

3. For the most part, the primary precedents include the Hague Convention on Land Warfare of 1907, which set the so-called "laws and customs of war on land." According to this convention, poison or poisoned weapons are forbidden and prisoners must be treated fairly and not tortured or mistreated. In addition, according to article 2J, "the attack or bombardment by whatever means, of towns, villages, dwellings, or buildings which are undefended is prohibited."

A second precedent was the Versailles Treaty of 1918, by which Kaiser Wilhelm was to be tried as a war criminal. A special tribunal of five judges from the United States, Great Britain, France, Italy, and Japan was to be convened. Germany was forced to recognize the right of the Allies to set up these trials and was ordered to hand over any person accused of war crimes. Also, the Germans were to "furnish all documents and information of every kind, the production of which may be considered necessary to ensure the full knowledge of the incriminating acts, the discovery of the offenders and the just appreciation of responsibility" (Falk, Kolko, and Lifton 1971, p. 42).

Additional precedents included the Geneva Protocol on Poison Gas and Bacteriological Warfare of 1925, the Pact of Paris (Kellogg-Briand Pact) of 1928, and the Geneva Convention on the Law of War of 1949, which was updated in the 1977 Geneva Protocols.

If future massacres and genocides are to be prevented, individuals who wage aggressive war, or plan and execute genocide, must be apprehended and held accountable. Although this is the first step in ending genocide, it unfortunately takes place after an act of genocide has been committed. Prevention is the key.

A number of proposals have suggested the creation of what have been called "genocide early warning systems" (Charny 1982; Kuper 1985, 1992; Littell 1991). Kuper (1992) claims that there are two major tasks to be performed during the early warning stage. The first is to "alert international public opinion" (p. 224), which involves gathering, processing, and disseminating information and then mobilizing coalitions to bring this information to world attention. The second task is to exert pressure on the offending party "in the hope that it can be prevailed upon to exercise restraint while the genocidal process is still under control."

Pressure is exerted through a variety of techniques, including petitions and representative missions to government officials. Since these are unlikely to have much impact, the next step is to launch campaigns against the offenders such as those undertaken by groups like Amnesty International and other nongovernmental organizations.[4] Even these are unlikely to deter a group or government determined to use genocide as a policy. If they fail, an "international alert" is declared, followed by securing the involvement of United Nations or other international organizations. This stage is crucial because, as Littell (1991) points out, "once the terrorists come to power they cannot be removed without outside intervention" (p. 310). It is of the utmost importance, therefore, to be able to identify the possibility of genocide in a society.

Five general indicators[5] might serve as portents of the potential for genocide.

1. The existence of instruments and mechanisms of recruitment. The printing, use, or distribution of anti-Semitic, racist, or other

---

4. A large number of organizations devote their efforts to stopping genocide or halting international violence. These include the Institute on the Holocaust and Genocide, located in Israel; the Montreal Institute for Genocide Studies, located at Concordia University; the Association of Holocaust Organizations, an umbrella group for many different Holocaust organizations; International Alert against Genocide and Mass Killing; International Commission of Jurists; International League for Human Rights; Human Rights Watch; Cultural Survival; and various other religious and ethnic group associations.

5. Littell (1991, pp. 314–15) identifies fifteen.

dehumanizing material for recruitment of members is a possible demonstration of genocidal possibility.

2. The use of the media or other means to distribute anti-Semitic, racist, or other dehumanizing appeals.

3. The use of mechanisms to achieve political power that involve techniques utilizing violence and intimidation, such as paramilitary training camps to teach the use of weapons, bombing, beating, and assassination.

4. The creation of an environment of unquestioning obedience to authority. The movement or state creates a "quasi-religious structure of authority and sanctions, with political hymns, shrines, martyrs, liturgies" (Littell 1991, p. 315), all designed to establish a situation in which an individual loses any semblance of identity and believes that he or she owes allegiance to the leader.

5. The use of secrecy and other methods to create an exclusionary organization that separates insiders from outsiders. These organizations utilize secret binding rituals established to cement the follower's relationship to the organization. Among these are rituals of induction and separation as well as the use of deception or disinformation to confuse the public and maintain extreme secrecy. Tactics may include infiltration and subversion of public and other institutions such as the police and schools.

When these indicators are present, the institutions created to deter atrocity and genocide must be prepared to act to prevent the assumption of power of terrorist groups or to intervene to save lives. In the long run, supporting democratic movements may be the most efficient method of preventing atrocity. Although democratic governments have also committed genocide, the idea of democratic prevention may be pursued by fostering and encouraging nations and groups to adhere to the covenanted internationalism discussed in the previous chapter.

The creation of some common rules, along with mechanisms to enforce adherence, should therefore be placed on the agenda. In an interdependent and fragile world all too prone to the abuse of human rights, nations and groups can apparently no longer be afforded unlimited self-determination. As Littell (1991) points out, if the Brazilian rain forest "provides 40 percent of the oxygen for the globe, do Brazilians have the right to destroy those forests?" (p. 312). Do certain obligations transcend the rights of special interests for profit or the sovereignty of the individual nation-state?

If this question is answered positively, then any conflict of interest must be worked out in international political deliberations in a truly international organization. Nations, as argued earlier, must relinquish some of their sovereignty. Governments can no longer be considered "legitimate" simply because they maintain order and are recognized by other governments. The governments of the world should cease to recognize those states that are responsible for violence to the environment or people. Moreover, as soon as likely or actual genocide or war crimes are identified in a particular group or state, the individuals who occupy leadership positions in that group or state must be apprehended and held accountable under international law. This can be accomplished by invoking the laws of war and creating a permanent tribunal, an entire judicial system to investigate, indict, and try war criminals.

The U.N. International Law Commission has already recommended that an International Criminal Court be established to take up such cases (Krieger 1993, p. 4). In fact, an Ad Hoc U.N. Criminal Tribunal was created in 1991 by the United Nations under articles 10, 11, 20, and 29 of the U.N. Charter to "hear all claims, render judgment and impose any justified punishment against Saddam Hussein, his political, military and economic advisors, and other unnamed defendants" (Kutner and Vanda 1991, p. 5). If these precedents were applied, for example, to the situation in Bosnia, it should be possible to prove that the Serbians' actions in Bosnia are violations of the laws of war and that the perpetrators should be apprehended and tried. As former secretary of state Lawrence Eagleburger stated at the international Conference on the Former Yugoslavia in Geneva, Switzerland, in December 16, 1992: "The fact of the matter is that we know that crimes against humanity have occurred, and we know when and where they occurred. We know, moreover, which forces committed those crimes, and under whose command they operated. And we know, finally, who the political leaders are to whom those military commanders were—and still are—responsible." Eagleburger proceeded to list some of the leaders and crimes. The U.S. State Department in its dispatches maintained an ongoing record of the activities (see, for example, U.S. State Department dispatches, September 28, November 16, 1992). In spite of all this evidence, no action has been taken to stop contemporary acts of genocide.

Even though the United Nations set up a War Crimes Commission in October 1992 to investigate the Bosnian situation, that commission has been criticized as ineffectual. The chairman of the panel is a retired Dutch academic, Fritz Kalshoven, who claims he was instructed "not to pursue Serbian politicians such as Slobodan Milosevic, President of Serbia, and Radovan Karadzic, head of the Bosnian Serbs" (Gutman 1993, p. 5). The commission issued one report on January 26, 1993, stating that "grave breaches" of humanitarian law have occurred but failing to indicate where or by whom they were committed. Kalshoven expressed his doubts that a war crimes tribunal, which was approved by the Security Council in May 1993, would be effective in the "present atmosphere," as he put it, and indicated that he was not "overly optimistic" trials would ever be held.

The commission has received little in the way of resources, including a budget of $690,000 for nine months, two staff members, and two secretaries. At Nuremberg, over 1,000 people were on the prosecution staff alone. The four commission members are not on salary but receive a per diem payment and travel expenses. A data bank has been set up to collate reports by U.N. members, but this was accomplished with the help of volunteers and funded by a $200,000 donation (Gutman 1993, p. 7B).

In addition, the identification of high-ranking Serbian officials as possible war criminals creates difficulties in the attempt to bring peace to the territory of the former Yugoslavia, for how do you negotiate a cease-fire, peace, or partition agreement with war criminals? In spite of the problems, however, if there is ever going to be a convincing demonstration of the world's desire to create institutions to stop the violence, the inaction must be replaced by action. The United Nations should proceed to indict and try the offenders identified by the U.S. reports. Once indicted as war criminals, the offending parties should be barred from leaving the immediate area of their home base, and it should be incumbent upon any signatory nation to apprehend these criminals and turn them over to the appropriate agency for trial. In addition, it should be the obligation of all nations to embargo certain materials and to not have commercial or other dealings with the perpetrators of war crimes. These should be the first steps toward controlling the violence. If they fail, then additional steps, outlined below, must be taken.

While it is, therefore, quite clear that certain Serbian actions are in violation of the laws of war, it is less clear whether they fit the Genocide Convention, the primary international document outlawing genocide.

GENOCIDE AND POLITICAL MASSACRES:
PROBLEMS OF DEFINITION AND INTENTIONALITY

If genocide and political massacres are ever going to be prevented and punished, it will be necessary to reformulate the U.N. definition of genocide to take account of the process by which genocidal possibility arises and to broaden the definition to include political massacres. This step will allow the creation, within the United Nations, of a set of institutions empowered to act when the genocidal possibility arises.

This suggestion is quite in line with the original conceptualization of Raphael Lemkin when he introduced the term "genocide" into our vocabulary in 1944 in his book, *Axis Rule in Europe*. According to Lemkin, "genocide" is derived from the Greek word "genus" (race, tribe) and the Latin word "cide" (killing), corresponding in its formulation to such words as tyrannicide and homicide. Lemkin defines genocide as "a coordinated plan of different actions aiming at the destruction of [the] essential foundation of the life of national groups, with the aim of annihilating the groups themselves. . . . Genocide is directed against individuals not in their individual capacity, but as members of the national group." He identifies two phases in the process of genocide: the "destruction of the national patterns of the oppressed group" and the "imposition of the national pattern of the oppressor" (pp. 79–80). Lemkin elaborates his definition at great length, pointing out that the Third Reich carried out genocide in seven areas: political, social, physical, cultural, economic, biological, and religious and moral. He proposed that the way to prevent genocidal actions was for the United Nations to adopt an international, multilateral treaty prohibiting genocide, which would then be incorporated into the constitutions and criminal codes of nation-states who were members of the United Nations.

The treaty or convention, as visualized by Lemkin, would protect the lives, liberty, and property of minority groups and would impose criminal liability on all individuals who committed, gave orders to commit, or incited genocide. In addition, he suggested that an international tribunal be established to examine allegations of genocide brought against government leaders. Finally, in order to prevent the occurrence of genocide during periods of war, an international nongovernmental organization, such as the Red Cross, was to be charged with the responsibility of supervising the treatment of civilians.

Lemkin's proposals were far-reaching and dramatic. They would have created an international tribunal to judge crimes and to pinpoint responsibility. Unfortunately, his early language and intent were diluted by the political debates prior to the December 9, 1948, adoption of the U.N. Convention on the Prevention and Punishment of the Crime of Genocide.

The tale of how Lemkin's original language was altered as his proposal traveled through the international and national political institutions is common fare in all works dealing with genocide and international law. Generally, the debates that took place prior to the final adoption of the convention give an early indication of the overall lack of impact the convention would have on international politics—it would not prevent or punish any crime of genocide. Major controversies erupted over what types of groups would be protected, how to measure the intention to commit genocide, how to implement punishment, and how much destruction was necessary to constitute genocide. In sum, the result was that political groups were excluded from the protection of the convention, and no mechanisms were established for enforcement. The delegates could not even agree on what constitutes genocide, and any moral or legal commitment to the eventual eradication of mass murder was absent.

The basic argument against including political groups under the convention was that membership in a political group is voluntary and not permanent, while membership in racial or religious groups is involuntary and generally permanent. The states opposing the inclusion of political groups also argued that their inclusion would weaken the convention and expose nations to external intervention in their domestic concerns. This would endanger the future of the convention because many nations would be unwilling to ratify it, fearing the possibility of being called before an international tribunal to answer charges. For example, opponents of the convention in the United States, as Smith (1992b) notes, "feared that the United States could be charged with genocide for its harsh treatment of African Americans and Native Americans. They reasoned that lynching could be construed as genocide since it involved the killing of a 'part' of a group for racial reasons, and that discrimination could be equated with 'mental harm' to a group, an act defined under the Convention as genocide" (pp. 229–30). Many of these basic arguments were verbalized in the debates involving U.S. attempts to ratify the Genocide Convention.

U.S. RATIFICATION OF THE GENOCIDE CONVENTION

On September 5, 1984, then president of the United States Ronald Reagan asked the U.S. Senate to ratify the Genocide Convention. His request came thirty-six years after the convention had originally been passed by the United Nations and thirty-nine years after the conclusion of World War II. When the convention was finally ratified by the U.S. Senate in 1986, "it had been before that body longer than any other treaty in United States history" (Smith 1992b, p. 227). The twisting road to ratification offers a clear view of the way state sovereignty has restricted the power of the United Nations to force its members to comply with the eloquent human rights provisions to which it has given verbal approval.

The convention was first sent to the Senate in 1949 by President Harry Truman. The 1950 hearings were, as Smith (1992b) points out, "acrimonious in the extreme, characterized by charges that the Convention was a 'sell-out' to the Communists, an attack on fundamental civil liberties, a grab for power by the President, and a threat to the powers of the states within the federal system" (p. 227). These charges were repeated whenever the convention was resubmitted or reconsidered, and no new hearings were held for twenty years.

The convention received no support from President Dwight Eisenhower and little from John Kennedy and Lyndon Johnson. President Richard Nixon did urge ratification, and unsuccessful hearings were held in 1970. It was not until Reagan's support in 1984 that the convention was again submitted. The Senate's ratification in 1986 was conditional, noting two reservations, five understandings, and one declaration, which were attached as integral parts of the treaty.[6] The most important condition was the rejection of the compulsory jurisdiction of the International Court of Justice, which clearly indicated that the United States had no intention of being bound by the convention and did not take international judicial institutions seriously.

During the Senate debates over ratification, this fear of international intervention was abundantly clear. Senator Jesse Helms (R-N.C.) argued, "I think

6. Reservations:

1. That "before any dispute to which the United States is a party may be submitted to the jurisdiction of the International Court of Justice under this article, the specific consent of the United States is required in each case."
2. "That nothing in the Convention requires or authorizes legislation or other action by the United States of America prohibited by the Constitution of the United States as interpreted by the United States."

Understandings:

1. "That the term 'intent to destroy, in whole or in part, a national, ethnical, racial, or religious group as such' appearing in Article II means the specific intent to destroy, in whole or in substantial part, a national, ethnical, racial or religious group as such by the acts specified in Article II."
2. "That the term 'mental harm' in Article II(b) means permanent impairment of mental faculties through drugs, torture or similar techniques."
3. "That the pledge to grant extradition in accordance with a state's laws and treaties in force found in Article VII extends only to acts that are criminal under the laws of both the requesting and the requested state and nothing in Article VI affects the right of any state to bring to trial before its own tribunals any of its nationals for acts committed outside a state." (Under this, the Nuremberg trials possibly would not have taken place because the idea of "conspiracy" does not exist in European law.)
4. "That acts in the course of armed conflicts committed without the specific intent required by Article II are not sufficient to constitute genocide as defined by this convention."
5. "That with regard to the reference to international penal tribunal in Article VI of the convention, the United States declares that it reserves the right to effect its participation in any such tribunal only by a treaty entered into specifically for that purpose with the advice and consent of the Senate." (Again the Nuremberg or Tokyo trials could not have been held unless approved by the U.S. Senate).

we should pass a Genocide Convention, but only if we can make it work so that our domestic affairs are not subjected to the supervision of international bodies, and that our security interests and those of our allies are not jeopardized" (U.S. Senate Committee on Foreign Relations 1985, p. 8). This statement provides a very clear illustration of the strength of the drive to protect national interests and sovereignty and reveals a rather unusual conceptualization of making the convention "work." What Senator Helms actually meant was "not work" since all provisions of enforcement were to be gutted from the convention, and it would be adopted as part of U.S. law only if the United States was not subject to its provisions. Clearly, if the same type of thinking were applied to domestic law, chaos and anarchy would reign supreme.

When asked by Senator Claiborne Pell (D-R.I.) why, when the United States is a party to at least eighty different treaties under which it accepts the jurisdiction of the International Court of Justice, it was necessary to attach reservations to the convention, Davis R. Robinson, legal adviser to the State Department, responded by arguing that the Senate might not pass it without the reservations. More importantly, however, he went on to cite the Nicaragua case:[7]

> We believe that the question of genocide could be a highly charged issue. Of course, we believe it would be preposterous that ever anybody could make any valid accusation against the United States that it had engaged in any acts or offenses involving genocide.
>
> Nonetheless, with the experience that we have recently undergone, and when combined with the practicalities, we think that a World Court reservation would be not only wise, but desirable at this point. (U.S. Senate Committee on Foreign Relations 1985, p. 12)

Consequently, although the convention was eventually ratified, it was accomplished in such a fashion as to guarantee that it would have little or no impact on national policy.

Finally, the Senate forbade the president to execute the treaty until implementing legislation was enacted. This legislation was enacted on January 25, 1988, when the Congress defined genocide as being within the criminal code of the United States (S. 1851). The legislation adopted the U.N. definition of genocide and then set penalties of a "fine of not more than $1,000,000 and imprisonment for life" for killing members of a group and "a fine of not more

---

7. In May 1984 the International Court of Justice rendered a preliminary decision against the United States (*Nicaragua v. United States*), which was charged with mining Nicaraguan harbors, and the United States refused to accept its jurisdiction.

than $1,000,000 or imprisonment for not more than twenty years, or both, in any other case." If a person "directly and publicly incites another to violate subsection (a) of this section," which defines the basic offense, he or she is to be fined "not more than $500,000 or imprisoned for not more than five years, or both." For these penalties to be imposed, the offense must be committed in the United States or the offender must be a U.S. citizen.

In spite of the convention's incorporation into U.S. law, the reservations and understandings attached to the convention may act to seriously undermine the credibility of the United States should it attempt to lead a coalition to prevent and punish genocide. In order to forestall the possibility that other states might invoke the record of U.S. indifference, it would be prudent for the United States to seriously consider repealing the understandings and reservations. Such an action might serve as a first step in developing a sincere commitment to the prevention of genocide and political massacres.

Even though the convention has not deterred, prevented, or punished any act of genocide, it has served symbolic notice on the world that genocide is not an acceptable activity. Without enforcement provisions and without a clear and generally applicable definition of genocide, however, action to prevent the occurrence of genocide is unlikely.

ISSUES OF DEFINITION

Lack of definitional clarity continues to plague the Genocide Convention. Some scholars have, in fact, argued that the definition of genocide found in the convention does not cover all the possible manifestations of the crime because the destruction of a large number of people may take forms other than killing, such as deportations or mass displacement, internment and enslavement with forced labor, denationalization by systematic terrorism, or torture.

A second stumbling block is the language concerning intent to commit genocide. If one adheres to a strict interpretation of the language of intent, then the Serbs are, for example, able to argue that their intent is not to commit genocide but to acquire territory, or as perpetrators often argue, to protect themselves from the threat raised by the Bosnian Muslims or Croatians. The concept of "intent" is ambiguous. If a group or nation intends to acquire another group's or nation's territory but ends up killing a large number of the people, it should still be liable for prosecution for both war crimes and genocide because one must examine the acts committed, not intent. If the interpretation is so broadened, then the conditions stated in article 2 of the Genocide Convention concerning intent to commit genocide are satisfied.

Under this and article 8 ("Any Contracting Party may call upon competent organs of the United Nations to take action under the Charter of the United Nations as they consider appropriate for the prevention and suppression of acts of genocide" [35:68]), combined with the Nuremberg Principles, there appears ample precedent for war crimes trials against the Serbs. In short, instead of emphasizing an obscure and impossible-to-define psychological state of intent, the convention should focus on an easily identifiable action or behavior and infer intent from that behavior.

Not only is there a problem with determining "intent," but, as Freeman (1991) points out, the United Nations also stipulates that the genocidal intent has to be to destroy a listed group "in whole or in part" (p. 187). This creates additional uncertainty as to the size of the "part" necessary to constitute genocide. The need for definitional specificity and the narrowing of Lemkin's original proposal lead to the quest for new conceptualizations of genocide.

Freeman (1991) refers to this dilemma as the "definitional problematic." The search for a clear definition is not merely an academic exercise since definitions are tied to politics and political action. How an idea is defined has important consequences for how it is implemented. As a result, a number of attempts have been made to reconceptualize genocide. Chalk and Jonassohn (1990), for example, have defined genocide as "a form of one-sided mass killing in which a state or other authority intends to destroy a group, as that group and membership in it are defined by the perpetrator" (p. 23). In this case, the definition is hardly an improvement over the U.N. definition since the question of intent not only remains but is raised to a preeminent level. Freeman's analysis, it seems to me, makes important strides in avoiding many of the problems of definitional ambiguity.

According to Freeman (1991), genocide is a "social process, initiated and implemented by various social agents in structured social situations. It consists of many different agents located in different positions in the social structure. The central genocidal relation is that of perpetrator domination and victim subordination" (p. 188). Genocide is made up of a series of relationships involving both power and violence. Generally, in modern times, the state has control of the forces of violence, and, therefore, states are "the most likely perpetrators of genocide, although genocide can also be committed by others with the connivance of states or by powerful social groups which states are too weak to control."

Since modern states are very powerful, often accumulating the necessary weaponry from other states, they are particularly well equipped to commit genocide. To move ahead with the planned destruction, the "perpetrator must prevent or overcome resistance by the victim, isolate the latter from potential allies, cut off escape routes and ensure an appropriate combination of collaboration, acquiescence and ignorance among the rest of the population." The modern state, or forces supported in one or another fashion by the state, is in a position to accomplish these ends. If genocide is most often committed by the nation-state or with its active support or collaboration, conditions of pluralism must exist within the state. But the pluralistic state provides only a possible setting for genocide. For genocide to occur, Freeman (1991) argues, a "genocidal ideology" is needed (p. 189)—a motivating factor. "Such ideologies construct genocide as natural, necessary, rational and/or obligatory. To understand genocide, we must understand what problems the perpetrators were trying to solve, why they defined their problems as they did, and in particular, why they defined the victim as part of the problem, and why genocide seemed to them a rational solution." Genocidal ideologies take many forms, including utopian fantasies and realistic projects for development or expansion. Often they dehumanize the potential victims, identifying them as animals, vermin, carriers of disease, or other threats. As discussed in chapter 11, these ideologies contrast the purity of the perpetrators with the corruption of the victims and argue that extermination is necessary to protect the perpetrators from the threat posed by the victims. Genocidal ideologies may find their roots in the myths and cultures of a society, or they may come into being to explain the action taken.

One "common precipitant of genocide is societal crisis" (Freeman 1991, p. 190) because those experiencing crisis call for blame to be allocated to explain it. Since modern states experiencing crises become vulnerable to groups that hope to gain from the crisis, as in the former Yugoslavia, nation-state-building may result in genocide.

Thus viewed, genocide is a relationship between victims and perpetrators involving "a complex set of social relations: different social agents in different social roles are motivated to perform different sorts of actions. Even the decision-making elites may not be unified: some may be true believers, others cynical careerists, and there may be factional power struggles within this group. Ideology may motivate the executives but theories of bureaucratic behavior and obedience to authority teach us that genocidal elites do not need to achieve high levels of ideological mobilization in order to implement genocidal policies" (Freeman 1991, pp. 191–92). It is important to recognize that genocide is not a pure, easily defined phenomenon and that events are not, as Freeman points out, "either genocidal or non-genocidal but more or less genocidal, and there is simply no cut-off point" (p. 193).

According to this conceptualization, genocide requires at least three ingredients:

1. Murderous elites motivated by a genocidal ideology.
2. Obedient perpetrators.
3. Acquiescent bystanders.

Throughout the ages, genocide has been justified by tribalism, nationalism, racism, religion, and science, and no historic epoch has had a monopoly on these conditions. Among scholars there is even some agreement regarding which historical events might be classified as genocides. A partial list includes the usual examples of the Armenian genocide and the Holocaust, as well as various activities of the former USSR in exterminating certain segments of its population. Additional cases include Paraguay's extermination of the Ache peoples from 1962 to 1972; Indonesia's killing in 1965–66 of ethnic Chinese and Communists; massacres in Burundi from 1965 to 1973; the Biafran War in 1967–70, in which the Ibos were slaughtered; and the genocide in Cambodia from 1975 to 1979.

While these examples can be classified fairly easily as genocides, there remain instances of large-scale killing that fall beyond the scope of even the reformulated definitions. Freeman's question concerning how many members of a group must be killed before the crime is labeled genocide remains. To remedy this ambiguity, it is necessary to add a new category that falls between assassination and genocide—political massacre.

POLITICAL MASSACRES

Left out of most definitions of genocide are political massacres, which do not fit the Genocide Convention's typologies. Political massacres are variously referred to as genocidal massacres, near genocide, or simply massacres. Generally, these fall somewhere between assassinations and genocide in the numbers of people killed and are more frequent than either assassination or genocide. Researchers for the PIOOM foundation, a "non-partisan Dutch based non-profit organization promoting, supporting and conducting interdisciplinary research on causes of gross violations of human rights" (Schmid and Jongman 1992, p. 12), have documented political massacres that took place in 1990 and 1991, concluding that "massacres occur on a weekly basis." They counted massacres in twenty-six countries and on all continents except Australia and North America. The listing is extensive, and the perpetrators are almost as widely divergent as the examples. The number of fatalities in each massacre "ranged from 10 . . . to 1,000." Without specifying further details, they point out that both "individual murder and genocide are outlawed," while massacres "fall into a no-man's land." They suggest that massacres should also be against the law and propose that a new category be developed with its own definition. They define a massacre as "the indiscriminate killing of persons, between 10 to 10,000, who are deliberately slain in a specific place at a particular time despite the fact that they are unarmed (or disarmed)" (Schmid and Jongman 1992, p. 12). This acknowledgment of political massacres would close the gap between genocide and assassination. If adopted by the United Nations along with the reconceptualization of the definition of genocide proposed by Freeman, it might make it easier to bring perpetrators to justice without the endless haggling over whether or not the number of people killed constitutes genocide.

Although this effort at redefinition would be a clear improvement, the nations of the world have shown scant desire to rectify this definitional weakness or any of the other weaknesses of the Genocide Convention.

WEAKNESSES OF THE CONVENTION

Even the United Nations has realized that the Genocide Convention has not been effective and has commissioned several reports (1973, revised in 1978) to examine its weaknesses (*Internet*, 1986, p. 6). In 1985 it commissioned another report on genocide, which was prepared by Ben Whitaker. The Whitaker Report pointed out that genocide had occurred both before and after the adoption of the convention and concluded that the convention had not been effective. It recommended a series of remedies:

> These are to explicitly include acts of "advertent omission" (within the Convention's meaning of "intent"); protection for "political groups"; the nonavailability of a "superior orders" defense; state responsibility and liability for damages and restitution; a tightened "non-extradition" clause; a Committee on Genocide (under Article VIII) with powers to investigate and communicate to the Secretary General; an anti-genocide educational plan; an early warning system; an International Court of Human Rights, endowing the World Court with criminal jurisdiction; and further study of "cultural genocide," "ethnocide" and "ecocide." (Hawk 1986, p. 3)

It is quite clear that independent scholars as well as the United Nations itself are well aware of the weaknesses of the Genocide Convention as a means to prevent and punish genocide. Most of the proposals for reform harken back to Lemkin's original formulation and link the idea of genocide to the precedents set under the laws of war. Despite this unusual consensus in defining the problem, the fact remains that, generally speaking, there has been no inclination to strengthen the international institutions devoted to the prevention of genocide and political massacres.

While bringing together the laws of war and the Genocide Convention and reformulating the definitions of genocide are important first steps toward a possible deterrent, the only real deterrent is to demonstrate to potential and actual perpetrators that the international community will not stand idly by and allow violence to be used as a tool in international politics. Since verbal and symbolic statements are not always successful, it is equally, if not more, important to create mechanisms to prevent future genocides or to avert the genocidal possibility.

Following this principle and invoking the Genocide Convention, the nations of the world have an obligation to stop genocidal violence through some form of humanitarian intervention.

HUMANITARIAN INTERVENTION

The basic idea of a right of states to intervene in the affairs of another state to save lives is controversial. The December 1992 intervention into Somalia under the auspices of the United Nations may, however, function to bring this right of humanitarian intervention back into the spotlight (Bayzler 1987; Teson 1988; Harff 1991; Kader 1991).

Humanitarian intervention was first discussed by the Dutch writer Hugo Grotius, who argued that a state could use force to prevent another state from mistreating its own citizens. However, as Slomanson (1990) notes, Grotius insisted that the state's oppression of its own citizens had to be "so ruthless and widespread that it would shock the sensibility of the international community" (p. 371). Although it seems perfectly logical to argue that nation-states should have the right to intervene in cases of massive abuse of human rights, humanitarian intervention is suspect among the nations of the world because in the 1800s some states used humanitarian intervention as an excuse to pursue their own political and economic ends.

In early 1827, for example, England, France, and Russia intervened militarily in the Greco-Turkish War for the ostensible purpose of ending atrocities. After the invasion, they announced the Treaty for the Pacification of Greece and proclaimed their primary motive as "putting an end to . . . daily fresh impediments to the commerce of the European States" (Slomanson 1990, p. 371). Other precedents for intervention have been cited, such as the 1849 intervention by the president of the United States with the sultan of Turkey on behalf of the Jews being persecuted in Damascus and Rhodes; French intervention in Lebanon in 1861; Allied intervention to stop Nazi atrocities; President Johnson's sending of 20,000 troops to the Dominican

Republic in 1965; and U.S. intervention in Panama and Nicaragua.[8] Generally speaking, there is no recognized or agreed to right of humanitarian intervention outside the framework of the United Nations. Determination of the necessity for intervention is to be made by the Security Council.

Beitz (1988, p. 182) and Bayzler (1987, pp. 598–607) suggest that intervention is justified if several overlapping criteria are met:

1. Large-scale atrocities or gross violations of basic human rights must be occurring in the offending society.
2. Humanitarian motives must take precedence over other motives, such as territorial acquisition.
3. Other possible remedies must be exhausted, and intervention must not cause significant harm elsewhere.

Even if these criteria were accepted by the nations of the world as triggers to cue action, humanitarian intervention might remain a rare and endangered species of international activity. Nation-states are generally unconcerned about the plight of other peoples unless there is some threat to their own interests. Thus, one must not forget that the most common response to violations of human rights and human dignity is to do nothing. Generally, states have been given the right to kill their populations because outside intervention would violate their sovereignty, and no state wants to set the precedent of intervention because it might find itself accused of human rights violations. In fact, the U.N. intervention in Somalia demonstrates that humanitarian intervention will only take place if the situation is perceived as not difficult to remedy, or, in the words of the then acting U.S. secretary of state, "not too costly." If an existing power with a relatively large army is slaughtering its population, it is unlikely that intervention to stop the slaughter will take place. In Somalia, anarchy was perpetuated by small bands of relatively lightly armed gunmen. As a result, the intervention was not seen as a violation of state sovereignty since, technically, there was no state—or at least no central government—and the intervening troops were under the auspices of the United Nations. Thus, no precedent for intervention was set. In other cases of

8. Since 1900, the United States has intervened militarily in Third World countries around twenty-five times. These interventions include Cuba, 1898–1902; Panama, 1903–14; Cuba, 1906–9; Nicaragua, 1912–25; Mexico, 1914–19; Haiti, 1915–34; Dominican Republic, 1916–24; Cuba, 1917–22; Panama, 1918–20; Nicaragua, 1926–33; Korea, 1950–53; Lebanon, 1958; Cuba, 1961; Congo, 1962–63; Vietnam, 1964–73; Dominican Republic, 1965; Cambodia, 1975; Iran, 1980; Nicaragua, 1981–91; Lebanon, 1983–84; Grenada, 1983; Libya, 1986; Panama, 1989–90; Iraq, 1990–91; Liberia, 1990; and Somalia, 1992 (Cingranelli 1993, pp. 236–37).

intervention, the United Nations is usually invited in by the state to attempt to restore stability.[9]

The concept of humanitarian intervention is further clouded by the fact that there are always different perspectives. What might appear to some to be a violation of human rights might be perceived by others as the culturally accepted way to behave. All observers, as I pointed out in chapter 13, do not agree that human rights standards are universal. In fact, it is this absence of protection from the genocidal possibility that is the precise reason why we must develop an overall transcendent ethic of life that is codified to provide the international political community with the power to enforce its provisions. The fact that this should prove a controversial proposal reveals that our collective memories of the history of genocide and political massacres have been constructed and reconstructed around the concepts of sovereignty and national interest, thus serving to reinforce the necessity of change if the cycle of human violence is to be broken.

CONCLUSION

At one time, prior to the rise of the nation-state, individual rights were not generally conceived since people lived in small communities, often at the whim of a ruler or local authority figure. Today individuals are face-to-face with the state, and, as we have seen, the state has repeatedly killed large numbers of its citizens while it continues to repress even larger numbers. The difficulty presented by the violence in Bosnia and elsewhere clearly demon-

9. At the time of this writing, the United Nations is involved in twelve different operations. These include U.N. truce supervision of Israel's borders with Lebanon, Syria, and Egypt; U.N. disengagement observer force in the Golan Heights between Israel and Syria; U.N. interim force in Lebanon near the border with Israel; U.N. military observer group in India and Pakistan supervising the cease-fire in Kashmir; U.N. peacekeeping force in Cyprus overseeing the Turkish-Greek cease-fire; U.N. Iraq-Kuwait observation mission in the demilitarized zone between the two nations; U.N. Angola verification mission observing the attempt to restore peace to Angola; U.N. observer mission in El Salvador supervising the end of the civil war in that country; U.N. mission in Western Sahara watching over disputed territory and trying to resolve the issue; U.N. protection force in Croatia, Bosnia-Herzegovina, which is having little effect in stopping the Serbs from taking over large amounts of territory; U.N. transitional authority in Cambodia, which is attempting to reconcile the factions but is getting little cooperation from the Khmer Rouge, who previously committed genocide against their own people; and U.N. operation in Somalia supervising transport of food to starving people (*Richmond Times-Dispatch*, December 6, 1992, p. A18).

strates how intractable the modern nation-state remains when faced with horrible crimes of war and genocide. No nation, it would seem, is willing to stand forthrightly behind "real" attempts to bring some stability to the increasingly unstable and dangerous new/old world of ethnic and nationalist hostility.

In the case of the former Yugoslavia, the United States and the European countries, either through the United Nations or NATO, should have acted with dispatch when the violence began. After the genocide was legitimated and sanctioned by the Serbs' capture of Muslim territory, no amount of negotiation can convince them to withdraw or give up their ambition to create a Serbian state. Will this feed other territorial aspirations? What should the world have done?

Through the United Nations, a series of progressive steps should have been taken, possibly including sanctions, threatening to supply the Bosnian Muslims with weapons, and imposing "no fly" and "no artillery" zones. If these failed, the next step would be the use of air power against the Serbian positions to demonstrate the resolve to stop the murder and torture. The last step would be the intervention of U.N. or NATO forces, in which the great powers such as the United States, Russia, France, Great Britain, and Germany would fully participate. But none of these steps were taken, or threatened, and the world once again watched and wrung its hands as another genocide was inscribed into the twentieth century's sad tale of death and destruction.

As long as nations and groups are willing to use force and pursue policies of genocide to achieve desired ends, internationally based means must be developed to demonstrate that such policies are not profitable. As Levi (1991) notes, "The efficacy of any law forbidding the use of force must therefore continue to depend upon the unpredictable outcome of every state's profit and loss calculation, which weighs expected benefits from the use of force against expected costs" (p. 295). If the world continues to see that genocide pays, that the expected consequences of genocide are the control of large amounts of territory and the creation of an independent, ethnically based state, the world will continue to see genocide pursued as a policy option. We have already defined genocide as a crime according to international and national law, yet we do not take steps to halt its occurrence. The world community, led by the United States, has to take the lead in drawing and enforcing a boundary around acceptable behavior. Otherwise, the situation will remain one in which genocide and mass killing triumph over the demands of civilization.

From 1945 until a few short years ago, the United States pursued a policy of containing what it perceived as aggressive Communist expansion. With the Soviet threat removed, it is now time to reformulate the policy of containment and bring it into the modern era of ethnonationalist violence. If we could devise a policy that "worked" in the seemingly unmanageable era of possible nuclear annihilation, why can we not design a policy to deal with the more common, though more pervasive, dangers of ethnonational violence and genocide?

The world is at yet another historic juncture. We have the opportunity to decide whether we want to live in a world of Hobbesian conflict or whether the nations of the world are willing to cede a portion of their sovereignty and power to international bodies empowered to stop the violence and create, perhaps for the first time, a hiatus in the ever-spiraling helix of human violence.

Epilogue

Memory, Hope, and Triumph over Evil

The power of memory lies in the fact that traditions have been built over many hundreds of years and generations have followed and believed in these traditions. Ideas of international cooperation, justice, and morality may seem, in an age of instant bromides and televised revelations of people's deepest emotional problems, archaic or perhaps overly idealistic. Unfortunately, idealism, in an age in which the dominant ethos is "get what you can while you can get it," has been turned into a pejorative. No longer are young people told to reach for Browning's unattainable ideal in the hope that, even if they fall short, they may have helped to better the human condition in some small way. Today one must be practical, one must be a selfish seeker of material gratification, or one is left behind in the race for success. Yet a world in which people do not have a sense of justice is a world in which evil has triumphed. In order to prevent that triumph, it is important to understand how our reconstructed memory contributes to the maintenance of evil and to begin to discern how we might generate new memories based on a new ethic.

War, violence, and death have been with humanity for as long as our memory exists. Situations involving extreme violence and crisis have always placed individual human beings in circumstances in which they may experience fear, terror, and death, but they also provide humans with an intensity of experience that is difficult to rival in everyday life. Klein (1984), for example, describes the feeling of a Marine walking point on a wartime patrol: "He loved the feeling of moving slowly through the jungle, becoming part of it, sensing imperfections—a jigsaw puzzle in which the pieces were constantly changing shape. He'd never done anything so well in his life" (p. 30).

Unfortunately, the celebration of this intensity of experience creates myths about the value of violence and the "goodness" of war. Myths to justify war have been created by religion and the state. As Mosse (1990) points out, the myth of the fallen soldier justified death in the service of the nation as the dead warriors assumed a Christlike status derived from the notion that they were serving and sacrificing themselves for the state or some other "cause" (p. 35).

In earlier times, prior to the rise of the nation-state, and even today, one may also sacrifice one's life for God or to defend the faith. Refusal to participate was and is attacked. War and violence are viewed as means to achieve noble ends, and those not wishing to participate are stigmatized. The cliché that "every generation must have its war" has become a truism. But why? The reality of war is no secret, even to those who have not personally experienced the irrationality and chaos. You can read about it in books such as Fussell (1989), and genocide, which often accompanies war, is no longer the "terrible secret" it was once thought to be. We now see events as they happen on television, yet we continue to perpetuate and participate in the extermination of our fellow human beings.

Against such seemingly persistent and powerful forces, what can an individual do to avoid becoming a participant in the destruction of the lives of others?

After so many years of reading about so many deaths, after thinking about the horrifying nature of the crimes committed against humanity, after teaching many students about genocide and pointing out their responsibility to think about preserving rather than destroying life, I am left with a feeling of disbelief and profound puzzlement. Something is missing. Steiner (1977) captures this feeling, which we discussed in chapter 3. At this very moment, repression, cruelty, and perhaps genocide are somewhere in process or being planned, and as it proceeds, you and I remain, if we are lucky, sheltered and relatively secure—although not entirely so, for sickness and violence are never completely out of sight—living, as Steiner puts it, "as if on another planet" (p. 157). Yet, as he notes, at any moment our personal situation might change and we might "drop out of humanity." Any writing about genocide and mass destruction should serve to make us "concretely aware" of how tenuous our lives are, and remind us that the "solution was not 'final,' that it spills over into our present lives." This is, indeed, a big order and one I doubt many of us will be able to approximate. In the end, it is probably the case that only the most powerful accounts of survivors are able to evoke the necessary empathic response from those who still believe they are untouched by ongoing atrocities.

Steiner suggests that reviewing this literature in the conventional sense is not enough unless "review" is defined as "seeing again." Perhaps he is correct. Perhaps only when all those who have not been ethnically cleansed, or finally solved, or any of the other euphemisms used to disguise mass murder, come to feel what the survivor felt, will they start to move in the direction of ending the incessant cycle of genocide. Perhaps it would benefit humanity if we followed Steiner's suggestion and, instead of reading or reviewing the literature of survivors, "re-copy the book, line by line, pausing at the names of the dead and the names of the children as the orthodox scribe pauses, when re-copying the Bible, at the hallowed name of God. Until we know many of the words by *heart* (knowledge deeper than mind) and can repeat a few at the break of morning to remind ourselves that we live *after*, that the end of the day may bring inhuman trial or a remembrance stranger than death" (1977, p. 168). Conceivably, a new form of empathic memory will then triumph over evil, because at that point it would be very difficult for any person, not totally numbed, not to be moved by the profound sadness one experiences when one surveys the fields of death. And perhaps once such memories are imprinted, as we imprint other covenants, other memories, it will become part of that national and individual memory that, no matter what the circumstance, causes an emotional response similar to that experienced when one is confronted by the symbols of national pride or the fact of individual accomplishment. After all of our other apparently futile attempts to stop the slaughter, it certainly would do no harm to imprint the reality of genocide on the memory.

But, as noted repeatedly throughout this work, embracing the memories of survivors is hardly sufficient. As long as policymakers continue to see genocide as a successful means to achieve political goals, it will be pursued as a viable policy option. Memory, as I noted in chapter 14, must be accompanied by political action.

If it is not, if we continue to dissemble and allow policymakers to slouch toward settlements that entail the ratification of genocide as a means to achieve political goals, the world will have welshed on its promise of "never again." It is important to remember that the consequences of inaction are often more devastating than the results of positive action to resolve suffering. We cannot continue to have it both ways. If genocide is being pursued, how can it be stopped unless the international community is willing to use force to humanitarianly intervene? Ultimately, we are once again left with the dilemma that we cannot resolve to abjure violence because we are then left undefended in a violent world. How can we be sure that any force of arms is turned to constructive rather than destructive ends? Surely, in an imperfect world, there are no guarantees.

In the modern world, events move at an astounding speed, and our consciousness cannot keep pace. We remain trapped in the memories of ancient hatreds and outdated international modalities such as sovereignty. Yet we have the ability, if not always the will, to change. In the past, notable individuals such as Raphael Lemkin charted the course that we have yet to navigate. We are, it seems to me, overdue to start the journey.

Finally, I hope the reader will allow me to close on a personal note. I have spent the better part of my academic life studying genocide and other forms of human cruelty. Once again, reading the accounts of horrible inhumanity, this time in the late twentieth century, I am saddened, pained, and outraged. Those of us who study death do so in the hope that it will preserve life; we do not want our subject to become so terribly relevant. The inhumanity of people to each other does not end. I think I now understand better how Primo Levi must have felt when, after surviving Auschwitz, he was forced to observe the events of the late twentieth century. So, as we continue to hope that the world will somehow summon the resolve to resist violence and end the scourge of genocide, there can be no more fitting conclusion than his reflections on the Warsaw ghetto uprising.

On April 17, 1983, approximately three years before his death, Primo Levi wrote a short essay about the Warsaw ghetto called "Defiance in the Ghetto" (in Levi 1989, pp. 167–71). "At a distance of forty years and in an ever more restless world, we do not want the sacrifices of the Warsaw Ghetto insurgents to be forgotten. They have demonstrated that even when everything is lost, it is granted to man to save, together with his own dignity, that of future generations" (pp. 170–71). We still have that possibility, but with every additional genocide, it becomes more difficult to grasp.

REFERENCES

Abramson, Paul. 1977. *The Political Socialization of Black Americans*. New York: Free Press.

Adam, Barry D. 1978. *The Survival of Domination*. New York: Elsevier.

American Forum for Global Education. 1989. *Annual Report*. Minneapolis: American Forum for Global Education.

Anger, Per. 1981. *With Raoul Wallenberg in Budapest*. New York: Holocaust Library.

Arendt, Hannah. 1965. *Eichmann in Jerusalem: A Report on the Banality of Evil*. Rev. and enl. ed. New York: Viking.

Aronson, Elliot. 1972. *The Social Animal*. New York: Viking.

Asher, Harvey. 1987. "Non-Psychoanalytic Approaches to National Socialism." In *Psycho/History: Readings in the Methods of Psychology, Psychoanalysis, and History*, edited by Geoffrey Cocks and Travis L. Crosby, pp. 267–83. New Haven: Yale University Press.

Atlas, James. 1988. "Survivor's Suicide." *Vanity Fair*, January, p. 83.

Auster, Albert, and Leonard Quart. 1988. *How the War Was Remembered: Hollywood and Vietnam*. New York: Praeger.

Aycoberry, Pierre. 1981. *The Nazi Question*. New York: Random House.

Ayer, A. J. 1956. *The Problem of Knowledge*. New York: Penguin Books.

Badran, Adnan. 1989. *At the Crossroads: Education in the Middle East*. New York: Paragon House.

Baird, Jay W., ed. 1972. *From Nuremberg to My Lai*. Lexington, Mass.: D. C. Heath.

Baker, Mark. 1981. *NAM*. New York: Berkley Books.

Barash, David P. 1988. *The Arms Race and Nuclear War*. Belmont, Calif.: Wadsworth Publishing.

Barber, J. D. 1965. *The Lawmakers: Recruitment and Adaptation to Legislative Life*. New Haven: Yale University Press.

———. 1985. *The Presidential Character: Predicting Performance in the White House*. 3d ed. Englewood Cliffs, N.J.: Prentice-Hall.

Barclay, Craig R. 1986. "Schematization of Autobiographical Memory." In *Autobiographical Memory*, edited by David C. Rubin, pp. 82–99. New York: Cambridge University Press.

Bardakjian, Kevork B. 1985. *Hitler and the Armenian Genocide*. Cambridge, Mass.: Zoryan Institute.

Baron, Lawrence. 1986. "The Holocaust and Human Decency: A Review of Research on the Rescue of Jews in Nazi Occupied Europe." In *Altruism and Prosocial Behavior*, edited by Elizabeth Midlarsky and Lawrence Baron, pp. 237–51, special issue of *Humboldt Journal of Social Relations* 13, nos. 1 and 2.

Barrier-Barry, Carol, and Robert Rosenwein. 1985. *Psychological Perspectives on Politics*. Englewood Cliffs, N.J.: Prentice-Hall.

Bar-Tel, Daniel. 1986. "Altruistic Motivation to Help: Definition, Utility, and Operationalization." In *Altruism and Prosocial Behavior*, edited by Elizabeth Midlarsky and Lawrence Baron, pp. 3–14, special issue of *Humboldt Journal of Social Relations* 13, nos. 1 and 2.

Bartlett, F. C. 1932. *Remembering: A Study in Experimental and Social Psychology.* New York: Cambridge University Press.

Bauer, Yehuda. 1987. "On the Place of the Holocaust in History: In Honor of Franklin H. Litell." *Holocaust and Genocide Studies* 2, no. 8:209–20.

Baum, Rainer. 1988. "Holocaust: Moral Indifference as *the* Form of Modern Evil." In *Echoes from the Holocaust,* edited by Alan Rosenberg and Gerald E. Myers, pp. 53–90. Philadelphia: Temple University Press.

Bayzler, Michael. 1987. "Re-Examining the Doctrine of Humanitarian Intervention in the Light of Atrocities in Kampuchea and Ethiopia." *Stanford Journal of International Law* 23, no. 2 (Summer): 588–607.

Becker, Elizabeth. 1986. *When the War Was Over.* New York: Simon and Schuster.

Becker, Ernest. 1975. *Escape from Evil.* New York: Free Press.

Becker, James M. 1973. "International and Cross-Cultural Experiences." In *Education for Peace: Focus on Mankind,* edited by George Henderson, pp. 103–24. Washington, D.C.: Association for Supervision and Curriculum Development.

Beitz, Charles R. 1988. "The Reagan Doctrine in Nicaragua." In *Problems of International Justice,* edited by Steven Luper-Foy, pp. 182–95. Boulder: Westview Press.

Bellow, Saul. 1991. *The Bellarosa Connection.* New York: Signet.

Beres, L. R. 1984. "U.S. Nuclear Strategy: Embracing Omnicide." Chapter 2 in *Reason and Realpolitik,* by L. R. Beres. Lexington, Mass.: Lexington Books.

———. 1985. "Genocide." *Policy Studies Review* 4, no. 2:397–406.

Berger, Alan L., ed. 1991. *Bearing Witness to the Holocaust, 1939–1989.* Lewiston, N.Y.: Edwin Mellen Press.

Berkhofer, Robert F., Jr. 1978. *The White Man's Indian.* New York: Random House.

Bettelheim, Bruno. 1980. *Surviving and Other Essays.* New York: Vintage Books.

Bettelheim, Bruno, and Morris Janowitz. 1964. *Social Change and Prejudice.* New York: Free Press.

Bickman, Leonard, and Mark Kamzan. 1973. "The Effect of Race and Need on Helping Behavior." *Journal of Social Psychology* 89, no. 3:73–77.

Bierman, John. 1981. *Righteous Gentile: The Story of Raoul Wallenberg, Missing Hero of the Holocaust.* New York: Viking.

Blackburn, Gilmer W. 1985. *Education in the Third Reich.* Albany: State University of New York Press.

Bodley, John H. 1982. *Victims of Progress.* 2d ed. Mountain View, Calif.: Mayfield Publishing.

Bolles, Edmund Blair. 1988. *Remembering and Forgetting: An Inquiry into the Nature of Memory.* New York: Walker and Company.

Bollinger, Dwight. 1980. *Language—The Loaded Weapon*. White Plains, N.Y.: Longman.

Bonss, Wolfgang. 1984. "Critical Theory and Empirical Social Research: Some Observations." In *The Working Class in Weimar Germany*, by Erich Fromm, pp. 1–38. Cambridge: Harvard University Press.

Boulding, Elise. 1988. *Building a Global Civic Culture: Education for an Interdependent World*. New York: Teachers College Press.

Bradley Commission on History in the Schools. 1988. *Building a History Curriculum: Guidelines for Teaching History in Schools*. Washington, D.C.: Educational Excellence Network.

Breslau, Karen. 1992. "Faultless to a Fault." *Newsweek*, May 11, p. 27.

Brewer, William F. 1986. "What Is Autobiographical Memory?" In *Autobiographical Memory*, edited by David C. Rubin, pp. 25–49. New York: Cambridge University Press.

Brock-Utne, Birgit. 1985. *Educating for Peace: A Feminist Perspective*. Elmsford, N.Y.: Pergamon Press.

Bronson, M., and J. Torney-Purta, eds. 1982. *International Human Rights, Society, and the Schools*. Washington, D.C.: National Council for Social Studies.

Brown, Lester. 1972. *World without Borders*. New York: Vintage Books.

Brown, Norman R., Steven K. Shevell, and Lance J. Rips. 1986. "Public Memories and Their Personal Context." In *Autobiographical Memory*, edited by David C. Rubin, pp. 137–58. New York: Cambridge University Press.

Brown, R., and Kulick, J. 1977. "Flashbulb Memories." *Cognition* 5:73–99.

Brown, Seyom. 1992. *International Relations in a Changing Global System*. Boulder: Westview Press.

Brzezinski, Zbigniew. 1993. *Out of Control*. New York: Charles Scribner's Sons.

Bullock, A. 1992. *Hitler and Stalin: Parallel Lives*. New York: Alfred A. Knopf.

Burnham, Irene H. 1938. *Not by Accident: The Story of Moses H. Gulesian's Career*. Boston: Christopher Publishing House.

Burns, John F. 1992. "Confessed Executioner Remembers the Little Girl." *Richmond Times-Dispatch*, November 27, pp. A1, A12, A13.

California State Department of Education. 1988. *History–Social Science Framework for California Public Schools, Kindergarten through Grade Twelve*. Sacramento: California State Department of Education.

Callero, Peter L. 1986. "Putting the Social in Prosocial Behavior: An Interactionist Approach to Altruism." In *Altruism and Prosocial Behavior*, edited by Elizabeth Midlarsky and Lawrence Baron, pp. 15–32, special issue of *Humboldt Journal of Social Relations* 13, nos. 1 and 2.

Calley, William L. 1972. "Lieutenant Calley: His Own Story." In *From Nuremburg to My Lai*, edited by Jay W. Baird, pp. 213–34. Lexington, Mass.: D. C. Heath.

Caputo, Philip. 1977. *A Rumor of War*. New York: Ballantine.

Cassirer, Ernst. 1946. *Language and Myth*. New York: Harper.

Chalk, F., and K. Jonassohn. 1990. *The History and Sociology of Genocide: Analyses and Case Studies*. New Haven: Yale University Press.

Charny, Israel W. 1982. *How Can We Commit the Unthinkable?* Boulder: Westview Press.

——. 1988. "Understanding the Psychology of Genocidal Destructiveness." In *Genocide: A Critical Bibliographic Review*, vol. 1, edited by Israel W. Charny, pp. 191–208. New York: Facts on File.

——, ed. 1991. *Genocide: A Critical Bibliographic Review*. Vol. 2. London: Mansell.

Chase, Allan. 1980. *The Legacy of Malthus*. New York: Alfred A. Knopf.

Cheles, Luciana, Ronnie Ferguson, and Michalina Vaughan, eds. 1991. *Neo-Fascism in Europe*. Chicago: Longman.

Cherrington, B. M. 1934. *Methods of Education in International Attitudes*. New York: Teachers College Press.

Chilton, Paul. 1986. "Nukespeak: Nuclear Language, Culture, and Propaganda." In *The Nuclear Predicament*, edited by Donna Gregory, pp. 127–42. New York: St. Martin's Press.

Chorover, Stephen. 1979. *From Genesis to Genocide*. Boston: MIT Press.

Cingranelli, David L. 1993. *Ethics, American Foreign Policy, and the Third World*. New York: St. Martin's Press.

Cocks, Geoffrey, and Travis L. Crosby, eds. 1987. *Psycho/History: Readings in the Methods of Psychology, Psychoanalysis, and History*. New Haven: Yale University Press.

Cohen, Ben. 1993. "Why Europe Failed to Halt the Genocide in Bosnia." *Washington Report on Middle East Affairs*, April/May, pp. 39–40.

Colegrove, F. W. 1899. "Individual Memories." *American Journal of Psychology* 10:228–55.

Connell, R. W. 1971. *The Child's Construction of Politics*. Melbourne, Australia: Melbourne University Press.

Connerton, Paul. 1989. *How Societies Remember*. New York: Cambridge University Press.

Conquest, R. 1986. *The Harvest of Sorrow*. New York: Oxford University Press.

Conway, Martin A. 1990. *Autobiographical Memory: An Introduction*. Philadelphia: Open University Press.

Curtiss, Richard H. 1993. "Bosnia 1993: Showdown for U.S., U.N., and Shape of the New World Order." *Washington Report on Middle East Affairs*, March, pp. 7–8, 70, 95.

Dallmayr, Fred. 1984. *Language and Politics*. South Bend, Ind.: University of Notre Dame Press.

Davies, Peter, ed. 1988. *Human Rights*. New York: Routledge.

Dawidowicz, Lucy S. 1975. *The War against the Jews*. New York: Bantam.

Delli Carpini, Michael X., and Scott Keeter. 1989. *Political Knowledge of the U.S. Public: Results from a National Survey*. Paper presented at the 1992 annual meeting of the American Association for Public Opinion Research.

Des Pres, Terrence. 1973. "Memory of Boyhood." *Sports Illustrated*, August 17, pp. 70–78.

——. 1976a. "Bleak Comedies: Lina Wertmüller's Artful Method." *Harpers*, June, pp. 26–28.

——. 1976b. *The Survivor: An Anatomy of Life in the Death Camps.* New York: Pocket Books.

——. 1977. "On the Verge of a New Morality: Wilson's Message for Humanists." *Horizon*, March, pp. 46–47.

——. 1978. "Czeslaw Milosz: The Poetry of Aftermath." *The Nation*, December, pp. 741–43.

——. 1981a. "Emblems of Adversity." *Harpers*, March, pp. 73–77.

——. 1981b. "Even a Limerick. . . ." *The Nation*, May, pp. 521–24.

——. 1988. *Praises and Dispraises: Poetry and Politics in the Twentieth Century.* New York: Viking.

Dimsdale, Joel E., ed. 1980. *Survivor, Victims, and Perpetrators: Essays on the Nazi Holocaust.* Washington, D.C.: Hemisphere Publishing.

Duster, Troy. 1971. "Conditions for Guilt-Free Massacre." In *Sanctions for Evil*, edited by Nevitt Sanford and Craig Comstock, pp. 25–36. Boston: Beacon Press.

Eagleburger, Lawrence. 1992. "The Need to Respond to War Crimes in the Former Yugoslavia." In *U.S. Department of State Dispatch* 3, no. 52 (December): 923–25.

Easton, David, and Jack Dennis. 1969. *Children in the Political System.* New York: McGraw-Hill.

Eatwell, Roger. 1991. "The Holocaust Denial: A Study in Propaganda Technique." In *Neo-Fascism in Europe*, edited by Luciana Cheles, Ronnie Ferguson, and Michalina Vaughan, pp. 120–46. Chicago: Longman.

Ebbinghaus, H. [1885] 1913. *Memory: A Contribution to Experimental Psychology.* Translated by A. A. Ruger and C. E. Byssenine. Reprint, Mineola, N.Y.: Dover.

Edelman, Murray. 1971. *Politics as Symbolic Action.* New York: Academic Press.

——. 1977. *Political Language: Words That Succeed and Policies That Fail.* New York: Academic Press.

——. 1988. *Constructing the Political Spectacle.* Chicago: University of Chicago Press.

Ehlert, Jeff, et al. 1973. "The Influence of Ideological Affiliation on Helping Behavior." *Journal of Social Psychology* 89, no. 2:315–16.

Ehman, Lee. 1980. "The American School in the Political Socialization Process." *Review of Educational Research* 50, no. 3:99–119.

Elder, Charles D., and Roger W. Cobb. 1983. *The Political Uses of Symbols.* Chicago: Longman.

Elias, Robert. 1986. *The Politics of Victimization.* New York: Oxford University Press.

"El Salvador Cover-Up Probe Gathers Steam." 1993. *Richmond Times-Dispatch*, March 21, pp. A1, A12.

Engelmann, Bernt. 1986. *In Hitler's Germany.* New York: Schocken Books.

Erikson, E. 1958. *Young Man Luther.* New York: W. W. Norton.

——. 1969. *Ghandi's Truth.* New York: W. W. Norton.

——. 1975. *Life History and the Historical Moment.* New York: W. W. Norton.

——. 1980. *Identity and the Life Cycle.* New York: W. W. Norton.

Falk, Richard A., Gabriel Kolko, and Robert Jay Lifton, eds. 1971. *Crimes of War*. New York: Random House.

Farias, Victor. 1989. *Heidegger and Nazism*. Philadelphia: Temple University Press.

Fein, Helen. 1979. *Accounting for Genocide*. New York: Free Press.

———. 1980. "Beyond the Heroic Ethic." *Society* 17 (March/April): 51–55.

———. 1992. *Genocide Watch*. New Haven: Yale University Press.

Fest, Joachim. 1970. *The Face of the Third Reich*. New York: Pantheon Books.

Fitzgerald, Joseph M. 1986. "Autobiographical Memory: A Developmental Perspective." In *Autobiographical Memory*, edited by David C. Rubin, pp. 122–33. New York: Cambridge University Press.

Fleming, Gerald. 1982. *Hitler and the Final Solution*. Berkeley: University of California Press.

Forbes, Gordon, et al. 1971. "Willingness to Help Strangers as a Function of Liberal Conservative or Catholic Church Membership: A Field Study with the Lost Letter Technique." *Psychological Reports* 28, no. 3:947–49.

Forrester, Mary Gore. 1982. *Moral Language*. Madison: University of Wisconsin Press.

Forsythe, David P. 1991. *The Internationalization of Human Rights*. Lexington, Mass.: Lexington Books.

Freeman, Michael. 1991. "The Theory and Prevention of Genocide." *Holocaust and Genocide Studies* 6, no. 2:185–99.

Freud, Sigmund, and J. Breuer. 1974. *Studies on Hysteria*. Vols. 15 and 16 of *The Standard Edition of the Complete Psychological Works of Sigmund Freud*, edited by J. Strachey. London: Hogarth Press.

Friedlander, Henry. 1980. "The Manipulation of Language." In *The Holocaust: Ideology, Bureaucracy, and Genocide*, edited by Henry Friedlander and Sybil Milton, pp. 103–13. Millwood, N.Y.: Kraus International Publications.

Friedman, Thomas L. 1990. *From Beirut to Jerusalem*. New York: Anchor Books.

Fromm, Erich. 1941. *Escape from Freedom*. New York: Holt, Rinehart and Winston.

———. 1950. *Psychoanalysis and Religion*. New Haven: Yale University Press.

———. 1961. *May Man Prevail?* New York: Doubleday.

———. 1964. *The Heart of Man*. New York: Harper and Row.

———. 1966. *Socialist Humanism*. New York: Doubleday.

———. 1967. *Man for Himself*. New York: Fawcett.

———. 1968. *The Revolution of Hope*. New York: Bantam.

———. 1970. *The Crisis of Psychoanalysis*. New York: Fawcett.

———. 1973. *The Anatomy of Human Destructiveness*. New York: Fawcett.

———. 1976. *To Have or To Be?* New York: Harper.

———. 1981. *On Disobedience and Other Essays*. New York: Seabury Press.

———. 1984. *The Working Class in Weimar Germany*. Cambridge: Harvard University Press.

———. 1986. *For the Love of Life*. New York: Free Press.

Fromm, Erich, and Michael Maccoby. 1970. *Social Character in a Mexican Village*. Englewood Cliffs, N.J.: Prentice-Hall.

Fromm, Erich, and Ramon Xirau, eds. 1968. *The Nature of Man.* New York: Macmillan.

Furlong, E. J. 1951. *A Study in Memory.* New York: Thomas Nelson.

Fussell, Paul. 1989. *Wartime: Understanding and Behavior in the Second World War.* New York: Oxford University Press.

Gagnon, Paul. 1988. "Why Study History?" *Atlantic,* November, pp. 43–61.

———. 1989. *Democracy's Half-Told Story: What American History Textbooks Should Add.* New York: American Federation of Teachers.

Galton, Francis F. *Hereditary Genius.* New York: D. Appleton.

George, A. L., and J. L. George. 1964. *Woodrow Wilson and Colonel House: A Personality Study.* Mineola, N.Y.: Dover.

Gibson, James. 1986. *The Perfect War.* New York: Vintage Books.

Gilbert, Miriam. 1989. "Scholarship versus Pedagogy: The Future of International Studies Education." *Political Science Teacher* 2, no. 1:4–5.

Goldstein, Leon J. 1976. *Historical Knowing.* Austin: University of Texas Press.

Gordon, Sarah. 1984. *Hitler, Germans, and the Jewish Question.* Princeton: Princeton University Press.

Gould, Stephen Jay. 1981. *The Mismeasure of Man.* New York: W. W. Norton.

Graber, G. S. 1978. *The History of the SS.* New York: David McKay.

Gray, Martin. 1971. *For Those I Loved.* Boston: Little, Brown and Company.

Greenstein, Fred I. 1960. "The Benevolent Leader: Children's Images of Political Authority." *American Political Science Review* 54 (December): 934–43.

———. 1965. *Children and Politics.* New Haven: Yale University Press.

———. 1975. "The Benevolent Leader Revisited: Children's Images of Political Leaders in Three Democracies." *American Political Science Review* 69 (December): 1371–98.

Grossman, Frances G. 1984. "A Psychological Study of Gentiles Who Saved the Lives of Jews during the Holocaust." In *Toward the Understanding and Prevention of Genocide,* edited by Israel Charny, pp. 202–16. Westport, Conn.: Greenwood Press.

Grosvenor, Gilbert M. 1989. "The Case for Geography Education." *Educational Leadership* 47:29–32.

Grunberger, Richard. 1971. *The Twelve-Year Reich.* New York: Holt, Rinehart and Winston.

Guroian, Vigen. 1992. "The Politics and Morality of Genocide." In *The Armenian Genocide: History, Politics, Ethics,* edited by Richard G. Hovannisian, pp. 311–39. New York: St. Martin's Press.

Gutman, Roy. 1993. *A Witness to Genocide.* New York: Macmillan.

Hahn, Carol. 1987. "The Right to a Political Education." In *Human Rights and Education,* edited by Norma Bernstein Tarrow, pp. 173–87. Elmsford, N.Y.: Pergamon Press.

Hallie, Philip P. 1979. *Lest Innocent Blood Be Shed.* New York: Harper and Row.

———. 1984/85. "Scepticism, Narrative, and Holocaust Ethics." *Philosophical Forum* 16, nos. 1–2 (Fall/Winter): 33–49.

Halsell, Grace. 1993. "Women's Bodies a Battlefield in War for 'Greater Serbia.'" *Washington Report on Middle East Affairs*, April/May, pp. 8–9.

Hampshire, Stuart. 1989. *Innocence and Experience*. Cambridge: Harvard University Press.

Harff, Barbara. 1991. "Humanitarian Intervention in Genocidal Situations." In *Genocide: A Critical Bibliographic Review*, vol. 2, edited by Israel Charny, pp. 146–72. London: Mansell.

———. 1992. "Recognizing Genocides and Politicides." In *Genocide Watch*, edited by Helen Fein, pp. 27–41. New Haven: Yale University Press.

Harff, Barbara, and Ted Gurr. 1987. "Genocides and Politicides since 1945: Evidence and Anticipation." *Internet on the Holocaust and Genocide* 13 (December): 1–7.

Harris, M. 1972. "The Effects of Performing One Altruistic Act on the Likelihood of Performing Another." *Journal of Social Psychology* 88, no. 1:65–73.

Harris, Marvin. 1973. *Cows, Pigs, Wars, and Witches: The Riddles of Culture*. New York: Vintage Books.

Hawk, David. 1986. "Some Recommendations of the Whitaker Report Are Achievable." *Internet on the Holocaust and Genocide* 5 (January): 3.

Hayes, Peter, ed. 1991. *Lessons and Legacies: The Meaning of the Holocaust in a Changing World*. Evanston, Ill.: Northwestern University Press.

Henderson, George, ed. 1973. *Education for Peace: Focus on Mankind*. Washington, D.C.: Association for Supervision and Curriculum Development.

Henningsen, Manfred. 1988. "The Politics of Symbolic Evasion: Germany and the Aftermath of the Holocaust." In *Echoes from the Holocaust*, edited by Alan Rosenberg and Gerald E. Myers, pp. 396–411. Philadelphia: Temple University Press.

Henry, Frances. 1984. *Victims and Neighbors: A Small Town in Nazi Germany*. Granby, Mass.: Bergin and Garvey.

———. 1986. "Heroes and Helpers in Nazi Germany: Who Aided Jews?" In *Altruism and Prosocial Behavior*, edited by Elizabeth Midlarsky and Lawrence Baron, pp. 306–19, special issue of *Humboldt Journal of Social Relations* 13, nos. 1 and 2.

Henry, Jules. 1965. *Culture against Man*. New York: Vintage Books.

Herken, G. 1987. *Counsels of War*. New York: Oxford University Press.

Herr, Michael. 1978. *Dispatches*. New York: Avon Books.

Herrmann, Douglas J., and Roger Chaffin, eds. 1988. *Memory in Historical Perspective*. Secaucus, N.J.: Springer-Verlag.

Hersh, Seymour. 1970. *My Lai 4: A Report on the Massacre and Its Aftermath*. New York: Vintage Books.

Hewson, Anne-Geale. 1982. "To Hell and Back: An Empirical Investigation of the Characteristics and Parameters of a Sense of Purpose in Life in Nazi Concentration Camps." In *Analecta Frankliana*, edited by Sandra A. Wawrytko, pp. 137–46. Knoxville, Iowa: Institute of Logotherapy.

Hilberg, Raul. 1985. *The Destruction of the European Jews*. 3 vols. New York: Holmes and Meier.

Hirsch, Herbert. 1971a. "The Political Socialization of State Legislators: A Re-Examination." In *Comparative Legislative Systems: A Reader in Theory and Research*, edited by Herbert Hirsch and M. Donald Hancock, pp. 98–106. New York: Free Press.

——. 1971b. *Poverty and Politicization: Political Socialization in an American Sub-Culture*. New York: Free Press.

——. 1985. "Why People Kill: Conditions for Participation in Mass Murder." *International Journal of Group Tensions* 15, nos. 1–4:41–57.

——. 1988. "Nazi Education: A Case of Political Socialization." *Educational Forum* 52, no. 4 (Fall): 65–76.

——. 1989. "Trivializing Human Experience: Social Studies Methods and Genocide Scholarship." *Armenian Review* 42, no. 4:71–81.

Hirsch, Herbert, and Armando Gutierrez. 1977. *Learning to Be Militant: Ethnic Identity and the Development of Political Militance in a Chicano Community*. San Francisco: R. and E. Research Associates.

Hirsch, Herbert, and Gail M. Hirsch. 1990. "Learning to Live Together: Political Socialization and the Formation of International Identity." *International Journal of Group Tensions* 20, no. 4 (Winter): 369–90.

Hirsch, Herbert, and Roger Smith. 1991. "The Language of Extermination in Genocide." In *Genocide: A Critical Bibliographic Review*, vol. 2, edited by Israel Charny, pp. 386–403. London: Mansell.

Hirsch, Herbert, and Jack Spiro, eds. 1988. *Persistent Prejudice: Perspectives on Anti-Semitism*. Fairfax, Va.: George Mason University Press.

Hitler, Adolf. [1925] 1943. *Mein Kampf*. Boston: Houghton Mifflin.

Hovannisian, Richard G., ed. 1987. *The Armenian Genocide in Perspective*. New Brunswick, N.J.: Transaction Books.

——. 1992. *The Armenian Genocide: History, Politics, Ethics*. New York: St. Martin's Press.

Howe, Irving. 1986. "Primo Levi: An Appreciation." Introduction to *If Not Now, When?*, by Primo Levi. New York: Penguin Books.

Hughes, Alan. 1975. *Psychology and the Political Experience*. New York: Cambridge University Press.

Hughes, H. S. 1983. *Prisoners of Hope*. Cambridge: Harvard University Press.

Hughes, Steven, and George Otero. 1989. "Global Education for the Secondary and College Student." *Political Science Teacher* 2 (Spring): 21–23.

Huneke, Douglas K. 1981/82. "A Study of Christians Who Rescued Jews during the Nazi Era." *Humboldt Journal of Social Relations* 9, no. 1:144–50.

——. 1985. *The Moses of Rovno*. New York: Dodd, Mead and Company.

——. 1986. "The Lessons of Herman Graebe's Life: The Origins of a Moral Person." In *Altruism and Prosocial Behavior*, edited by Elizabeth Midlarsky and Lawrence Baron, pp. 320–32, special issue of *Humboldt Journal of Social Relations* 13, nos. 1 and 2.

Hunt, Michael. 1987. *Ideology and U.S. Foreign Policy*. New Haven: Yale University Press.

Hyman, Herbert. 1959. *Political Socialization*. New York: Free Press.

Isaac, Jules. 1964. *The Teaching of Contempt: Christian Roots of Anti-Semitism*. New York: Holt, Rinehart and Winston.

Isaacs, Arnold R. 1984. *Without Honor: Defeat in Vietnam and Cambodia*. New York: Vintage Books.

———. 1988. "Writing about the Holocaust: A Survey of What We Know." *Washington Post Book World*, January 17, p. 11.

Isenberg, Michael T. 1985. *Puzzles to the Past: An Introduction to Thinking about History*. College Station: Texas A & M University Press.

Janis, Irving L. 1982. *Groupthink*. Boston: Houghton Mifflin.

Janis, Irving L., and Leon Mann. 1977. *Decision Making*. New York: Free Press.

Jaros, Dean, Herbert Hirsch, and Frederick J. Fleron, Jr. 1968. "The Malevolent Leader: Political Socialization in an American Sub-Culture." *American Political Science Review* 62 (June): 564–75.

Jegstrup, Elsebet. 1986. "Spontaneous Action: The Rescue of the Danish Jews from Hannah Arendt's Perspective." In *Altruism and Prosocial Behavior*, edited by Elizabeth Midlarsky and Lawrence Baron, pp. 260–84, special issue of *Humboldt Journal of Social Relations* 13, nos. 1 and 2.

Jennings, M. Kent, and Richard G. Niemi. 1974. *The Political Character of Adolescence: The Influence of Families and Schools*. Princeton: Princeton University Press.

———. 1981. *Generations and Politics*. Princeton: Princeton University Press.

Johnson, George. 1991. *In the Palaces of Memory*. New York: Alfred A. Knopf.

Kader, David. 1991. "Progress and Limitations in Basic Genocidal Law." In *Genocide: A Critical Bibliographic Review*, vol. 2, edited by Israel Charny, pp. 141–45. London: Mansell.

Kammen, Michael. 1991. *Mystic Chords of Memory: The Transformation of Tradition in American Culture*. New York: Alfred A. Knopf.

Kandel, I. L. [1935] 1970. *The Making of Nazis*. Reprint, Westport, Conn.: Greenwood Press.

Karnow, Stanley. 1983. *Vietnam: A History*. New York: Viking.

Kelman, Herbert C., and V. Lee Hamilton. 1989. *Crimes of Obedience: Toward a Social Psychology of Authority and Responsibility*. New Haven: Yale University Press.

Kemp, Anthony. 1991. *The Estrangement of the Past*. New York: Oxford University Press.

Keneally, Thomas. 1982. *Schindler's List*. New York: Penguin Books.

Kenrick, Donald, and Grattan Puxon. 1972. *The Destiny of Europe's Gypsies*. Portsmouth, N.H.: Chatto, Heinemann.

Kiernan, Ben. 1985. *How Pol Pot Came to Power*. London: Verso.

Klein, Joe. 1984. *Payback: Five Marines and Vietnam*. New York: Ballentine Books.

Kniep, Willard. 1989. *Education 2000: A National Model Schools Network*. Minneapolis: American Forum for Global Education.

Knowlton, James, and Truett Cates, trans. 1993. *Forever in the Shadow of Hitler?:*

Original Documents of the Historikerstreit, the Controversy Concerning the Singularity of the Holocaust. Atlantic Highlands, N.J.: Humanities Press International.

Knutson, Jeanne N. 1972. *The Human Basis of the Polity.* Chicago: Aldine.

Kren, George M. 1988. "The Holocaust: Moral Theory and Immoral Acts." In *Echoes from the Holocaust,* edited by Alan Rosenberg and Gerald E. Myers, pp. 245–61. Philadelphia: Temple University Press.

Krieger, David. 1993. "Individual Accountability for International Crimes." *Internet on the Holocaust and Genocide* 42 (February): 4.

Kundera, Milan. 1981. *The Book of Laughter and Forgetting.* New York: Penguin.

Kuper, Leo. 1982. *Genocide: Its Political Use in the Twentieth Century.* New Haven: Yale University Press.

———. 1985. *The Prevention of Genocide.* New Haven: Yale University Press.

———. 1989. "Reflections on Education against Genocide." Special supplement to *Internet on the Holocaust and Genocide* 19 (September).

———. 1992. "Reflections on the Prevention of Genocide." In *Genocide Watch,* edited by Helen Fein, pp. 135–61. New Haven: Yale University Press.

Kurtz, Lester R. 1988. *The Nuclear Cage: A Sociology of the Arms Race.* Englewood Cliffs, N.J.: Prentice-Hall.

Kutner, Luis, and Ned P. Vanda. 1991. "Draft Indictment of Saddam Hussein." *Denver Journal of International Law and Policy* 20, no. 1:91–97.

Laber, Jeri. 1993. "Bosnia: Questions about Rape." *New York Review of Books,* March 25, pp. 3–6.

LaFarge, Phyllis. 1987. *The Strangelove Legacy: The Impact of the Nuclear Threat on Children.* New York: Harper and Row.

Lambert, Wallace E., and Otto Klineberg. 1967. *Children's Views of Foreign Peoples.* New York: Appleton-Century-Crofts.

Landau, Saul. 1988. *The Dangerous Doctrine: National Security and U.S. Foreign Policy.* Boulder: Westview Press.

Landes, David S. 1983. *Revolution in Time: Clocks and the Making of the Modern World.* Cambridge: Harvard University Press.

Landis, B., and Edward S. Tauber, eds. 1971. *In the Name of Life: Essays in Honor of Erich Fromm.* New York: Holt, Rinehart and Winston.

Lane, Robert E. 1962. *Political Ideology.* New York: Free Press.

———. 1969. *Political Thinking and Consciousness.* New York: Markham Publishing.

Lang, Jochen von. 1984. *Eichmann Interrogated: Transcripts from the Archives of the Israeli Police.* New York: Vintage Books.

Langer, Lawrence. 1991. *Holocaust Testimonies: The Ruins of Memory.* New Haven: Yale University Press.

Lasswell, H. D. 1930. *Psychopathology and Politics.* Chicago: University of Chicago Press.

———. 1936. *Politics: Who Gets What, When, How.* New York: McGraw-Hill.

———. 1948. *Power and Personality.* New York: W. W. Norton.

Latane, B., and J. M. Darley. 1970. "Social Determinants of Bystander Intervention in Emergencies." In *Altruism and Helping Behavior*, edited by J. Macaulay and L. Berkowitz, pp. 13–28. New York: Academic Press.

Laufer, Robert S. 1989. "The Aftermath of War: Adult Socialization and Political Development." In *Political Learning in Adulthood*, edited by Roberta Sigel, pp. 415–57. Chicago: University of Chicago Press.

LeBlanc, Lawrence J. 1991. *United States and the Genocide* Convention. Durham: Duke University Press.

Leming, J. S. 1985. "Research on Social Studies Curriculum and Instruction: Interventions and Outcomes in the Socio-Moral Domain." In *Review of Research in Social Studies Education*, edited by W. B. Stanley, pp. 123–33. Washington, D.C.: National Council for the Social Studies.

Lemkin, Raphael. 1944. *Axis Rule in Europe*. Washington, D.C.: Carnegie Endowment for World Peace.

Lerner, A. W. 1970. "The Desire for Justice and Reaction to Victims." In *Altruism and Helping Behavior*, edited by J. Macaulay and L. Berkowitz, pp. 205–29. New York: Academic Press.

Lerner, Richard M. 1992. *Final Solutions: Biology, Prejudice, and Genocide*. University Park: Pennsylvania State University Press.

Levi, Primo. 1984. *The Periodic Table*. New York: Summit Books.

——. 1986a. *If Not Now, When?* New York: Penguin Books.

——. 1986b. *The Monkey's Wrench*. New York: Summit Books.

——. 1986c. *Survival in Auschwitz* and *The Reawakening*. New York: Summit Books.

——. 1987. *Moments of Reprieve: A Memoir of Auschwitz*. New York: Penguin Books.

——. 1988. *The Drowned and the Saved*. New York: Summit Books.

——. 1989. *The Mirror Maker*. New York: Schocken.

Levi, Werner. 1991. *Contemporary International Law*. Boulder: Westview Press.

Liddell Hart, B. H. 1971. *Why Don't We Learn from History?* New York: Hawthorn Books.

Lifton, Robert Jay. 1973. *Home from the War*. New York: Simon and Schuster.

——. 1979. *The Broken Connection*. New York: Simon and Schuster.

——. 1986. *The Nazi Doctors*. New York: Basic Books.

——. 1987. *The Future of Immortality and Other Essays for a Nuclear Age*. New York: Basic Books.

Lifton, Robert Jay, and Eric Markusen. 1990. *The Genocidal Mentality: Nazi Holocaust and Nuclear Threat*. New York: Basic Books.

Lindeman, Mark, and William Rose. 1993. *The Role of the United States in a Changing World*. Guilford, Conn.: Dushkin Publishing Group.

Linton, Marigold. 1975. "Memory for Real-World Events." In *Explorations in Cognition*, edited by D. A. Norman and E. E. Rumelhart, pp. 376–404. Salt Lake City: Freeman.

——. 1986. "Ways of Searching and the Contents of Memory." In *Autobiographical Memory*, edited by David C. Rubin, pp. 50–67. New York: Cambridge University Press.

Littell, Franklin H. 1991. "Early Warning: Detecting Potentially Genocidal

Movements." In *Lessons and Legacies: The Meaning of the Holocaust in a Changing World*, edited by Peter Hayes, pp. 305–15. Evanston, Ill.: Northwestern University Press.

Locke, D. 1971. *Memory.* New York: Anchor Books.

Loewenberg, Peter. 1983. *Decoding the Past.* New York: Alfred A. Knopf.

London, Perry. 1970. "The Rescuers: Motivational Hypotheses about Christians Who Saved Jews from the Nazis." In *Altruism and Helping Behavior*, edited by J. Macaulay and L. Berkowitz, pp. 241–50. New York: Academic Press.

Lowe, Roland, and Gary Richter. 1973. "Relationship of Altruism to Age, Social Class, and Ethnic Identity." *Psychological Reports* 33, no. 2:567–72.

Luper-Foy, Steven, ed. 1988. *Problems of International Justice.* Boulder: Westview Press.

Lyon, Charles. 1972. "The Case of General Yamashita." In *From Nuremberg to My Lai*, edited by Jay W. Baird, pp. 139–49. Lexington, Mass.: D. C. Heath.

McCollough, Thomas E. 1991. *The Moral Imagination and Public Life.* Chatham, N.J.: Chatham House.

Mace, James E. 1988. "The Politics of Famine: American Government and Press Response to the Ukrainian Famine, 1932–1933." *Holocaust and Genocide Studies* 3, no. 1:75–94.

Mackenzie, W. J. 1978. *Political Identity.* Manchester: Manchester University Press.

McNeill, William H. 1986. *Mythhistory and Other Essays.* Chicago: University of Chicago Press.

Mann, Erika. 1938. *School for Barbarians.* New York: Modern Age Books.

Marlowe, D. A. 1983. *Cohesion, Anticipated Breakdown, Endurance in Battle: Considerations for Severity and High Intensity Combat.* Washington, D.C.: Walter Reed Army Institute of Research.

Matthews, Donald R. 1960. *U.S. Senators and Their World.* New York: Vintage Books.

Mehlinger, Howard, et al. 1976. *Global Studies for American Scholars.* Washington, D.C.: National Education Association.

Merkl, Peter. 1980. *The Making of a Stormtrooper.* Princeton: Princeton University Press.

Meyer, Karl E. 1993. "The Roots of Bosnia's Anguish." *Washington Report on Middle East Affairs*, April/May, p. 61.

Midlarsky, Elizabeth, and Lawrence Baron, eds. 1986. *Altruism and Prosocial Behavior*, special issue of *Humboldt Journal of Social Relations* 13, nos. 1 and 2.

Midlarsky, Elizabeth, Eva Kahanna, and Robin Corley. 1986. "Personal and Situational Influences on Late Life Helping." In *Altruism and Prosocial Behavior*, edited by Elizabeth Midlarsky and Lawrence Baron, pp. 217–33, special issue of *Humboldt Journal of Social Relations* 13, nos. 1 and 2.

Midlarsky, Manus. 1986. "Helping during the Holocaust: The Role of Political, Theological, and Socioeconomic Identifications." In *Altruism and Prosocial Behavior*, edited by Elizabeth Midlarsky and Lawrence Baron, pp. 285–305, special issue of *Humboldt Journal of Social Relations* 13, nos. 1 and 2.

Milgram, Stanley. 1974. *Obedience to Authority*. New York: Harper and Row.

——. 1977. *The Individual in a Social World*. Reading, Mass.: Addison-Wesley.

Miller, Donald E., and Lorna T. Miller. 1993. *Survivors: An Oral History of the Armenian Genocide*. Berkeley: University of California Press.

Miller, Judith. 1990. *One, by One, by One: Facing the Holocaust*. New York: Simon and Schuster.

Mills, C. Wright. 1984. "Situated Actions and Vocabularies of Motive." In *Language and Politics*, edited by Michael Shapiro, pp. 13–24. New York: New York University Press.

Minear, Richard H. 1971. *Victor's Justice: The Tokyo War Crimes Trials*. Princeton: Princeton University Press.

Mink, Louis O. 1987. *Historical Understanding*. Edited by Brian Fay, Eugene O. Golob, and Richard T. Vann. Ithaca, N.Y.: Cornell University Press.

Moffic, H. Steven. 1988. *What's in a Name?: Labelling and Group Tensions in the United States*. Paper presented at the Conference of the International Organization for the Study of Group Tensions, Princeton, N.J., June 10–12.

——. 1989. "Labelling and Group Tensions in the United States." *International Journal of Group Tensions* 19, no. 2:152–64.

Monez, Thornton. 1973. "Working for Peace: Implications for Education." In *Education for Peace: Focus on Mankind*, edited by George Henderson, pp. 11–42. Washington, D.C.: Association for Supervision and Curriculum Development.

Moon, Thomas. 1925. *Syllabus on International Relations*. New York: Macmillan.

Moore, Barrington, Jr. 1978. *Injustice: The Social Bases of Obedience and Revolt*. New York: M. E. Sharpe.

Mosse, George L. 1975. *The Nationalization of the Masses*. New York: Meridian.

——. 1978. *Toward the Final Solution*. New York: Harper and Row.

——. 1990. *Fallen Soldiers*. New York: Oxford University Press.

Neissed, Ulric. 1986. "Nested Structure in Autobiographical Memory." In *Autobiographical Memory*, edited by David C. Rubin, pp. 71–81. New York: Cambridge University Press.

Nelson, Jack L. 1980. "The Uncomfortable Relationship between Moral Education and Citizenship Instruction." In *Moral Development and Politics*, edited by Richard Wilson and Gordon Schochet, pp. 256–85. New York: Praeger.

Neumann, George Bradford. 1926. *A Study of International Attitudes of High School Students*. New York: Teachers College Press.

Niemi, Richard. 1973. "Political Socialization." In *Handbook of Political Psychology*, edited by Jeanne N. Knutson, pp. 117–38. San Francisco: Jossey-Bass.

Nietzsche, Friedrich. 1956. *The Birth of Tragedy and the Genealogy of Morals*. New York: Doubleday.

——. 1957. *The Use and Abuse of History*. Translated by Adrian Collins. New York: Bobbs-Merrill.

——. 1980. *On the Advantage and Disadvantage of History for Life*. Hawthorne, N.Y.: Walter de Gruyter.

Nolte, Ernst. 1993. "Between Historical Legend and Revisionism?: The Third Reich in the Perspective of 1980." In *Forever in the Shadow of Hitler?: Original Documents of the Historikerstreit, the Controversy Concerning the Singularity of the Holocaust*, translated by James Knowlton and Truett Cates, pp. 1–15. Atlantic Highlands, N.J.: Humanities Press International.

Norton, Anne. 1988. *Reflections on Political Identity*. Baltimore: John Hopkins University Press.

Oakeshott, Michael. 1983. *On History and Other Essays*. Cambridge, Mass.: Basil Blackwell.

Office of the U.S. Chief of Council for Prosecution of Axis Criminality. 1946. *Nazi Conspiracy and Aggression*. Washington, D.C.: Government Printing Office.

Oliner, Pearl M. 1983. "Putting 'Community' into Citizenship Education: The Need for Prosociality." *Theory and Research in Social Education* 11 (Summer): 65–81.

———. 1986. "Legitimating and Implementing Prosocial Education." In *Altruism and Prosocial Behavior*, edited by Elizabeth Midlarsky and Lawrence Baron, pp. 391–410, special issue of *Humboldt Journal of Social Relations* 13, nos. 1 and 2.

Opton, Edward M., Jr. 1971. "It Never Happened and Besides They Deserved It." In *Sanctions for Evil*, edited by Nevitt Sanford and Craig Comstock, pp. 49–70. Boston: Beacon Press.

Orwell, George. 1954. "Politics and the English Language." In *A Collection of Essays*, by George Orwell, pp. 156–71. New York: Harcourt Brace Jovanovich.

———. 1961. *1984*. New York: New American Library.

Osborn, Lynn R. 1970. "Language, Poverty, and the North American Indian." In *Language and Poverty*, edited by Frederick Williams, pp. 229–47. Chicago: Markham Publishing.

Ouellette, André, and David Livermore. 1993. *Minorities: Addressing an Emerging International Security Issue*. Policy Planning Staff Paper, no. 9313. Ottawa, Canada: Policy Planning Staff, External Affairs, and International Trade.

Pattison, E. M. 1984. "Psychoanalysis and the Concept of Evil." In *Evil Self and Culture*, edited by M. E. Nelson and Michael Eigen, pp. 61–87. New York: Human Sciences Press.

Pike, Lewis, and Thomas Barrows. 1976. *Other Nations, Other Peoples: A Survey of Student Interests and Knowledge, Attitudes, and Perceptions*. Washington, D.C.: U.S. Department of Health, Education, and Welfare.

Piliavin, I. M., J. Rodin, and J. A. Piliavin. 1969. "Good Samaritanism: An Underground Phenomenon?" *Journal of Personality and Social Psychology* 13, no. 1:289–99.

Pocock, J. G. A. 1984. "Verbalizing a Political Act: Toward a Politics of Speech." In *Language and Politics*, edited by Michael Shapiro, pp. 25–42. New York: New York University Press.

Poliakov, Leon. 1971. *The Aryan Myth*. New York: New American Library.

Rapaport, David. 1971. *Emotions and Memory*. Madison, Conn.: International Universities Press.

Ravitch, Diane, and Chester Finn. 1987. *What Do Our Seventeen-Year-Olds Know?* New York: Harper and Row.

Reiser, Brian J., John B. Black, and Peter Kalamanides. 1986. "Strategic Memory Search Processes." In *Autobiographical Memory*, edited by David C. Rubin, pp. 100–121. New York: Cambridge University Press.

Renn, Walter F. 1983. "Confronting Genocide: The Depiction of the Persecution of the Jews and the Holocaust in West German History Textbooks." In *Contemporary Views on the Holocaust*, edited by Randolph L. Braham, pp. 157–77. Norwell, Mass.: Kluwer-Nijhoff.

Renshon, Stanley. 1989. "Psychological Perspectives on Theories of Adult Development and the Political Socialization of Leaders." In *Political Learning in Adulthood*, edited by Roberta Sigel, pp. 203–64. Chicago: University of Chicago Press.

Ribot, T. 1882. *Diseases of Memory: An Essay in the Positive Psychology*. Translated by W. H. Smith. Boston: Appleton.

Roberts, Adam, and Richard Guelff, eds. 1989. *Documents on the Laws of War*. New York: Clarendon.

Robertson, James Oliver. 1980. *American Myth, American Reality*. New York: Hill and Wang.

Robinson, John A. 1986a. "Autobiographical Memory: A Historical Prologue." In *Autobiographical Memory*, edited by David C. Rubin, pp. 19–23. New York: Cambridge University Press.

——. 1986b. "Temporal Reference Systems and Autobiographical Memory." In *Autobiographical Memory*, edited by David C. Rubin, pp. 59–88. New York: Cambridge University Press.

Rosenberg, Alan. 1988. "The Crisis in Knowing and Understanding the Holocaust." In *Echoes from the Holocaust*, edited by Alan Rosenberg and Gerald E. Myers, pp. 379–95. Philadelphia: Temple University Press.

Rosenblatt, Roger. 1984. *Children of War*. New York: Anchor Press.

Roth, John K. 1984/85. "How to Make Hitler's Ideas Clear?" In *Philosophical Forum* 16, nos. 1 and 2:82–94.

Rothgeb, John, Jr. 1993. *Defining Power: Influence and Force in the Contemporary International System*. New York: St. Martin's Press.

Rubenstein, Richard. 1978. *The Cunning of History*. New York: Harper and Row.

——. 1988. "Luther and the Roots of the Holocaust." In *Persistent Prejudice: Perspectives on Anti-Semitism*, edited by Herbert Hirsch and Jack Spiro, pp. 31–42. Fairfax, Va.: George Mason University Press.

Rubin, David C., ed. 1986. *Autobiographical Memory*. New York: Cambridge University Press.

Russell, B. 1921. *The Analysis of Mind*. New York: Allen and Unwin.

Ryan, William. 1976. *Blaming the Victim*. New York: Vintage Books.

Sachar, Abram. 1983. *The Redemption of the Unwanted*. New York: St. Martin's Press.

Samuel, R. H., and R. Hinton Thomas. 1949. *Education and Society in Modern Germany*. Westport, Conn.: Greenwood Press.

Sanders, Jonathan. 1988. "Never Say Never." *New Leader*, January, p. 19.

Sanford, Nevitt, and Craig Comstock. 1971. *Sanctions for Evil*. Boston: Beacon Press.

Sapir, Edward. 1960. *Culture, Language, and Personality*. Berkeley: University of California Press.

Sauvage, Pierre. 1986. "Ten Things I Would Like to Know about Righteous Conduct in Le Chambon and Elsewhere during the Holocaust." In *Altruism and Prosocial Behavior*, edited by Elizabeth Midlarsky and Lawrence Baron, pp. 252–59, special issue of *Humboldt Journal of Social Relations* 13, nos. 1 and 2.

Schaar, John. 1961. *Escape from Authority: The Perspectives of Erich Fromm*. New York: Harper.

———. 1981a. "The Case for Patriotism." In *Legitimacy in the Modern State*, by John Schaar, pp. 285–312. New Brunswick, N.J.: Transaction Books.

———. 1981b. "Violence in Juvenile Gangs: Some Notes and a Few Analogies." In *Legitimacy in the Modern State*, by John Schaar, pp. 273–83. New Brunswick, N.J.: Transaction Books.

Scheer, Robert. 1983. *With Enough Shovels: Reagan, Bush, and Nuclear War*. New York: Random House.

Schell, Jonathan. 1987. *The Real War*. New York: Pantheon Books.

Schmid, A. P., and A. J. Jongman. 1992. "Contemporary Massacres." *Internet on the Holocaust and Genocide* 41 (December): 12.

Schneider, Frank W., and Zig Mokus. 1974. "Failure to Find a Rural-Urban Difference in Incidence of Altruistic Behavior." In *Psychological Reports* 35, no. 2:294.

Schwartz, David C., and Sandra Kenyon. 1975. *New Directions in Political Socialization*. New York: Free Press.

Schwartz, Edward. 1980. "Traditional Values, Moral Education, and Social Change." In *Moral Development and Politics*, edited by Richard Wilson and Gordon Schochet, pp. 221–36. New York: Praeger.

Sebaly, Kim. 1987. "Education about Human Rights: Teacher Preparation." In *Human Rights and Education*, edited by Norma Bernstein Tarrow, pp. 207–21. Elmsford, N.Y.: Pergamon Press.

Sennett, Richard. 1980. *Authority*. New York: Alfred A. Knopf.

Sereny, Gitta. 1974. *Into That Darkness*. New York: Vintage Books.

Shafer, Suzanne M. 1987. "Human Rights Education in Schools." In *Human Rights and Education*, edited by Norma Bernstein Tarrow, pp. 191–205. Elmsford, N.Y.: Pergamon Press.

Shapiro, Michael. 1984. *Language and Politics*. New York: New York University Press.

Shirer, William L. 1960. *The Rise and Fall of the Third Reich*. New York: Simon and Schuster.

Sigel, Roberta, ed. 1989. *Political Learning in Adulthood*. Chicago: University of Chicago Press.

Simpson, Elizabeth L. 1971. *Democracy's Stepchildren*. San Francisco: Jossey-Bass.

Slomanson, William R. 1990. *Fundamental Perspectives on International Law*. St. Paul, Minn.: West Publishing Company.

Smith, B. A. 1985. *Politics and Remembrance*. Princeton: Princeton University Press.

Smith, Bradley F. 1977. *Reaching Judgement at Nuremberg*. New York: New American Library.

Smith, M. E. 1952. "Childhood Memories Compared with Those of Adult Life." *Journal of Genetic Psychology* 80, no. 2:151–82.

Smith, Roger. 1992a. "The Armenian Genocide: Memory, Politics, and the Future." In *The Armenian Genocide: History, Politics, Ethics*, edited by Richard G. Hovannisian, pp. 1–20. New York: St. Martin's Press.

——. 1992b. "Exploring the United States' Thirty-Five-Year Reluctance to Ratify the Genocide Convention." *Harvard Human Rights Journal* 5 (Spring): 227–33.

——. 1987. "Human Destructiveness and Politics: The Twentieth Century as an Age of Genocide." In *Genocide and the Modern Age*, edited by Isidor Walliman and Michael Dobkowski, pp. 21–39. Westport, Conn.: Greenwood Press.

——, ed. 1971. *Guilt, Man, and Society*. New York: Anchor Books.

Sniderman, P. 1975. *Personality and Democratic Politics*. Berkeley: University of California Press.

Snow, Donald M. 1993. *Distant Thunder: Third World Conflict and the New International Order*. New York: St. Martin's Press.

Sontag, Susan. 1978. "Disease as a Political Metaphor." *New York Review of Books*, February 23, pp. 29–33.

Sorokin, P. A. 1950. *Altruistic Love: A Study of American "Good Neighbors" and Christian Saints*. Boston: Beacon Press.

Speer, Albert. 1970. *Inside the Third Reich*. New York: Macmillan.

Staub, Ervin. 1989. *The Roots of Evil*. New York: Cambridge University Press.

Steiner, George. 1971. *In Bluebeard's Castle*. New Haven: Yale University Press.

——. 1977. *Language and Silence*. New York: Atheneum.

Steiner, John M. 1976. *Power, Politics, and Social Change in National Socialist Germany*. Paris: Mouton Publishers.

Stewart, Abigail J., Carol Franz, and Lynne Layton. 1988. "The Changing Self: Using Personal Documents to Study Lives." *Journal of Personality* 56 (March): 41–74.

Stone, William F., and Paul E. Schaffner. 1988. *The Psychology of Politics*. Secaucus, N.J.: Springer-Verlag.

Storr, Anthony. 1991. *Human Destructiveness*. New York: Ballantine.

Study Commission on Global Education. 1987. *The United States Prepares for Its Future*. Washington, D.C.: Global Perspectives in Education.

Tarrow, Norma Bernstein, ed. 1987. *Human Rights and Education*. Elmsford, N.Y.: Pergamon Press.

Task Force on International Education, National Governors' Association. 1989. "America in Transition: The International Frontier." Washington, D.C.

Taylor, Telford. 1970. *Nuremberg and Vietnam: An American Tragedy*. New York: Bantam Books.

——. 1992. *The Anatomy of the Nuremberg Trials*. New York: Alfred A. Knopf.

Tec, Nechama. 1984. "Sex Distinctions and Passing as Christians during the Holocaust." *East European Quarterly* 18, no. 1:113–23.

——. 1986. *When Light Pierced the Darkness: Christian Rescue of Jews in Nazi-Occupied Poland.* New York: Oxford University Press.

Teson, Fernando R. 1988. *Humanitarian Intervention: An Inquiry into Law and Morality.* New York: Transnational Publishers.

Thompson, Kenneth W. 1980. *Morality and Foreign Policy.* Baton Rouge: Louisiana State University Press.

Timerman, Jacobo. 1981. *Prisoner without a Name, Cell without a Number.* New York: Vantage Books.

Todorov, Tzvetan. 1984. *The Conquest of America: The Question of the Other.* New York: Harper and Row.

Tolley, Howard. 1973. *Children and War.* New York: Teachers College Press.

Torney-Purta, Judith. 1987. "Human Rights and Education Viewed in a Comparative Framework: Synthesis and Conclusions." In *Human Rights and Education,* edited by Norma Bernstein Tarrow, pp. 223–33. Elmsford, N.Y.: Pergamon Press.

Trial of the Major War Criminals before the International Military Tribunal. 1947–49. 42 vols. Nuremberg, Germany.

Tutorow, Norman E., ed. 1986. *War Crimes, War Criminals, and War Crimes Trials: An Annotated Bibliography and Source Book.* New York: Greenwood Press.

U.S. Senate Committee on Foreign Relations. 1985. *Hearing on the Prevention and Punishment of the Crime of Genocide.* 99th Cong., 1st sess., March 5.

Vidal-Naquet, Pierre. 1992. *Assassins of Memory: Essays on the Denial of the Holocaust.* New York: Columbia University Press.

Waller, Douglas. 1993. "The CIA's New Spies." *Newsweek,* April 12, pp. 30–32.

Weber, Max. 1946. "Bureaucracy." In *From Max Weber: Essays in Sociology,* edited by H. H. Gerth and C. Wright Mills, pp. 27–55. New York: Oxford University Press.

Weinstein, Fred. 1980. *The Dynamics of Nazism.* New York: Academic Press.

Weissbrodt, David. 1988. "Human Rights: An Historical Perspective." In *Human Rights,* edited by Peter Davies, pp. 1–20. New York: Routledge.

Wells, H. 1963. *The Failure of Psychoanalysis—From Freud to Fromm.* New York: International Publishers.

Wheeler, Stanton. 1966. "The Structure of Formerly Organized Socialization Settings." In *Socialization after Childhood,* edited by Orville Brim and Stanton Wheeler, pp. 51–116. New York: John Wiley.

Whitaker, B. 1985. *Revised and Updated Report on the Question of the Prevention and Punishment of the Crime of Genocide.* Document E/CN, 4/5SUB/1985/6, July 2. New York: United Nations.

White, Hayden. 1973. *Metahistory: The Historical Imagination in Nineteenth Century Europe.* Baltimore: Johns Hopkins University Press.

Wiesel, Elie. 1960. *Night.* New York: Bantam Books.

——. 1978. *One Generation After.* New York: Pocket Books.

Williams, Frederick. 1970. *Language and Poverty.* Chicago: Markham Publishing.

Wilson, Richard, and Gordon Schochet, eds. 1980. *Moral Development and Politics.* New York: Praeger.

Wolin, Sheldon. 1985. "Under Siege in the German Ivory Tower." *New York Times Book Review,* July 18, p. 12.

Woodward, C. Vann. 1989. *The Future of the Past.* New York: Oxford University Press.

Wundheiler, Luitgard N. 1986. "Oskar Schindler's Moral Development during the Holocaust." In *Altruism and Prosocial Behavior,* edited by Elizabeth Midlarsky and Lawrence Baron, pp. 333–56, special issue of *Humboldt Journal of Social Relations* 13, nos. 1 and 2.

Yates, F. A. 1966. *The Art of Memory.* New York: Routledge and Kegan Paul.

Young, James E. 1988. *Writing and Rewriting the Holocaust: Narrative and the Consequences of Interpretation.* Bloomington: Indiana University Press.

Ziemer, Gregor. 1972. *Education for Death.* New York: Octagon Books.

Zuccotti, Susan. 1987. *The Italians and the Holocaust.* New York: Basic Books.

INDEX

sacres," 124–25; "analysis of obedience," 171

Hampshire, Stuart, 17, 35

Hart, Liddell, 34

Heroism, notions of, 63–66, 69, 85

Hilberg, Raul, 127

Himmler, Heinrich, 129

History, construction of, 10, 13, 15, 17, 19–22, 25, 32, 34, 70, 78, 162

Holocaust, 2, 26–31, 33, 35, 39, 57, 75, 78, 81, 87–88, 148; survivors of, 39–65, 73

Humanitarian intervention, 207–13; and notions of sovereignty, 208; in Somalia, 208

Human rights, 207–13

Huneke, Douglas K., 153

If Not Now, When? (Levi), 50–51, 53

Individual identity, 3, 60, 66, 96, 133–34, 141, 145; construction of, 134–56; and collective self, 138–40, 145; and self-concept, 141

International Conference on the Former Yugoslavia, 5

International identity, 162–69, 178–80

Internationalism, 166–67

International political community, 184, 209

Isenberg, Michael T., 10, 18–19, 34

Israel, 32–33, 61

Jews, 100–102, 131, 148–57

Kalshoven, Fritz, 196–97

Kammen, Michael, 25–26, 33

Karnow, Stanley, 77

Kelman, Herbert C., 124–26, 171; "crime of obedience," 124; "sanctioned massacres," 124–25; "analysis of obedience," 171; "global perspective," 173

Kemp, Anthony, 20–22

Klineberg, Otto, 137, 163–64

Kren, George M., 175

Lambert, Wallace E., 137, 163–64

Language, utilization of, 3, 28–29, 69–70, 97–108, 126–28, 139–40, 164

Laufer, Robert S., 142–44

Laws, notion of, 176–78

Lemkin, Raphael, 125, 197–99, 206

Levi, Primo, 43–55, 57–59, 62, 73, 78, 105

Lifton, Robert J., 53, 72, 77, 80–93, 105, 127, 130, 144, 154; "notions of hope," 83–84; "nuclearism," 84, 88, 90; "numbing," 85–86, 89–90, 127, 130, 144; "technicism," 86; "species mentality," 87, 92, 170, 172–73; "genocidal mentality," 87–88, 90–92, 170; "deterrence," 88, 90–91; "dissociation," 89, 91–92; "doubling," 89–92, 144–46

Littell, Franklin H., 194–95

Luther, Martin, 100

McCollough, Thomas E., 174; "moral imagination," 174

McNeil, William H., 25

Markusen, Eric, 87–92, 130, 144, 170–73; "species mentality," 87, 92, 170, 172–73; "genocidal mentality," 87–88, 90–92, 170–71; "nuclearism," 88, 90; "deterrence," 88, 90–91; "dissociation," 89, 91–92; "doubling," 89–92, 144

Memory: the politics of, 3–4, 9–11, 23, 26–36, 75, 87, 96, 111, 121–22, 82; the construction of, 4, 17, 20–22, 25, 39, 55, 70, 82, 132, 136, 146, 163, 182–83; historical perspectives of, 11–12; personal, 13–15, 153–54; preservation of, 69–70

Milgram, Stanley, 90, 124–25, 129, 146, 173

Miller, Judith, 27–30
Mills, C. Wright, 98
Modern nation-state, 67–69, 75–76,
   99–102, 110, 123, 128–32, 135–42,
   161–67, 175, 177–85, 203, 207–13
Moffic, H. Steven, 103
*Moments of Reprieve: A Memoir of
   Auschwitz* (Levi), 47, 54
Myths, the construction of, 3, 9, 24–27,
   29, 35, 98–103, 108, 126–28, 131, 139,
   164, 182–83; cultural, 128, 131–32

National identity, 26, 35, 96, 99, 120,
   122, 131, 133, 163, 182
Nationalism, 161–70, 182
Nazi Doctors, The, (Lifton), 80, 87
Nazi Germany, 26–30, 59–61, 88–92,
   100, 104–5, 108
Neumann, George Bradford, 162–64
Nietzsche, Friedrich, 2, 35
Norms: cultural, 131–32
Nuclear weapons, 84, 87–91, 105,
   107–8
Nuremberg Military Tribunals (NMT),
   187–89, 191–92
Nuremberg Principles, 187–89

Obedience, 100, 105–8
Objectivity, notions of, 75, 85, 134

Paradigm(s), 17, 72; supersessive,
   20–22; positivist, 72
Periodic Table, The, (Levi), 51–52
Political massacres, 184–85, 205–7
Politics, the discipline of, 68–69, 135
Power, uses of, 68–69, 135–36, 167,
   175–76, 210
Presidents Commission on the Holo-
   caust (U.S.), 28–29
"Psychic numbing," 80, 86, 89
Psychoanalytic theory, 57–59, 140
Psychological conditions, 128, 132

Racism, 101–3
Rapaport, David, 11, 14
Rape, 5–6
Rationalization, 29–30, 127–32
Reawakening, The, (Levi), 48–50
Relativization, 30
Religion, 111, 120, 131, 164–65, 177
Rescuers, the characteristics of,
   150–54
Responsibility: collective, 124; individ-
   ual, 124–26, 129–30, 155, 171–72
Revisionism, 30–32, 121
Ritualistic behavior, 106, 25
Robertson, James Oliver, 25
Roots of Evil, The, (Staub), 124
Rosenberg, Alan, 174
Rosenblatt, Roger, 165
Rouge, Khmer, 141
Routinization, 125–26
Rust, Bernard, 116–17

Sauvage, Pierre, 151
Schaar, John, 168
Shifting blame, 29
Socialization: the process of, 3, 96–100,
   108, 125; agents of, 109–21, 178–80;
   political, 134–56, 163, 166–78
Social science methods, 72, 80–82, 85,
   135; empirical, 74–78, 81; positivistic,
   74–78, 81, 93; interpretative, 77–78,
   80
Staub, Ervin, 124, 138, 140–41, 145
Steiner, George, 17–18, 97, 104–5, 108
Storr, Anthony, 173, 175–76
Survival, notions of, 57–70, 85, 144
Survival in Auschwitz (Levi), 44–45
Survivor, The, (Des Pres), 70

Taylor, Telford, 71
Tec, Nechama, 148–52
Tokyo war crimes trial, 190–92
Totalitarian states, 111, 121